DEMOCRATIC GOVERNANCE

DEMOCRATIC GOVERNANCE

James G. March
Johan P. Olsen

THE FREE PRESS

New York   London   Toronto   Sydney   Tokyo   Singapore

The Free Press
A Division of Simon & Schuster Inc.
1230 Avenue of the Americas
New York, N.Y. 10020

Printed in the United States of America

printing number

1 2 3 4 5 6 7 8 9 10

Text design by Carla Bolte

Library of Congress Cataloging-in-Publication Data

March, James G.
    Democratic governance / James G. March and Johan P. Olsen.
      p. cm.
    Includes index.
    ISBN 0-02-874054-8
    1. Democracy.   2. Representative government and representation.   I. Olsen, Johan P.
II. Title.
JC423.M3557   1995
321.8—dc20
                                                    95-2849
                                                     CIP

CONTENTS

ACKNOWLEDGMENTS

In more than the usual way, this book is testimony to the pleasures (and complications) of international collaboration. We have worked with each other for more than twenty-five years, traveling innumerable times between Norway and California in quest of time to talk and opportunities to write. This enduring collaboration would have been impossible without the support for such endeavors provided by our research patrons in the Spencer Foundation, the Stanford Graduate School of Business, the Norwegian Centre in Organization and Management, the Center for Advanced Study in the Behavioral Sciences, the Scandinavian Consortium for Organizational Research, and the Norwegian Research Council.

We have also had the advantage of many good students and colleagues. Although the list of people from whom we have extracted intellectual sustenance is too long to include here, some effects persist longer and are more pervasive than others; so it seems appropriate to acknowledge the long-lasting influence of our early exposure to the ideas and friendships of Robert A. Dahl and Stein Rokkan. Roderick Kramer, Nils Brunsson, Andreas Føllesdal, B. Guy Peters, and Philip Tetlock made important contributions to specific sections of the book; and Richard Barnett, Mary Diane Burton, and Chris Mazzeo provided much appreciated bibliographic help.

We are grateful for the contributions of an old friend, Robert Wallace, who has been our editor at The Free Press for many years and has been a stable link to the wondrous world of publishing through several corporate transformations. He and his associates, particularly Edith Lewis, Elena Vega, and Catherine Wayland, have provided welcome therapy through the trauma of publication.

And we are, of course, hopelessly in debt to our friends and wives, Jayne Dohr March and Helene Olsen, who still tolerate us.

James G. March
Johan P. Olsen

Chapter One

AN INTRODUCTION

For thousands of years, students and practitioners of politics have tried to understand, justify, and improve political life. The list is an honor roll of political philosophers from Solon and Confucius to Gandhi and Rawls. It is also a list of politicians, tyrants, and ordinary citizens trying to comprehend, construct, and control a system of political order. Their concerns are embedded not only in their teachings but also in the institutions of government they have crafted—the practices, rules, norms, identities, beliefs, accounts, and capabilities that constitute modern polities. We wish to continue those traditions of concern.

A FOCUS ON DEMOCRACY

Although many issues of governance have applications in many different kinds of political systems, our focus is on democracies. A focus on democracy is not precise. "Democracy" has become a term of such general legitimacy and indiscriminate use as to compromise its claim to meaning (Duncan and Lukes, 1963; Davis, 1964; Barker, 1984; Offe and Preuss, 1991). Even if we ignore the more obviously perverse uses of the term, the democracy of Aristotle differs from the democracy of James Madison, and both differ from the democracy of Jürgen Habermas or Hannah Arendt. The practices of democratic governance differ among contemporary democratic systems,

1

as each differs from its own antecedents. Democracy is a culture, a faith, and an ethos that develop through interpretation, practice, wars, and revolutions. It discovers new meanings and new possibilities in new experiences and ideologies. As a result, democratic traditions involve a richly evolving collection of diverse beliefs, processes, and structures that are neither easily characterized in concise terms nor summarized in a single systematic philosophy of governance (Næss, 1968; Sartori, 1987; Dahl, 1989).

Nevertheless, the focus on democracy is limiting. Democracy is a distinct political order and a particular form of human coexistence, providing a distinct historical-institutional context for governance. It is an accumulation of concrete institutional practices, rules, and procedures that are tied to democratic ideals. While not completely unambiguous, democratic ideals provide a yardstick for assessing how various societies are governed and criteria for justifying and criticizing existing forms of government and proposals for social reforms. Those ideals secure their essential character from confidence in the ability of ordinary men and women to govern themselves and shape their futures.

An essential part of the democratic vision is a commitment to personal liberty and individual responsibility in its exercise (Mill, 1956). Democratic communities recognize substantial areas of ordinary life as private and impose constraints on private individual and group actions only reluctantly and with great care. These rights to liberty are protected not only by the political system but also by the habits and obligations of citizens. Democratic citizens defend the private spheres of others and protect the freedom to pursue private lives and aspirations to the extent to which individual actions do not impinge on the rights of others to do likewise. They are also committed to limiting the intrusion of their own free actions on the rights of others (Cohen and Arato, 1992).

A second essential part of the democratic vision is the idea of popular sovereignty and political equality. Responsibility for governance lies in the first instance with those who are formally designated as governors, but it lies ultimately with a sovereign community of free and equal citizens (Wolin, 1981). This democratic vision assumes a willingness to accept that when it comes to how society should be organized and governed, that is, in deciding which principles and rules should order common affairs and be binding for all members of the community, all adult members of society should participate and count as equals. Significant differences among individuals are to be subordinated to their equal rights and responsibilities to participate in the system of governance (Cohen, 1971).

A third essential part of the democratic vision is faith in the role of individual and collective human reason in human affairs. The meanderings of history are seen as capable of being affected by the intentions of ordinary citizens acting after reasoned deliberations. Institutions are seen to be subject to human will (Wolff, 1970, p. 76; Rawls, 1971, p. 102). It is a vision of a self-chosen life. Of course, such grand visions and commitments give ample room for competing interpretations of, and struggles over, their contents and applications, as well as over what it takes in terms of institutions and identities to implement them; but the democratic faith has developed within an ethos of human will, reason, and control (Habermas, 1981, 1989).

A fourth essential part of the democratic vision reflected here is an emphasis on procedural reliability and stability, on the rule of law and the regulation of arbitrary power. Democracy is undermined by prolonged failures to achieve substantive justice, but it is much more quickly made illegitimate by failures to sustain a system of institutions and rules (e.g., free elections, independent judiciary) that are associated with protections from arbitrariness. As a result, a major feature of democracy is that it tolerates and encourages differences among individuals in values and interests while sustaining a diffuse confidence in democratic procedures and their outcomes (Locke, 1690; Muller, Jukam, and Seligson, 1982; Klosko, 1993).

A FOCUS ON GOVERNANCE

This book is intended not to elaborate what is known about democracy's present inadequacies and uncertainties, nor to make predictions about its future, but to outline a framework for thinking about democratic governance. The contribution is as modest as the vision is grand. The ideas are not particularly novel. They are even, perhaps, self-evident. Taken together, however, they raise questions regarding some parts of standard current thinking about governance.

The democracies of today are products of yesterday. They involve structures of institutions, beliefs, practices, interests, and resources that have evolved over hundreds of years in special circumstances. Democratic governance first arose in a small city-state and developed its modern forms over the past two hundred or three hundred years in a few countries with relatively small populations, relatively substantial wealth, and relative geographic, social, and economic autonomy. Democratic polities have developed through processes of wars, revolutions, and political compromises reflecting the realities of political, economic, and social power. Groups with strong resources have created, maintained, and transformed privileges based on their own strength and the strength of their allies. The traditions and institutions of governance have been forged in those contexts. They carry those histories.

The present context, however, is different from much of that history. It is a context of large, complex, interconnected social systems. It is a context of communication, information, and military technologies that change important premises of government. It is a context of persistent fundamentalism and differentiation in religious, ethnic, and national identities juxtaposed with increasingly interpenetrated cultures. It is a context of global economic competition along with global consciousness of disparities in wealth and well-being. It is a context of highly elaborated and differentiated knowledge in which what is knowable and accessible is a function more of social and technological organization than of intellect. It would be truly remarkable if a set of ideas about governance that developed in a context so different from the modern one should prove to fit present conditions. Assumptions about democratic governance that were self-evident to Plato and Aristotle, or to Bentham and Mill, are not so self-evident now. Times have changed. And although almost anything that could be said now has been said before, ideas about governance have also changed.

One great metamorphosis in thinking about politics took place during the late sixteenth and early seventeenth centuries. A conception of the political order as divine, natural, hierarchical, and beyond human control was replaced by a conception of order as political, secular, and social. The preeminence of religious institutions in defining frameworks for constructing and maintaining political accounts was challenged by secular institutions (Collins, 1989). The political order came to be seen as a matter of choice, based on human will, calculation, and power, and society came to be seen as a collection of independent individuals bound together by consent and contract (Herzog, 1989). A belief in human agency and the malleability of society left political actors with confidence in their ability to control events and to build a social order in accordance with the dictates of their desires. Accounts constructed around the assumption that God has created and ordered the world according to immutable laws gave way to accounts emphasizing human will and power (Rice, 1970). Political actors became responsible for political history. Governance became the province of mortals who served the polity. Political institutions became instruments of progress.

In recent years visions based on such democratic optimism and conceptions of modernity have become less prevalent. It is unclear what democratic progress now means (Alexander and Sztompka, 1990; Giddens, 1991). Confidence in the capabilities or ordinary citizens has been undermined by experience with the limitations of public discourse and opinion formation (Page and Shapiro, 1993, p. 40). Confidence in the political system as an agent of the public has been undermined by consciousness of the corruption and irresponsibility of state power. Confidence in the triumph of enlightenment has been undermined by the ease with which appeals to ethnic, gender, religious, and national loyalties overcome commitments to reason. This aura of pessimism is partly a reflection of a more general fin-de-siècle mood of broadening introspection, of pessimism and a feeling of decline, but it is also a reflection of more specific problems with democratic governance.

PROLEGOMENON

Contemporary thinking about democratic governance builds primarily on premises of individualism and self-interest. Ideas of governors pursuing an autonomous public virtue and collective purpose have been subordinated to ideas of negotiation, political coalition, and competition (Viroli, 1992). A vision of statecraft as the art of acting according to duty, justice, and reason on behalf of a community of citizens has been superseded in large part by a language emphasizing exchanges among rational self-interested citizens. Exchange metaphors for understanding and managing collective action capture some important elements of social life, and well-designed systems for exchange may often be more consistent with modern realities than are dreams of reasoned discussion. Nevertheless we, in company with many others, believe that individualism and exchange theories of democracy provide incomplete bases for thinking about governance. We believe that the theory of human behavior that underlies such theories is also incomplete, that it reflects only a partial theory of history and human action, one that should be supplemented with a view of governance that has come to be called an institutional perspective.

From an institutional perspective a democratic polity is constituted by its basic practices and rules, as well as by individual purposes and intentions. Political action is organized through the interdependent obligations of political identities. Governance involves affecting the frameworks within which citizens and officials act and politics occurs, and which shape the identities and institutions of civil society. A discussion of modern, democratic governance in these terms is primarily a discussion of how those institutional frameworks can be organized to achieve democratic ideals and how institutions are constituted and changed within the processes they define (Ostrom, 1990).

Institutions are manifested in a wide variety of forms. Our primary interest in this book is in formally organized institutions, practices, and rules that are embedded in organized systems of authority, resources, and meaning. We ask how political institutions are structured, how they work, how they change, how they are governed, and how governance might be made honorable, just, and effective. We ask how individuals and societies can achieve political institutions that sustain and elaborate democratic values, beliefs, and identities, how they can make politics civil, accountable, capable, and transformative. The book is romantic in its imagination of governance as having something to contribute to the commonweal and shared aspirations for a good life, but it recognizes the complications in fulfilling democratic ideals. It is cautious in the hopes that it provides for deliberate control of human destiny, but it embraces the idea that we should try.

Chapter Two

PERSPECTIVES ON GOVERNANCE

Governance presumes a perspective on politics and government, a way of thinking about how things happen in a polity. We contrast two different modern views of governance. The first is an exchange perspective built around ideas of coalition building and voluntary exchange among self-interested political actors. It assumes that individual action depends on the answers to three questions: What are the alternatives? What are the consequences that will follow from each alternative? What is the value, in terms of preferences of the decision maker, of the consequences? Collective action is based on exchanges among individuals acting on the basis of the answers to such questions. The second view is an institutional perspective built around ideas of identities and conceptions of appropriate behavior. It assumes that individual action depends on the answers to three different questions: What kind of a person am I? What kind of a situation is this? What does a person such as I do in a situation such as this? Collective action is based on combinations of answers to those questions.

EXCHANGE PERSPECTIVES

Politics can be seen as aggregating individual preferences into collective actions by some procedures of rational bargaining, negotiation, coalition formation, and exchange (Riker, 1962; Coleman, 1966a,

7

1966b; Downs, 1967; Niskanen, 1971; Taylor, 1975). Ideas of politics as involving rational exchange are connected both to a long tradition of political thought and to current intellectual, political, and ideological fashion. Exchange visions of politics and governance have roots in the doctrines of Greek political theory and seventeenth-century social contract theory. They currently dominate a large fraction of the academic and policy discussions of governance. As we shall suggest below, these ideas seem to us incomplete, but they represent a familiar and coherent supplement to those with which we will be primarily concerned. Far from foolish or malevolent, they illuminate important truths about the governance of political systems.

Exchange Conceptions of Political Action

In an exchange conception, governance is seen as neutral among potential human preferences. It involves the facilitation of voluntary exchanges among political actors rather than the pursuit of a particular moral imperative or a particular constellation of individual wants. Theories in which exchange is the basis for living together are characteristic of many liberal traditions emphasizing political orders based on voluntary agreements among autonomous individuals. They seem almost self-evidently part of contemporary Western social and political life. The standard metaphors are metaphors of interests, bargaining, and coalition formation (Taylor, 1975; Riker, 1982).

Exchange theories of politics are special cases of rational actor theories of human behavior. They presume that individuals pursue their interests by considering alternative bargains in terms of their anticipated consequences for individual preferences and choosing those combinations of bargains that serve their preferences best. Political actors are imagined to have preferences, or interests, that are consistent, stable, and exogenous to the political system. Individual political actors are seen as assessing the probable consequences of any proposed policy (exchange) in terms of their own preference functions and agreeing only to those that promise subjective improvement for themselves relative to continuing the status quo. Collective action requires a willingness on the part of sufficient numbers of political actors to make a change. It depends on the negotiation of bargains and side-payments among potential trading partners (Harsanyi, 1977; Coase, 1994).

Modern exchange theories of politics are theories of bounded rationality. They assume that reality is only dimly perceived. Not all alternatives are considered, and not all consequences are known with certainty. As a result, theories of choice are theories of search, theories of the process by which actors reduce ignorance about available alternatives and their consequences (Cyert and March, 1963; March, 1988a). The presumption, not always stated, is that search activities reduce the disparity between what is believed to be true and what is actually true. Rational theories of search presume that since search is costly, rational actors will not insist on knowing everything but will act on the basis of incomplete information. They assume that investments in search will be made up to the point at which the expected marginal return from search is equal to its expected marginal cost in terms of other opportunities forgone.

Modern theories of rational exchange are also, for the most part, theories of strategic behavior. That is, they do not imagine a shared preference function or common will as a basis for action within a collectivity. Rather, they assume that there is conflict of interest among individual actors and that collective action stems from the coercion of mutual self-interest, not from shared values or preferences. Along the way to self-interested bargains, conflict produces a host of strategic actions—lying, cheating, and stealing—that are guided by calculations of their utility for the individual actor (Riker, 1982, 1984, 1986).

The ability of any particular actor to realize his or her desires in such a system of exchange depends on what the desires are, what exchangeable resources that actor possesses, and what political rights he or she has. Wants that are consistent with the wants of others are more easily satisfied than wants that compete with others. The greater the exchangeable resources (initial endowments) and the more rights to political voice, the stronger the trading position. One side of the exchange story emphasizes the Pareto-improving qualities of exchange and gains from trade—the achievement of outcomes that make at least some people better off and no one worse off than before the exchanges (Axelrod and Keohane, 1985; Shepsle, 1986;

Garrett and Weingast, 1993). A second side of the exchange story emphasizes the coercive qualities of "voluntary" exchange when initial endowments are unequal, in which case "exchange" means that one group of actors imposes its will on other groups by virtue of its trading advantage (Moe, 1990; Krasner, 1991; Sened, 1991; Olsen, 1992b).

Exchange Conceptions of Political Change

For the most part, rational actor ideas about political development interpret institutional and political change as driven largely by anticipated or experienced changes in the social and physical environment. Institutions come to match their environments (Shepsle, 1989). One variant of the matching idea sees changes as reflecting the imposition of the future on the present. Theories of rational action, including theories of rational conflict (e.g., game theory), theories of strategic action, and theories of power all assume that forms and procedures are shaped by expectations and intentions. Human expectations and wills enact the future (Shepsle and Weingast, 1987). A second variant of the matching idea portrays the present as a residue of the past. In theories of learning, culture, and natural selection, the present encapsulates the past. Present institutions are summaries of past experience (Baum and Singh, 1994).

The argument is not always made explicit, but the spirit is Spencerian. A process that encodes experience in a reasonably systematic and adaptive way is assumed to lead to improvement in fit and ultimately to the one best fit. Observed institutional structures are assumed to exist and persist because they are (or become) well adapted to their environments, producing favorable results. The basic idea is that expectations about the future and experiences of the past are efficient in converting environmental requirements into institutional forms and practices. Thus, it can be assumed that a population of institutions will come to match its environment and that differences between any two populations of institutions are attributable to differences between their environments. In such a formulation, institutional structure is implicit in the constraints of an exogenous environment (Moe and Caldwell, 1993).

Modern students of governance in the voluntary exchange tradition are of two minds with respect to whether this process can be assumed to result in a unique, stable match between institutions and environments. For some of them—particularly those who wish to describe political institutions as necessary solutions to exogenous political problems—the efficiency of historical processes is vital. The institutional rules, coalitions, and policies that evolve have to be seen as implicit in the political situation that exists. Such a position treats governance as part of an inexorable process, without an independent role (Downs, 1957; Shepslc and Weingast, 1987). A somewhat milder version of the position would emphasize the "long-run" efficiency of history but would allow for some "short-run" perturbations that might be of interest to "short-run" historians (Moe, 1984, 1990).

For others—particularly those who would give some role to conscious governance—a political solution is subject to, but not uniquely specified by, constraints. Although institutional and normative rights and rules limit the set of possible political coalitions, practices, and policies, they do not determine them completely. Although distributions of preferences and resources among the politically active make some imaginable programs impossible to achieve, those distributions are consistent with a number of alternative outcomes. And although features of the environment require some response, they do not compel a unique response (March and Olsen, 1984; Krasner, 1988). The resulting indeterminacy in outcomes within a particular environmental context provides a possible role for deliberate political manipulation. It directs attention to such things as agenda effects, the order of presentation of alternative policies or coalitions (Riker, 1980, 1993; Kingdon, 1984). Some such confidence in the indeterminacy of environmental matching is necessary for political theorists who want to imagine that governance is something other than an elaborate human orchestration of necessary adjustments of political systems to environmental requirements.

Exchange Conceptions of Governance

The core artistry of politics in an exchange perspective is the crafting of winning coalitions and policies. A political system is judged by the ability of its institutions and practices to discover and implement changes in policies that leave at least one person better off and no person worse off, as measured by individual subjective preference functions (the Pareto-improving criterion). Democratic governance is seen as converting individual wants and resources into collective action by discovering and implementing policy coalitions that arrange Pareto-improving exchanges among citizens.

This process of coalition and policy formation depends on three features of the political world that are seen as exogenous to governance, as vital to the practice of politics but outside its ken. The first is the structure of rights and rules within which the process occurs. In this tradition, rights and rules may be seen as rational solutions to a longer-term meta game, but they are not generally treated as subject to contemporary conscious choice or influence (Axelrod, 1984; Sugden, 1986; Kreps, 1990; North, 1990). The second feature is the distribution of preferences (interests) among political actors. The process responds to preferences, but it neither creates nor affects them (Becker and Stigler, 1977). The third feature is the distribution of resources and capabilities among actors. As in any other voluntary exchange process, the outcomes of political bargaining and coalition formation depend critically on the distribution of exchangeable resources and capabilities. That distribution may be seen as subject to public policy, but it is treated as exogenous to the coalition formation and exchange process (Coase, 1994).

Governance within an exchange tradition is seen as the management of political exchange within those three constraints. Instead of imagining that political actors are always fully activated and always fully cognizant of all of their interests and the interests of others, they can be seen as operating within a reduced set of activated concerns and consciousnesses (Keohane, 1984; Coleman, 1990; Moe, 1990). Numerous opportunities exist for affecting the specific coalition that is organized or policy that is chosen, for discovering new possibilities for voluntary exchange and trade. The process by which some identities and interests become salient and others lose salience is, from this perspective, a central process of governance (Hall, 1989; Goldstein and Keohane, 1993). Similarly, governance involves influencing the process by which conflict is defined along some possible lines of cleavage rather than others (Schattschneider, 1960), and the process by which some alternatives are considered rather than others (Bachrach and Baratz, 1962; Kingdon, 1984; Stone, 1988). These conceptions of efficient voluntary exchange, contracts, and coalitions are now almost conventional in political thought.

ADVOCATES AND GOVERNORS

As long as preferences, resources, rights, and rules do not uniquely determine the coalition to be formed or the policy to be adopted, there is a role for conscious governance that attempts to influence the particular set of coalitions, programs, and policies that are realized, and through them the ultimate social outcomes that are achieved. We can distinguish two versions of governance in the exchange tradition. The first is what might be called the role of the *advocate*. The role of the advocate is to improve the chance that particular policies will be pursued by a winning coalition. An individual who looks for others to form a coalition to further his or her interests, or who engages in strategic action designed to improve the prospects for being on a winning coalition or for having the winning coalition adopt favorable policies, is intervening to further a particular set of interests.

The second role is what might be called the role of the *governor*. The role of the governor is to improve conditions for discovering and arranging winning coalitions. Unlike the advocate, the governor does not seek to organize a winning coalition around a particular preferred set of policies. Rather, the governor seeks to reduce limitations on the capabilities of political actors to organize winning coalitions. Thus, a strategy of information restriction that is attractive to some particular individual bargainer, or advocate, will not generally be attractive to a governor.

Exchange-based political institutions are justified by their successes in achieving political efficiency within existing constraints and opportunities, particularly the constraints imposed by constitutions, the distributions of individual preferences and resources, and the opportunities introduced by the shifting capabilities of institutions. Such successes are not routine. The complexity of modern society makes it easy for individuals and groups to overlook policies and exchanges that might be Pareto-preferred to existing arrangements. The design and realization of political agreements involves affecting complicated and often ambiguous understandings. Even more, shifts in individual tastes and changes in the capabilities of institutions, reflected particularly in improvements in the technology and organization of collective action, continually threaten the stability and efficiency of political coalitions and policies.

It is possible to imagine that competition among advocates effectively performs the role of governor, that ambition and cleverness in the service of contending interests assure an efficient process of discovery and implementation. Such a proposition, however, is a speculation to be demonstrated rather than assumed, and ordinary experience and observations speak against it. There are information restrictions on the search for possible coalitions and on the coordination and implementation of agreements. The political brokerage function often seems unable to discover winning coalitions, or slow to do so. It strains credulity and contradicts what is known about evolutionary and adaptive processes in general to imagine that existing political procedures are optimal solutions to the information problems of coalition discovery and implementation (Baum and Singh, 1994).

Within this view, the role of governance, therefore, is twofold: On the one hand, it is to reduce the chance that viable policies are overlooked, either because they are not considered or because information on their viability is misleading. On the other hand, it is to reduce the chance that an inferior policy portfolio preempts a superior one by virtue of some quirk in the process (e.g., the order of presentation). The problems and objectives are familiar both to standard books on parliamentary procedure and to modern game-theoretic treatments of majority-rule games.

For a political process to claim efficiency within this tradition it must assure that collective political actions represent the final step in a complex process in which all possible coalitions and policies have, in some sense, been discovered, that there exists no unconsidered coalition and policy portfolio that would have been chosen if considered. In order to make such assurances, it is necessary that the rewards for collusive suppression of a potentially winning set of policies be less than the rewards of political victory for at least one necessary party to the collusion; that the rewards for the effort of discovering and negotiating winning coalitions and policies be great enough to guarantee that all such policies are, in fact, considered; and that any potentially winning coalition and policy portfolio have sufficient access to the political system to be considered actively by the relevant political actors. Such assurances cannot be made in the real world of politics, but efforts to approximate them produce the paraphernalia of modern politics—for example, political organizations, interest groups, lobbyists, the media. They constitute the indispensable institutional apparatus of a modern political system of exchange.

Voluntary exchange political systems depend on political brokerage for the discovery and negotiation of Pareto-improving political deals. The effectiveness of political brokerage depends on some fairly elementary factors (March, 1970). First, it depends on the size of the polity. The greater the number of political actors, the greater the brokerage requirements. Second, it depends on the political experience, education, and income of individuals. The greater the average political experience, education, and income of political actors, the more the brokerage function can be assumed by individuals rather than by special brokers. Third, it depends on the munificence of resources in the system. The greater the spare resources, the less brokerage time and talent required. Fourth, it depends on collective political experience. As a political system gains experience with political brokerage within a particular society, it becomes more competent at identifying and arranging trades. Fifth, it depends on social and political institutions that facilitate the enforcement of political bargains. Enforcement of political agreements depends on trust in their execution, trust that can be generated by a set of relations among individuals, as in a small homogeneous society, or by broad acceptance of a legal and administrative system.

Thus, with fixed rewards for political brokerage, exchange politics will function better in small polities than in large ones; better in polities populated by well-educated, rich individuals with extensive political experience than in those with less-educated, less experienced, and poorer citizens; better in good times than in bad; better in older democracies than in younger ones; and better where there is shared confidence in understandings than where there is not. Alternatively, we can observe that to maintain a fixed quality of the political process, governors must invest more in brokerage in large polities than in small ones, more in poor polities than in rich ones, more in inexperienced, poorly educated polities than in experienced, well-educated ones, more in bad times than in good, more in younger democracies than in older ones, and more where trust is low than where it is high. Unfortunately, it appears to be true that for the most part modern political systems do precisely the opposite.

BUILDING COALITIONS

Within the rational exchange framework, governance involves contributing to the discovery and implementation of winning coalitions among individuals whose desires are consistent with one another. The process of *discovery* is normally seen as involving search. Self-interested political actors look for others with complementary interests. They try to inhibit the discovery of complementarities that might exist between their partners and their competitors. At the same time, self-interested brokers of political coalitions look for coalitions to arrange, hoping to secure for themselves some fraction of the Pareto-improvement that they affect. The process of *implementation* is dominated by the difficulties of enforcing coalition agreements when the exchanges involved are made over time, may be difficult to specify in advance, may involve different people at different times, and may have to accommodate a shifting distribution of resources (Weingast and Marshall, 1988). The twin processes of discovery and implementation lead to a history of coalitions and public policies.

Since the processes by which coalitions are discovered and implemented can be specified in several different ways, it is hard to say anything very general about them. It would be convenient if it were possible to assume historical efficiency, that is, that a coalition uniquely appropriate to environmental conditions would necessarily appear ultimately. However, the conditions for a unique equilibrium are fairly restrictive. Under rather general conditions, the discovery and implementation of political coalitions fail to reach a stable equilibrium, reach one of many quasi-stable local equilibria, or take so long to reach a stable equilibrium that the chance that the external conditions will remain unchanged is nil (Riker, 1980; Shepsle, 1986). As a result, the winning coalitions and resulting policies that will be realized in particular historical moments are not uniquely determined by the constraints or prior conditions but appear to depend on somewhat indeterminate paths of coalition discovery and implementation. It is precisely these indeterminacies that make governance an important concern within exchange theories of politics.

SHAPING POLICIES

The central process involved in building a political coalition is the creation of an agreement among political actors that specifies the trades among them. These agreements may involve a variety of understandings, threats, and promises, but they are typically imagined to be organized around a set of public policies that will be adopted by a coalition if it is successful in gaining power. Thus, contemporary theories of politics are theories of policy construction. Each potential policy, program, or manifesto is a portfolio of commitments to action. It is supported by a coalition having certain political resources and rights to political authority. A necessary, but not sufficient, condition for a policy to be adopted is that its portfolio have support from individuals with political rights adequate to satisfy the rules defining a winning coalition (e.g., in a majority-rule system, that it be able to secure a majority vote).

Types of coalition policies. There are three quite different pure forms of such policies (March, 1994b). The first is a policy that finds support among a group of like-minded people. All want the same thing, what they want is captured by the policy, and their combined political resources are adequate to ensure its adoption and implementation. If we ignore, as we should not ultimately, various forms of strategic action that complicate the simple picture, this kind of policy seems a straightforward manifestation of the shared-interest spirit of politics.

The second pure form of policy is one that reflects a weighted average of the wants of similar people. The wants of each are arrayed along some continuum, the policy reflects the weighted average of the winning coalition members' wants where the weights are proportional to their political resources, and the resulting policy is acceptable to members of a coalition having collective resources adequate to win. There are strategic issues that complicate this picture also, but this kind of policy seems a straightforward manifestation of the preference-pooling or power-weighting spirit of politics (Dahl, 1956).

The third pure form of policy is a policy portfolio that finds support among a group of people, each of whom is indifferent to the policies desired by others. Each of the individual wants is captured by one element in the portfolio, and the combined political resources of the coalition are adequate to ensure the adoption and implementation of the portfolio, provided there are no defections. Through such a portfolio, a political actor with a special interest in a smoke-free environment may join with another who has a special interest in a football stadium to make what amounts to a contract to support each other's proposals. Once again, there are complications of strategic behavior, but in a general way this kind of policy seems a straightforward manifestation of the logrolling spirit of politics (Ferejohn, 1974, 1986).

Logrolls combine individuals with complementary interests into viable coalitions, but they are invitations to disappointment. Support that is strategic (as most support in a logroll is) tends to be unreliable. Coalitions that are created to make a decision cannot be relied on to deal effectively with postdecision complications. Logrolls create a need for trust, but they are structured in such a way as to remove a primary basis for trust—the sharing of values. They involve individuals who are mutually indifferent to each other's concerns and are bound together simply by the incentive structure of the coalition. Perhaps for this reason, logrolls appear to be less common in politics than might be expected (Weingast and Marshall, 1988).

Each of these forms can be seen as a variation on an exchange perspective. Clearly, any conception of coalition through exchange gives an advantage to coalitions involving individuals with complementary demands. A coalition among like-minded people is probably the most efficient, provided the like-mindedness can be sustained. A coalition among individuals with mutually indifferent demands is a close contender. Preference pooling (the second form) is more complicated but can be seen as a variation on a Newtonian power model in which resources are exchanged to gather power, and advantage goes to individuals with resources desired by others.

Complications in policy coalitions. These simple forms of policy port-folios are considerably complicated in practice by a host of real-world features. As examples, we mention three critical complications: First, most portfolios are mixtures of talk and action. The talk includes declarations of intent, proclamations of public virtue, and assertions of public policy whose main impact is on the symbolic standing of particular values or groups. The action includes specific allocations of resources, specific implemented regulations, and specific creations of institutions. Both talk and action are impor-tant politically, and their relative importance varies over time, over political actors, and over kinds of policies. Some things can be said politically but not done; others can be done but not said (Brunsson, 1985, 1989).

Second, winning coalitions involve the mobilization of resources as well as the possession of them. Political actors have many de-mands on their attention. Not everything can be attended to. Some people and issues have easier access to some political arenas than to others. As a result, a winning coalition in one arena at one time is quite likely to be a losing coalition in another arena or at another time. Policies are adopted but not implemented. Inconsistent policies are adopted. This instability is experienced as frustrating to almost all political actors, but it gives a certain advantage to those who can maintain attention persistently over time and space (Cohen, March, and Olsen, 1972; March and Olsen, 1976).

Third, political bargains often involve trades across time in which the exact terms are difficult to specify in advance and the capabilities of the partners to fulfill expectations in the future are uncertain. This produces some characteristically ambiguous features of political exchange. Since political actors have highly unpredictable needs for future support, they are likely to be willing to "bank" favors—to offer current support in return for vaguely specified expectations of possible future support. Since such favors are subject to substantial ambiguity and discounting over time, politics can become a vast in-surance scheme in which many more favors are provided than are requested (March, 1981b).

Exploiting indeterminacies. The willingness and capability of citizens to object to the policies and practices of coercive governmental institutions play a critical role in regulating governmental power. The significance of consent has been demonstrated repeatedly in modern times, particularly in societies with pretensions to democracy. Even such powerful instruments of coercion as armies, secret police, and prisons are dependent on some measure of popular tolerance. Consent is provided, however, in a world in which the indeterminacies produced by ambiguity, attention, and the mixture of talk and action are embedded in a broader property of policy portfolio politics. None of these forms of policy guarantees that any viable policy will be found or that, if a viable policy is found, only one such policy will be found. The number of alternative policy portfolios and the number of alternative possible coalitions are both very large. The number of *winning* combinations of portfolios and coalitions is much smaller—indeed may be zero. It is unlikely to be precisely one.

Because winning coalitions and associated policies are unlikely to be unique, the definition and discovery of alternatives can be shaped so as to influence which winning coalition is actually formed and which policy is actually enacted. Opportunities for shaping the discovery and implementation of winning coalitions and policies are not limited to formal authorities, of course, and one of the responsibilities of governance is to provide competitive arenas for the development of coalition and policy options. Students of governance are particularly concerned with identifying techniques for developing and maintaining an inventory of alternative coalitions and policies and for focusing political attention on a few alternatives within that inventory (Kingdon, 1984; Baumgartner and Jones, 1993).

Many of these techniques, however, give an advantage to existing governmental authorities. They can exploit the power of government to proclaim, interpret, and enforce specific policy solutions. The same coercive capabilities that allow legislatures, courts, and governmental agencies to function as effective instruments of the rule of law and popular sovereignty generally give them the capability to manage choices within the set of viable policy alternatives. They bind future actions through laws, enforceable contracts, and path-dependent histories. They can preempt consideration of many alternatives, as long as the advantages of coordinated collective action are substantial and the level of prior agreement on a particular alternative is small.

The institutions and realities of democracy described here narrow the meaning of consent as a defining principle. In particular, the requirement of consent is different from a requirement of prior conscious approval. Governance is made significant not by the fact that governments can do whatever they choose, because they cannot, but by the fact that there are policies and practices that will be accepted if proclaimed and enforced even though they will not be chosen through undirected debate or majority vote. Similarly, actions that secure the consent of the governed at one time effectively limit the options for objection by the governed at a subsequent time. In any democracy, the vast majority of ongoing collective rules are consented to in a way that gives a substantial advantage to the status quo. This "first mover" advantage also exists within the process of debate and voting. Control over the agenda and over the sequence of presentation of alternatives is an important factor in determining the policies adopted within a legislative system (Riker, 1980, 1993).

POLITICAL RIGHTS AND RULES

In a rational exchange definition of a political order, there is conflict of interest among political actors. Individuals are self-interested and seek the best possible personal outcome, given the distribution of preferences and resources. They participate in politics in order to make favorable bargains. Through politics, preexisting interests are organized into winning coalitions that improve the lot of their members. Political systems embody a structure of rights, rules, norms, and procedures that regulate this process of bargaining, coalition, and exchange (North, 1990; Garrett and Weingast, 1993). Rights and rules include rights to legitimate formal authority and the rules determining a winning coalition, especially the extent to which the requirements for victory depend not only on the level of popular support but also on the nature of the proposed public policy. They include rules regulating the conversion of nonpolitical resources (e.g., money) into political resources (e.g., votes). They include rules enforcing agreements among coalition partners. Political rules for regulating political exchange are manifested not only in formal institutions but also within the political culture of the community. Differences in the position of the rule of law, the sanctity of elections, and the honesty of officials are not due entirely to differences in formal rules but come from political traditions. In some societies, people obey traffic laws, pay taxes, and abandon public office gracefully after political defeat. In others, they do not.

Rules regulating legitimate authority. Systems of democratic governance organize consent through a system of constitutional rights and rules that regulate the formation of coalitions and specify the bases of legitimate power. For example, democracies provide current citizens with a right to vote and make decisions by some procedure that counts votes without regard to the identity of the voter. The details of the rules vary from one system to another in important ways, and so consequently do the resulting processes. Governance within a parliamentary system based on single-member constituencies with plurality elections is different from governance within a list system of proportional representation. And both are different from governance within a system of single-party rule or a plebiscitary monarchy.

Much of the technical discussion of governance within a voluntary exchange vision confines itself to a minimal specification of rules, typically to a one person/one vote, majority-rule system and to minimal restrictions on exchange beyond the Pareto-preferred criterion rules. Most theorists of democratic political orders, on the other hand, would expand the specification to include an assortment of other rules. For example, Dahl (1980) mentions several fundamental rights and rules necessary for a democratic process: open inquiry, discussion, enlightened understanding, equal consideration, effective participation, and a decision reached by some system of voting that respects the essential equality of the citizens.

Rules regulating coalition formation. Systems of voluntary political exchange require some shared understanding of what are, and are not, exchangeable commodities. In general, the rules of politics make policy support an exchangeable commodity. It is normally, though not always, assumed to be appropriate for two political actors to enter into an agreement by which each is bound to support some specific project of the other. Similarly, it is normally assumed to be appropriate to enter into more general agreements by which each member of a group is bound to support the policies adopted by a majority of the group. On the other hand, money is not a legitimately exchangeable commodity in political coalition-building in most democratic systems. It is not normally appropriate to trade political action for money or to trade policy support for money. Although such exchanges occur often and in some cases appear to be endemic (e.g., bribery of voters or officials in some systems, political campaign contribution investments in legislators in others), they are generally viewed as illegitimate or unfortunate.

Modern political systems have clouded the prohibition of political trading in money (i.e., the distinction between political corruption and political bargaining) by emphasizing the creation of policy portfolios that have direct financial consequences for individual citizens. Certain kinds of actions that offer concrete financial rewards to coalition members (e.g., the buying of support) are discouraged in many polities, but other kinds (e.g., redistributional taxation, subsidies) are not. The usual distinction is between explicit particularistic alienation of a political right by an individual citizen, which is ordinarily discouraged, and implicit revocable leasing of a right by a group of citizens, which is more likely to be condoned.

Rules regulating political contracts. Realizing the terms of political trade requires the enforcement of trading agreements. Political actors interact as strangers united by contracts and alliances. Institutional rules secure their obedience because they reduce uncertainty and transaction costs, and make it possible to capture gains of trade. Some assurance must be provided that the person making the first "payment" can be confident of receiving the agreed-upon "return." The prototype is the simultaneous exchange of hostages, but that procedure is often awkward or impossible, so in practice parties seek some guarantor, often the state.

Effective guarantees of agreements with exchange systems depend on the existence of a reliably enforceable contract between the parties or the existence of a high level of trust. Political negotiation involves trades that are difficult to specify completely at the time they are made, for example, the exchange of specific support now for some unspecified support at some unspecified future date. Formal contracts are difficult to write. The result has been a heavy dependence on political trust, along with considerable doubt about its existence. Some traditional political institutions, most notably political parties and parliamentary codes of procedure, can be seen as making the enforcement of agreements more reliable (Krehbiel, 1991; Cox and McCubbins, 1993; Gilligan and Krehbiel, 1993).

Contemporary political systems have further complicated this already relatively fragile structure of rules for exchange. The complications are seen most vividly in discussions of the so-called implementation problem, the concatenation of political maneuver after formal adoption of a law or policy (Pressman and Wildavsky, 1974; Bardach, 1977; Brodkin, 1990). The rule of law and informal political understandings are strained by the inclination of the political system to be continually reinterpreting and renegotiating political agreements. This strain, in turn, leads to political "contracts" that must be negotiated with only modest expectation of the reliability of exchanges over time, a feature that particularly reduces the options for organizing coalitions that involve long-term commitments.

Rules as solutions to an optimization problem. It is tempting to imagine that the processes by which the rules of politics have evolved make them optimal solutions to problems of institutional design. Insofar as we can assume that the processes of rule evolution shape rules in a uniquely optimal way, we are inclined to give a privileged position to existing rules. Different rules will arise in different contexts, reflecting different solutions to different problems—each uniquely appropriate to its own situation. They can be seen as encoding historical experience in a way that gives them greater intelligence than can be understood explicitly by contemporary analysts. As a result, we look for rational intelligence in existing rules, and finding some plausible rational interpretation of them, come to view such an interpretation as having validity (McCubbins, Noll, and Weingast, 1987; Weingast and Marshall, 1988).

Such presumptions have had appeal not only for generations of conservative political theorists but also for their contemporary cousins, rational choice theorists of political institutions and functionalist theorists of society. Since there is intelligence in the processes of rationality, learning and selection, the instinct to look for manifestations of that intelligence in existing rules and institutions seems unexceptionable. But, as we shall observe below, the optimal matching of rules and institutions to environments can not be guaranteed.

Limits to Exchange Criteria for Governance

Any treatment of governance must include substantial elements of an exchange perspective to be plausible. Individual political actors sometimes pursue objectives and calculate consequences. Processes of change sometimes lead to relatively stable, unique equilibria. A significant part of governance consists in negotiating and sustaining winning coalitions based on mutually acceptable exchanges, and in facilitating such political brokerage by others. Many features of rights, rules, and resources can be treated as given exogenously, taken for granted and not explained.

Nevertheless, we think those perspectives are seriously incomplete, that they need to be modified and supplemented. From the point of view of political theory, efficient exchange visions of governance are particularly limited by the criterion for collective action that the theory postulates. Legitimate collective action is restricted to Pareto-preferred deviations from the status quo, and any such deviations are seen as desirable. There are numerous objections to exclusive emphasis on such a criterion as a definition of politics, most notably:

1. Among the large number of dramatically different "Pareto optimal solutions," the one that an efficient exchange process discovers is notoriously dependent on the initial distribution of endowments (resources, capabilities). Disparities in wealth, power, and competence make voluntary trades suspect as a basis for social action (Anderson, 1990, p. 122). Major considerations of the appropriateness of initial endowments are sacrificed to relatively minor considerations of finding voluntary trades. This treatment of initial endowments not only puts distributional questions off the political agenda, it exaggerates the importance of current citizens. It sustains initial inequities and subordinates political actors of the future to those of the present.

2. The inviolate position of voluntary exchange is questionable (Walzer, 1983). Most theories of government assume the appropriateness of restrictions on voluntary trade in the name of the inalienability of certain rights and restrictions on intersector (e.g., economic-political or economic-judicial) exchange. And involuntary exchanges, based on some form of interpersonal comparison of preferences and judgments about the commonweal, are usually seen as fundamental to political action.

3. In some circumstances an exchange-based political system—even if operating perfectly in a technical sense—will lead to unfortunate results in a moral sense (Polanyi, 1944). Many students of political philosophy insist on a moral criterion for collective action, asking that a system of governance contribute not only to voluntary exchange of prior endowments but also to justice, a good society, beauty, harmony. There is no guarantee that virtue is correlated perfectly with the distribution of endowments (Sen, 1990).

4. The emphasis on self-interested exchange as the basis for interpersonal relations has the potential advantage of being consistent with a self-seeking human nature, but it has the potential disadvantage of creating or accentuating that nature. Some philosophies of human existence portray self-interest as the highest moral principle (Mandeville, 1755; Smith, 1776), but the more common claim is that the pursuit of self-interest is an unavoidable limitation of human motivation. From the latter point of view, a focus on self-interested exchange is a necessary accommodation to a flawed human nature. If human nature is seen less as an immutable gift from God than as a consequence of the expectations we have for it, political institutions cannot take human nature as a given but must accept responsibility for their involvement in its creation.

By emphasizing the arrangement of Pareto-improving coalitions and policies, exchange theories tend to lose sight of those aspects of governance that focus on the development and transformation of constraints, on the ways the rights, rules, preferences, and resources that structure political outcomes are created, sustained, and reformed. They eliminate from the agenda for research and discussion much of what political science has traditionally found interesting (Moe, 1990; Petracca, 1991).

INSTITUTIONAL PERSPECTIVES

Historically, analyses of politics and political systems have involved more an interweaving of metaphors than a coherent theory or even an arena for competition among alternative theories. Those analyses have taken the traditions of Aristotle and Tocqueville combined with those of Hobbes and Bentham and grafted onto those roots elements of the ideas of Freud, Marx, Durkheim, Adam Smith, and Darwin. In recent years this pragmatic approach to ideas has been expressed most conspicuously in efforts to reconcile the exchange conception of politics just outlined with an institutional conception that builds on jurisprudential, sociological, and psychological conceptions of identity, and modern organization theory. In textbook writings about political institutions the term "institution" often refers only to systems that are organized formally, such as a national legislature or courts. We use the term in a more general sense to refer not only to legislatures, executives, and judiciaries but also to systems of law, social organization (such as the media, markets, or the family), and identities or roles (such as "citizen," "official," or "individual").

The Basic Ideas

Contests over the meaning of the word "institutional" are easy to see not only among academic disciplines and research traditions but also within them (March and Olsen, 1984).* The word is clearly evocative enough to have captured attention, but "institutional" seems more notable for its capacity to engender variations and typologies of meaning than for its precision. Nevertheless, most people who write about institutions or the new institutionalism in social science

---

*Consider, for example, the treatments in political science (Evans, Rueschemeyer, and Skocpol, 1985; Shepsle and Weingast, 1987; Lepsius, 1988; March and Olsen, 1989; Shepsle, 1989; Moe, 1990; Apter, 1991; Grafstein, 1992; Steinmo, Thelen, and Longstreeth, 1992; Weaver and Rockman, 1993; Orren and Skowronek, 1994), sociology (Meyer and Rowan, 1977; Scott, 1987; Thomas *et al.*, 1987; Hechter, Opp, and Wippler, 1990; Powell and DiMaggio, 1991), anthropology (Douglas, 1986), economics (Furubotn and Richter, 1984, 1993; North, 1990; Eggertsson, 1990), and law (Broderick, 1970; MacCormick and Weinberger, 1986; Smith, 1988).

share a few key ideas. An institutional supplement to voluntary exchange conceptions of politics and governance is built around:

1. A view of *human action* as driven less by anticipation of its uncertain consequences and preferences for them than by a logic of appropriateness reflected in a structure of rules and conceptions of identities.
2. A view of *change and history* as matching institutions, behaviors, and contexts in ways that take time and have multiple, path-dependent equilibria, thus as being responsive to timely interventions to affect the meander of history and susceptible to deliberate efforts to improve institutional adaptiveness.
3. A view of *governance* as extending beyond negotiating coalitions within given constraints of rights, rules, preferences, and resources to shaping those constraints, as well as constructing meaningful accounts of politics, history, and self that are not only bases for instrumental action but also central concerns of life.

In an institutional perspective, governance involves creating capable political actors who understand how political institutions work and are able to deal effectively with them (Anderson, 1990, pp. 196–97). It involves building and supporting cultures of rights and rules that make possible the agreements represented in coalition understandings. It involves building and supporting identities, preferences, and resources that make a polity possible. It involves building and supporting a system of meaning and an understanding of history.

Institutional Conceptions of Political Action

Institutional theories supplement exchange theories of political action in two primary ways: First, they emphasize the role of institutions in defining the terms of rational exchange. Rational action depends on subjective perceptions of alternatives, their consequences, and their evaluations. Pictures of reality and feelings about it are constructed within social and political institutions (March and Simon, 1958; Cyert and March, 1963). Second, without denying the reality of calculations and anticipations of consequences, institutional conceptions see such calculations and anticipations as occurring within a broader framework of rules, roles, and identities (North, 1981, 1990; Shepsle and Weingast, 1987; Shepsle, 1989, 1990). At the limit, self-interested calculation can be seen as simply one of many systems of rules that may be socially legitimized under certain circumstances (Taylor, 1985, ch. 7; Nauta, 1992).

INSTITUTIONAL BASES OF RATIONAL EXCHANGE

In exchange theories, political action (decision-making, resource allocation) is a result of bargains negotiated among individual actors pursuing individual interests. Institutional theories focus on the behavioral and social bases of information and preferences in rational choice. They picture preferences as inconsistent, changing, and at least partly endogenous, formed within political institutions. Interests are seen as shaped by institutional arrangements and maintained by institutional processes of socialization and co-optation (Selznick, 1949; Lipset and Rokkan, 1967; Eisenstadt and Rokkan, 1973; Wildavsky, 1987; Sunstein, 1990; Greber and Jackson, 1993). Institutional theories similarly emphasize the ways in which institutions shape the definition of alternatives and influence the perception and construction of the reality within which action takes place. Institutional capabilities and structures affect the flow of information, the kinds of search undertaken, and the interpretations made of the results (Cyert and March, 1963; March and Olsen, 1989; Olsen and Peters, 1995a).

Awareness of the embedding of rationality in an institutional context has led to a considerable restructuring of theories of rational exchange, including political theories based on an exchange perspective. This restructuring has come to picture rational exchange as framed by and dependent on political norms, identities, and institutions. Insofar as political actors act by making choices, they act within definitions of alternatives, consequences, preferences (interests), and strategic options that are strongly affected by the institutional context in which they find themselves. Exploring the ways in which institutions affect the definition of alternatives, consequences, and preferences; the cleavages that produce conflict; and the enforcement of bargains has become a major activity within modern choice theory (Laitin, 1985).

RULES AND IDENTITIES

Institutional conceptions of action, however, differ from rational models in a more fundamental way. The core notion is that life is organized by sets of shared meanings and practices that come to be taken as given. Political actors act and organize themselves in accordance with rules and practices that are socially constructed, publicly known, anticipated, and accepted. Actions of individuals and collectivities occur within these shared meanings and practices, which can be called identities and institutions (Meyer and Rowan, 1977; March and Olsen, 1984, 1989; North, 1986). Institutions and identities constitute and legitimize political actors and provide them with consistent behavioral rules, conceptions of reality, standards of assessment, affective ties, and endowments, and thereby with a capacity for purposeful action (Douglas, 1986; Thompson, Ellis, and Wildavsky, 1990).

In the institutional story, people act, think, feel, and organize themselves on the basis of exemplary or authoritative (and sometimes competing or conflicting) rules derived from socially constructed identities and roles. Along the way, political institutions create rules regulating the possession and use of political rights and resources. Even the conception of an autonomous agent, with a particularistic way of self-understanding, feeling, acting, and expression, is a conception of an acquired identity, a socialized understanding of self and others (Taylor, 1985, p. 205). In such an institutional perspective, the axiomatics for political action begin not with subjective consequences and preferences but with rules, identities, and roles; and a theory that treats intentional, calculative action as the basis for understanding human behavior is incomplete if it does not attend to the ways in which identities and institutions are constituted, sustained, and interpreted (Friedrich, 1950; Tussman, 1960; March, 1994b).

Action is taken on the basis of a logic of appropriateness associated with roles, routines, rights, obligations, standard operating procedures, and practices (Burns and Flam, 1987). Appropriateness refers to a match of behavior to a situation. The match may be based on experience, expert knowledge, or intuition, in which case it is often called "recognition" to emphasize the cognitive process of pairing problem-solving action correctly to a problem situation (March and Simon, 1993, pp. 10–13). The match may be based on role expectations, normative definitions of a role without significant attribution of moral virtue or problem-solving correctness to the resulting behavior (Sarbin and Allen, 1968, p. 550). The match may also carry with it a connotation of essence, so that appropriate attitudes, behaviors, feelings, or preferences for a citizen, official, or farmer are those that are essential to being a citizen, official, or farmer—essential not in the instrumental sense of being necessary to perform a task or socially expected, nor in the sense of being an arbitrary definitional convention, but in the sense of that without which one cannot claim to be a proper citizen, official, or farmer.

Action as rule-based. Political institutions and rules matter. Most people in politics and political institutions follow rules most of the time if they can (Searing, 1991). The uncertainties they face are less uncertainties about consequences and preferences than they are uncertainties about the demands of identity. Rules and understandings frame thought, shape behavior, and constrain interpretation. Actions are expressions of what is appropriate, exemplary, natural, or acceptable behavior according to the (internalized) purposes, codes of rights and duties, practices, methods, and techniques of a constituent group and of a self.

The legal system, one of the key institutions of democratic polities, seeks to subject human conduct to rules that are general, stable, known, understandable, operational, and neither contradictory nor retroactive, rather than to the discretion and arbitrary power of authorities or those with exchangeable resources (Fuller, 1971). Institutionalized identities create individuals: citizens, officials, engineers, doctors, spouses (Dworkin, 1986). Institutionalized rules, duties, rights, and roles define acts as appropriate (normal, natural, right, good) or inappropriate (uncharacteristic, unnatural, wrong, bad).

The impact of rules of appropriateness and standard operating procedures in routine situations is well known (March and Simon, 1958; Cyert and March, 1963). But the logic of appropriateness is by no means limited to repetitive, routine worlds. It is also characteristic of human action in ill-defined, novel situations (Dynes, 1970;

Quarantelli and Dynes, 1977). Civil unrest, demands for comprehensive redistribution of political power and welfare, as well as political revolutions and major reforms often follow from identity-driven conceptions of appropriateness more than conscious calculations of costs and benefits (Lefort, 1988; Elster, 1989b). Appropriateness has overtones of morality, but it is in this context primarily a cognitive concept. Rules of action are derived from reasoning about the nature of the self. People act from understandings of what is essential, from self-conceptions and conceptions of society, and from images of proper behavior. Identities define the nature of things and are implemented by cognitive processes of interpretation and forming accounts (March and Olsen, 1989).

Rule-following can be viewed as contractual, an implicit agreement to act appropriately in return for being treated appropriately. Such a contractual view has led game theorists and some legal theorists to interpret norms and institutions as meta-game agreements (Shepsle, 1990; Gibbons, 1992), but the term "contract" is potentially misleading. The terms are often unclear enough to be better called a "pact" (Selznick, 1992) than a "contract," and socialization into rules and their appropriateness is ordinarily not a case of willful entering into an explicit contract (Van Maanen, 1976).

As a result, identities and rules assure neither consistency nor simplicity (Biddle, 1986; Berscheid, 1994). Defining an identity and achieving it require energy, thought, and capability. Fulfilling an identity through following appropriate rules involves matching a changing (and often ambiguous) set of contingent rules to a changing (and often ambiguous) set of situations. As a result, institutional approaches to behavior make a distinction between a rule and its behavioral realization in a particular instance (Apter, 1991; Thelen and Steinmo, 1992, p. 15). As they try to understand history and self, and as they try to improve the often confusing, uncertain, and ambiguous world they live in, individuals and collectivities interpret what rules and identities exist, which ones are relevant, and what different rules and identities demand in specific situations or spheres of behavior. Individuals may have a difficult time resolving conflicts among contending imperatives of appropriateness and among alternative concepts of the self. They may not know what to do. They also may know what to do but not have the capabilities to do it. They are limited by the complexities of the demands upon them and by the distribution and regulation of resources, competencies, and organizing capacities, that is, by the capability for acting appropriately.

The elements of openness in the interpretation of rules mean that while institutions structure politics, they ordinarily do not determine political behavior precisely. The processes through which rules are translated into actual behavior through constructive interpretation and available resources have to be specified. Processes of constructive interpretation, criticism, justification, and application of rules and identities, are processes familiar to the intellectual traditions of the law (Dworkin, 1986; Sunstein, 1990; Teubner, 1993). Such processes give specific content in specific situations both to such heroic identities as patriot or statesman and to such everyday identities as those of an accountant, police officer, or citizen (Kaufman, 1960; Van Maanen, 1973; Spradley and Mann, 1975).

Identities and emotions. Emotion is an aspect of human behavior. People have feelings. They experience joy and sorrow. They love and hate, cry and laugh. They feel anxiety, remorse, exhilaration, fear, regret, anticipation. They have emotional pains and excitements to which they respond and which they try to control. They have attachments that link their own emotions to others. Despite their manifest importance, emotions fit into rational theories of politics only with difficulty. They are treated as part of the irreducible irrational error of human existence, perhaps buried in biology. Like other persistent irrationalities, they create a problem for the theory. If it is to be believed that competitive pressures tend to eliminate irrationalities in the genetic and social bases of behavior, the conspicuous endurance of emotions and emotionality is prima facie a puzzle.

Emotions are more easily accommodated in theories of identity-based action, though such theories tend to endorse a conception of emotions different from that of some psychological and biological students of the phenomenon. Institutions organize hopes, dreams, and fears, as well as purposeful actions. Institutionalized rules proscribe or prescribe emotions and expression of emotions (Flam, 1990a, 1990b). Sentiments of love, loyalty, devotion, respect, and friendship, as well as hate, anger, fear, envy, and guilt are made appropriate to particular identities in particular situations. In this conception, emotions are rule-based interpretations of identity. The reason girls exhibit joy at different times and in different ways from boys is because the codes of gender identity provide rules about emotion or the expression of emotions. The distinction between emotions and their expression is a source of dispute in emotion research: Do emotions exist independent of their expression or communication? The answer from the point of view of most students of rule-based, identity-based action is that there may well be some sense in postulating emotions as existing prior to and independent of their expression, but emotion is heavily influenced by the rules surrounding its expression. The dictum "Real men don't cry" can be interpreted as an identity rule about feelings or as an identity rule about communicating feelings.

In either case, an identity-based theory of politics encompasses feelings as an important component of identity. The identities of public officials (like those of professionals) are often interpreted as requiring a censoring of feelings. The interpretation is not quite correct. What such identities commonly require is the subordination of *private* feelings, the feelings associated with personal identities. Most public identities, in fact, mandate appropriate feelings. Witness, for example, the speeches of judges to convicted criminals, the reaction of political leaders to civic outrages, the welcomes by public officials to championship football teams, and the ritualized emotional celebration of military, legislative, and judicial victories.

Rules, shared meanings, and cultures. Institutional conceptions of politics emphasize shared meaning as a basis for political systems and for governance of them. There are, however, two varieties of shared meanings, both important, that are sometimes confused. The first is shared meanings about values, perspectives, and worldviews, understandings about the nature of things. These shared meanings are often associated with a homogeneous "culture." They underlie systems of governance that emphasize mutual sympathy, trust, and awareness among citizens. Shared values and mutual trust lead to government through consensus and congruence.

The second variety of shared meanings emphasizes institutions. Institutions are collections of interrelated practices and routines, sometimes formalized into formal rules and laws and sometimes less formally specified. Those practices and routines, as well as their interpretations, must be built on shared understandings of the behaviors they mandate or permit, but such understandings do not necessarily require the kind of shared values and cognitive frames reflected in homogeneous cultures. Institutions buffer and regulate conflict of values and cognitions. As a result, institutions are substitutes for deeper levels of agreement. They are likely to be particularly elaborated in heterogeneous societies in which formal rules, bureaucratic control, and formal contracts substitute for informal coordination based on shared values and cognitions.

The longer-run dynamics of the relation between shared understandings of values and shared understandings of practices and routines are not easy to specify. Several quite different stories can be told. First, it seems clear that a certain amount of value consensus is essential to shared routines, and a certain amount of shared understanding of rules is essential to maintaining value understandings. Second, it also seems likely that shared understandings of practices and routines tend to substitute for shared understandings of values and identities. As capabilities for acting coherently without shared values are elaborated and improved through systems of laws and rules, experience with social and individual rehearsals and reinforcements of shared values is reduced. This, in turn, is likely to require agreement on a broader structure of routines. Third, it also seems likely that an escalation of routinization and heterogeneity will be echoed by a similar process involving escalation of informality and homogeneity. Value understandings and trust substitute for and lead to reduced elaboration of and experience with formal rule systems, thus to a decay in the sharing of their interpretation and in their effectiveness.

Identities, interests, and the common good. Some of the more celebrated differences between exchange theories of politics and institutional theories concern the concept of the "common good," the idea that individuals might—in some circumstances—act not for the sake of individual or group interest but for the sake of the good of the community. Exchange traditions downplay the significance, or meaning, of the common good and doubt the relevance of social investment in citizenship. The assumption is that self-oriented interests cannot (and should not) be eliminated or influenced. The object is to provide an arena for voluntary exchange among them. If leaders wish to control the outcomes of this self-seeking behavior, they should do so by designing incentives that—as much as possible—induce self-interested individuals to act in desired ways (Hart and Holmström, 1987; Levinthal, 1988). Political norms are seen as negotiated constraints on fundamental processes of self-serving rationality rather than as constitutive (Coleman, 1986; Shepsle, 1990).

From this perspective, a community of virtuous citizens is Gemeinschaftschwärmerei—a romantic dream (Yack, 1985). The fantasy in some democratic thought that modern society can be held together by, and that conflicts can be resolved through, reference to either a moral consensus or a shared conception of the common good is deemed to be wrong as a description and pernicious as an objective. For example, although both Habermas (1992a, 1992b, 1994) and Rawls (1993) seem to suggest that citizens may share some aims and ends that do not make up a comprehensive doctrine, as well as basic rules for regulating their political coexistence in the face of persistent disagreements and different ways of life, they criticize models that overburden citizens ethically by assuming a political community united by a comprehensive substantive doctrine. The dream can be seen not only as romantic but also as dangerous. Developing a community based on a shared moral purpose and a common identity has been the aspiration of tyrants, and the use of government to manage desires, beliefs, and identities can make governmental responsiveness to those elements a democratic fraud (Perry, 1988; Sunstein, 1990).

Nevertheless, virtually all institutional theories of politics give importance to the idea of community. Humans (or their institutions) are seen as able to share a common life and identity and to have concern for others. Either what is good for one individual is the same as what is good for other members of the community, or actions are supposed to be governed by consideration of the community as a whole. Although the idea of a common good is plagued by the difficulty of defining what is meant by the term and by the opportunities for exploitation of individual gullibility that lie in an uncritical embrace of hopes for community values, many institutional theorists criticize presumptions of autonomous, individual, self-interested be-havior that are standard in the rational tradition (Mansbridge, 1990; Mulhall and Swift, 1992; Chapman and Galston, 1992).

Good government is seen as impossible if citizens and officials are concerned only with their self-interest and ignore the common good. Governance relying only on self-interest, incentives, and a bal-ance of power among interests is too contingent and may collapse under the pressure of changing circumstances or shifts in the balance of power (Rawls, 1987). Proper citizens are assumed to act in ways consistent with common purposes that are not reducible to the ag-gregation of their separate self-interests (Spragens, 1990). Good citi-zens are pictured as willing to reason together. They deliberate on the basis of a sense of community that is itself reinforced by the processes of deliberation. From this perspective, the real danger to a polity comes when no controlling standard of obligation is recog-nized and politics becomes the unchecked pursuit of interests (Wolin, 1960). As a result, the processes by which identities, roles, and interests are created, nurtured, transformed, and implemented are a critical concern of governance, and the civic basis of identities is intrinsic to the concept of a person, citizen, or public official. Giv-ing priority to private interests and preferences is seen not merely as a corruption of the political process but also as a corruption of the soul and a fall from grace. Social identities are among the building blocks of the self. Anyone incapable of achieving an identity based on constitutive attachments—if such a person could be imagined—should be described not as a free and rational agent but as a being without character or moral depth, a nonperson (Sandel, 1982, 1984).

In large parts of this tradition, citizenship or membership in the polis is the most important and inclusive identity. It is the highest form of association, responsible for the common good of society. Being a citizen and holding public office are constitutive belongings integrating and shaping other allegiances and particular identities derived from social affiliations like the family, voluntary associa-tions, class, or one's market position. Citizens and officeholders are presumed to act according to norms associated with their roles rather than in pursuit of personal advantage and interests. They are presumed to respond to the dictates of their identities (Walzer,

1983; Barber, 1984; Mouffe, 1992). Realizing that such education and indoctrination may not be completely effective, that individuals may not always fulfill their citizenship identities, democracies also seek to provide concrete incentives that make being a good citizen attractive to a self-interested individual. The hope of governance is to encourage ordinary people, with their usual mix of identities and interests, to attend to the obligations of citizenship.

The folding of communitarian values into institutional theories of politics is almost universal in modern discussions of political democracy, and it leads to a tendency to confuse two related but distinct notions. The first notion is the idea that political democracy requires a sense of *community*. Exactly what constitutes a sense of community varies from one communitarian author to another, but a common element is the idea that individuals might (and should) have empathic sympathy for the feelings and desires of others and in some circumstances might (and should) subordinate their own individual or group interests to the collective good of the community (Sabine, 1952; Olsen, 1990). The second notion is the idea that democracy is built upon visions of *civic identity* and a framework of rule-based action—what we have called a logic of appropriateness. Embedded in this notion are ideas about the duties and obligations of citizenship and office, the commitment to fulfill an identity without regard to its consequences for personal or group preferences or interests. The self becomes central to personhood, and civic identity becomes central to the self (Turner, 1990).

The two notions share some common presumptions, but they have quite different perspectives about the fundamental basis for democratic action. The communitarian ideal of shared preferences, including a preference for the common good, presumes that individual action is based on individual values and preferences. The model is a model of individual, consequential, preference-based action. Strategies for achieving democracy emphasize constructing acceptable preferences. The civic identity ideal presumes, on the other hand, that action is rule-based, that it involves matching the obligations of an identity to a situation. Pursuit of the common good is not so much a personal value as a constitutive part of democratic political identities and the construction of a meaningful person. The community is created by its rules, not by its intentions. Strategies for achieving democracy emphasize molding rules and identities and socializing individuals into them (Elster and Slagstad, 1988; Elster, 1989a). In this sense, the argument over individual interests and the collective good with which we began this section is often framed incorrectly. In a rule-based polity, the potential conflict is not between the individual pursuit of preferences based on conceptions of private gain and the individual pursuit of preferences based on conceptions of collective good. The conflict is, in the first instance, between a preference-based consequential logic and an identity-based logic of appropriateness; and, in the second instance, between the claims of particularistic identities and the claims of citizenship and officialdom.

The distinctions are worth maintaining. When they are confounded, there is a tendency to see the problems of modern polities as lying primarily in the value premises of individual preference-based action rather than in a structure of political rules, institutions, accounts, and identities. In fact, many of the greatest dangers to the democratic polity come not from individual self-seeking but from deep, group-based identities that are inconsistent with democracy, for example, strong feelings of ethnic, national, religious, and class identities. Efforts to build a personal set of communitarian values enhancing concern for the common good will be of little use—even if successful—if antidemocratic action stems primarily not from preferences and their associated values but from commitments to identities that are inconsistent with democratic institutions.

Institutional Conceptions of Political Change

Although their many different manifestations allow numerous variations on theories of history, institutional and exchange conceptions of politics tend to mirror a grand debate in historical interpretation. On one side in that debate is the idea that politics follows a course dictated uniquely by exogenous factors. From such a perspective, history is efficient in the sense that it matches political institutions and outcomes to environments uniquely and relatively quickly. This side of the debate is typical of exchange theories, theories of rational choice, and many versions of comparative statics drawn from them. Exchange theories of political change are largely theories of the adjustment of political bargains to exogenous changes in interests, rights, and resources. When values change, political coalitions change. For example, when attitudes with respect to the role of women in society shifted, so also did political parties. When resources are redistributed, political coalitions change. For example, when the age composition of society shifted in the direction of older citizens, so also did political programs. The presumption is that political bargains adjust quickly and in a necessary way to exogenous changes.

On the other side of the debate is the idea that history follows a slower, less determinate, and more endogenous course. From such a perspective, history is a path-dependent meander. This side of the debate is typical of institutional theories. Students of political institutions are generally less confident of the efficiency of historical processes in matching political outcomes to exogenous pressures. They see the match between an environment of interests and resources on the one hand and political institutions on the other as less automatic, less continuous, and less precise. They see a world of historical possibilities that includes multiple stable equilibria. They see the pressures of survival as sporadic rather than constant, crude rather than precise. They see institutions and identities as having lives and deaths of their own, sometimes enduring in the face of apparent inconsistency with their environments, sometimes collapsing without obvious external cause (Krasner, 1988; March and Olsen, 1989).

HISTORY AS EFFICIENT

Seeing political institutions as instruments for political action and assumptions about efficient institutional histories are appealing to democratic theorists. Competitive selection is seen as a mechanism securing historical efficiency. If institutions do not adapt, they are expected to deteriorate and wither away as people stop observing, and as governments stop enforcing, the rules. Although the precise way in which this selection takes place and institutions came to match their environments is often left obscure, some version of a matching theory is an important part of traditional comparative statics as applied to political institutions. Why do political institutions differ from one country to another? Because the social and economic environments of the countries differ. How are differences in specific institutions to be explained? By pointing to specific differences in their environments.

As long as history is efficient in this way, variations in institutional structures can be predicted without identifying the underlying processes of change (Furubotn and Richter, 1984). It is not necessary to decide whether the primary mechanism is rational choice, adaptation of individual institutions, or variation and selection among unchanging institutions. There is no need to understand either the actions of reformers trying consciously to adapt an institution to its environment or the institutional processes by which changes are effected. The specific ways in which institutions orchestrate their transformation may be of interest to a student of political interpretation and dramaturgy, but the outcome itself is dictated by environmental conditions. Such confidence in efficient histories is one of the reasons that students of populations of institutions are often relatively unconcerned about establishing that any particular story of adaptation is uniquely capable of explaining their observations.

In modern theories of efficient histories, the pressures of the environment are most commonly related to technical capabilities, the effectiveness of an institution in using operational and organizational technologies to meet physical, political, and economic demands. Some versions of transaction cost economics, for example, seek to predict organizational form from the costs to organizers of alternative forms, assuming that the processes of history will eliminate more costly forms. The most common modern story involves the shaping of political and economic institutions to match global variations and changes in the scale of organization and technologies of communication and coordination.

Institutional survival is also often related to the ability to match "institutionalized environments," norms and beliefs about how an institution should be organized and run. Those norms are particularly compelling in highly developed social systems where an institution depends on a network of relations with other institutions that simultaneously depend on it. Forms and practices sustain themselves through epidemics of legitimacy. Professional associations and associations of similar institutions create and approve standard practices and thereby make them necessary. An institution survives because its structures, processes, and ideologies match what society finds appropriate, natural, rational, democratic, or modern (Meyer and Rowan, 1977; Meyer and Scott, 1983; Thomas *et al.*, 1987; Scott and Meyer, 1994).

In these conceptions of history, politics is an instrument for matching the institutions of a society to an exogenous social, economic, technical, and normative environment. Changes in the environment produce dislocations in the political system, which are translated into new political interests and resource distributions, which, in turn, are translated into new political coalitions, institutions, and policies. For example, as normative fashions in procedures for dealing with criminals change in a population of political systems, each individual system experiences a transformation of political institutions and policies that brings judicial and penal institutions into step with social norms.

HISTORY AS INEFFICIENT

The conditions under which political development is driven quickly to a unique outcome in which the match between a political system and the political environment has some properties of unique survival advantage seem relatively restricted (Kitcher, 1985; Baum and Singh, 1994). There is no guarantee that the development of identities and institutions will instantaneously or uniquely reflect functional imperatives, normative concerns, or demands for change (Carroll and Harrison, 1994). Political institutions and identities develop in a world of multiple possibilities. Moreover, the path they follow seems determined in part by internal dynamics only loosely connected to changes in their environments (Amenta and Carruthers, 1988; Wood, 1992).

Even in an exogenous environment, there are lags in matching an environment, multiple equilibria, path dependencies, and interconnected networks of diffusion. Besides, environments are rarely exogenous. Environments adapt to institutions at the same time as institutions adapt to environments. Institutions and their linkages coevolve. They are intertwined in ecologies of competition, cooperation, and other forms of interaction. And institutions are nested, so that some adapting institutions (e.g., bureaus) are integral parts of other adapting institutions (e.g., ministries).

The complications tend to convert history into a meander (March, 1994a). The path of development is produced by a comprehensible process, but because of its indeterminate meander the realized course of institutional development is difficult to predict very far in advance. There are irreversible branches, involving things like experimentation, political alliances, communication contacts, and fortuitous opportunities. Wars, conquests, and occupation are significant in changing political directions and organization (Tilly, 1975, 1993; Giddens, 1985). The direction taken at any particular branch sometimes seems almost chance-like, however decisive it may be in its effect on subsequent history (Brady, 1988; Lipset, 1990).

In general, neither competitive pressures nor current conditions uniquely determine institutional options or outcomes (Herzog, 1986; North, 1990). Institutional forms also depend on the historical path of their development (Berman, 1983). The proposition is a general one in evolutionary theory. In discussing optimization ideas in evolutionary theory, Oster and Wilson (1984, p. 284) conclude: "As systems become more complex, the historical accidents play a more and more central role in determining the evolutionary path they will follow." Political technologies and practices are stabilized by positive local feedback leading to the endurance of institutions, competency traps, and misplaced specialization (Levitt and March, 1988). The adaptation of identities and institutions to an external environment is shaped and constrained by internal dynamics, by which identities and institutions modify themselves endogenously.

Inefficient histories have implications for theories of political development. Much of the style of political science is basically comparative statics, the exploration of the ways in which individual behavior, institutional practices, and cultural norms match the demands of the environments in which they are found. The basic strategy is to predict features of the units of adaptation (individuals, institutions, cultures) from attributes of their environments. The "invisible hand" of efficient historical development is imagined to provide the link. Meandering, locally adaptive histories are inconsistent with that strong "functionalist" tone of many modern interpretations of comparative institutions and institutional change. Such ideas attribute differences among institutions not only to differences among their contemporary environments but also to differences among their histories of interaction with changing path-dependent environments.

The course of a meandering history is created by the sequence of particular historical branches that are realized along the way. Since small, precise changes can be imagined to produce large, permanent effects, "timely interventions" at historical junctures may make a difference. The possibilities have attracted people from cattle breeders to philosophers of science, from environmental and political activists to consultants in strategic management. If small, well-timed interventions can be multiplied by spontaneous historical forces, the possibilities for governance may be substantial; but control of political history is limited by the kinds of branches that arise fortuitously. The ability to create change, therefore, does not guarantee that any arbitrary change can be made at any time or that changes will ultimately turn out to have consequences consistent with prior intentions (March, 1981a). There is no assurance that occasions will arise to achieve any particular desired outcome through opportunistic exploitation of moments in history, and institutions that have been established to serve specific interests have sometimes meandered in ways that serve them poorly in the long run (Rothstein, 1992).

Institutional Conceptions of Governance

From an institutional perspective, democratic governance is more than the management of efficient political coalition-building and exchange within prior constraints. It also involves influencing the process by which the constraints are established (Wendt, 1994). It involves molding social and political life—shaping history, an understanding of it, and an ability to learn from it. To speak of governance as affecting history is to assume that history is neither completely determined nor entirely random, that human control is imaginable. To speak of governance as affecting an understanding of history is to assume that interpretations of history are not inherent in the events of history, that neither civic contentments nor civic discontents are completely determined by objective conditions. To speak of governance as sustaining an ability to learn from history is to assume that history can be made to serve the society.

The constraints of identities, capabilities, and accounts are subject to change in two principal senses. First, the constraints are often defined in terms of necessary change. The transformation of a human into a fish or a democratic government into a totalitarian one is excluded by the conception of what it is to be a human or a democracy. But the transformation of a human from a child to an adult is part of the "constraint" of being human, and the transformation of a democratic government from the control of one party to another is part of the "constraint" of being democratic. As a result, governance that seeks to shape children into adults or social democratic regimes into conservative regimes faces a remarkably easier task than would be involved in trying to convert humans into fishes or democracies into totalitarian regimes. Changes that are defined as natural, normal, or legitimate are easier to accomplish than those that are not.

Second, the constraints are themselves transformed at varying rates. What it means to be human or democratic changes. The meanings of political and social identities—democrat, citizen, English, liberal, bureaucrat—are contested. There are debates over what an identity is or can be, what accounts are appropriate and valid, what capabilities matter and how they should be distributed. The constraints of identities, accounts, and capabilities change slowly within institutional contexts (families, churches, educational systems, armies, political movements, mass media) that are themselves changing. Some parts of those constraints change more rapidly than others. Those parts of the constraints that are slowest to change can be described as "core" elements of meaning, as long as it is recognized that their "coreness" is observable primarily through their slow rate of change.

From an institutional perspective, therefore, the craft of governance is organized around four tasks:

1. Governance involves *developing identities* of citizens and groups in the political environment. Preferences, expectations, beliefs, identities, and interests are not exogenous to political history. They are created and changed within that history. Political actors act on the basis of identities that are themselves shaped by political institutions and processes. It is the responsibility of democratic government to create and support civic institutions and processes that

facilitate the construction, maintainance, and development of democratic identities, and to detect and counteract institutions and processes that produce identities grossly inconsistent with democracy and therefore intolerable from a democratic point of view.

2. Governance involves *developing capabilities* for appropriate political action among citizens, groups, and institutions. Democracy requires that political actors act in ways that are consistent with and sustain the democratic system, fulfilling the expectations of the relevant rules, norms, and duties, and adapting them to changing experience. Acting appropriately and learning from experience, however, require not only a will to do so but also an ability. Capabilities define potentials to affect politics, to exercise rights, and to influence the course of history. Democratic governance must accept responsibility not only for responding to the distribution of capabilities in the polity but also for modifying that distribution to make it more consistent with the requirements of democratic identities.

3. Governance involves *developing accounts* of political events. Accounts define the meaning of history, the options available, and the possibilities for action. Accounts are used both to control events and to provide reassurance that events are controllable. Meanings and histories are socially constructed. Political myths are developed and transmitted. Accounts of what has happened, why it happened, and how events should be evaluated provide a key link between citizens and government. They underlie democratic efforts to secure control and accountability. Democratic governance involves contributing to the development of accounts and procedures for interpretation that improve the transmission, retention, and retrieval of the lessons of history and the use of such accounts to improve democracy.

4. Governance involves *developing an adaptive political system,* one that copes with changing demands and changing environments. It involves creating accounts of history that make learning possible and providing resources and capabilities adequate for executing, interpreting, and learning from experiments. Manipulating the level of risk taking, or the salience of diversity relative to unity, or the amount of institutional slack are conspicuous examples of ways by which history can be affected by changing the level of variation or the effectiveness by which lessons and opportunities of the environment are exploited.

The remainder of this book outlines some ideas about how such an institutional perspective on governance is implemented within a democratic context. We ask whether it is imaginable that citizens can realize political institutions that not only work but justify their commitment to them. What sort of citizens and institutions does it take to constitute a democratic society? How can such institutions and citizens be fostered?

Chapter Three

DEVELOPING POLITICAL IDENTITIES

Democracy is partly a structure of laws and incentives by which less-than-perfect individuals are induced to act in the common good while pursuing their own. It is also a set of institutions within which individual potentials, identities, and preferences are created and elaborated (Mill, 1969, p. 139; Brief and Motowidlo, 1986; Organ, 1988; Kramer, 1993). Any one individual has a potential for accommodating many identities (Gould, 1988; West, 1988) and elaborating many alternative interpretations of those identities, thus of all kinds of action (Bloom, 1990, pp. 6, 113). Ordinary individuals are capable both of heroic sacrifices in the name of others and of extraordinary selfishness. They are capable of considerable self-discipline in the name of duties and responsibilities, as well as uncompromising venality. Civility can be developed; it can also be corrupted (West, 1988).

Individuals come to define political identities and to mold those identities to a specific set of historical and political experiences and conditions. Religious movements, great social and economic transformations, war, conquest, and migration all leave their marks (Tilly, 1975; Flora, 1983), but political identities also evolve endogenously within a political process that includes conflict, public discourse, civic education, and socialization. In the context of political life, citizens struggle to understand "who they are, where they come from historically, what they stand for, and what is to be done about the perils and possibilities that lie ahead of them as a people" (Wolin, 1989, p. 14). In the course of that struggle, they elaborate self-restraints and obligations as they embrace, challenge, and transform the political order.

Democratic government is responsible for providing a milieu of education, reflection, interpretation, and action within which these developments occur (Reich, 1988; Offe, 1989; Mansbridge, 1990; Offe and Preuss, 1991). There are limits. The differences among individuals and cultures are large enough to discourage the thought that any arbitrary individual can be endowed with any arbitrary identity (Hoffmann, 1993, p. 66). And the idea of political authorities as a source of moral or civic education for a community strikes some people as a horror (MacIntyre, 1984, p. 195; Dunn, 1990, p. 91). Nevertheless, the self is not only a premise of politics but also one of its principal creations (Sandel, 1982, 1984). Individuals come to define themselves in terms of their identities and to accept the rules of appropriate behavior associated with those identities. They learn how loyalties, affections, obligations, and meanings are attached to identities. They seek the competencies required to fulfill their identities.

What institutional arrangements make it possible for individuals to act as democratic citizens and officials, and how such institutions, citizens, and officials can be fostered (Mill, 1962; MacIntyre, 1984, pp. 165, 171)? How is an ethos of civic virtue, duty, and obligation maintained in a society of free individuals? How do political identities develop? How is it possible to assure integrity, competence, and reasoned debate? How can citizens, officials, and political institutions be civilized without being enslaved (Mill, 1956, 1962; Pateman, 1970; Pitkin, 1981).

REQUIREMENTS OF CIVILIZED SOCIETY

In its original meaning "to civilize" meant to evoke consciousness of the civic, or collective, character of human existence. In that sense, a central requirement of democracy is a commitment to the civilization of citizens, public officials, institutions, and political processes (Mill, 1969, pp. 102, 139). History suggests that producing a civil society is possible but not easy, particularly in a large state. It involves reinforcing, exploiting, and linking three fundamental features of democratic political development:

1. The shaping of a *sense of solidarity* that connects the individual citizen to a broad political community of others and organizes other belongings in a way that enriches that community. A secure sense of belonging is part of a psychological sense of well-being. In situations involving conflict, it is as tangible a factor as territory or property. Protecting and enhancing the identity associated with belonging is sometimes more important than survival (Bloom, 1990, p. 114).

2. The shaping of *specific identities* (character, habits of thought, senses of reality, and codes of conduct) that fit into and support a democratic political order. To improve the cognitive and moral qualities of public life, the polity needs to civilize individual action, to create a buffer between an individual's own immediate interests, passions, and needs and that individual's beliefs and behavior as a citizen or official. Being a citizen or official binds an individual to act under some critical circumstances to confirm the private self by confirming a public self.

3. The shaping of *institutions* to civilize expressions of solidarity and confrontation of conflict among identities. Democracy presumes a balancing of the claims of community with the claims of individual autonomy. It presumes political institutions and processes that induce citizens to serve the common good. Democratic institutions transform inconsistencies among identities and preferences into discourse in pursuit of shared understanding, channeling disagreements into reasoned discussion and empathetic exploration of possible compromises and mutual interests.

Civilized Solidarities

Individuals, groups, institutions, political orders, and communities develop senses of solidarity with groups of similar others. Citizens belong to a community of citizens bonded to each other by a sense of common condition and destiny. Solidarity allows citizens to develop and interpret meanings, feelings, and social bonds, while maintaining individual autonomy. It is a base for mobilizing citizens to defend the political system and a frame within which internal conflicts can be resolved. At the same time, however, solidarity is a threat to democracy and to civilized politics. National solidarity organized around the polity blends into unthinking patriotism and bellicosity. Solidarity often supports and is often supported by rules of exclusion that define who is outside the group or community and contribute to intolerance and temptations to abandon democratic procedures.

NATIONAL SOLIDARITY

Much of contemporary political practice revolves around the idea of a national political identity. Despite expectations that modernization might culminate in new supranational allegiances, the last part of the twentieth century has seen a strong resurgence of national- and ethnicity-based politics in many parts of the world. National identity is a sense of solidarity that has both integrative and divisive effects. It encourages a sense of commonality and shared destiny that permits a political system of cooperation and trust. At the same time, however, solidarity is built on ideas of differentiation from and exclusion of those who do not belong. Since the earliest city-state democracies, rights and freedoms have been exclusionary, enforcing a basic distinction between insiders and outsiders and creating a double standard of behavioral rules and morals—one for fellow citizens and a different one for others (Nauta, 1992, p. 24). Freedom for citizens has implied neither legal (civil) freedom for noncitizens resident within the community nor the rights of citizenship for those outside the community (Finley, 1973, p. 54).

Ideas of national identity are different from, but tightly linked with, ideas of the nation-state (Smith and Østerud, 1994). Although elements of national consciousness—including consciousness related to ethnic identification—antedated the rise of the nation-state in some places, they were generally subordinated to other identifications. An emphasis on national political identity was an instrument in the solidification of the nation-state, both in Europe, where national identity replaced a relatively complex set of overlapping combinations of allegiances, and in the European colonial empires in Asia, Africa, and South America, where it became the basis first for colonial administrative order and subsequently for decolonization.

National consciousness was primarily a social construction (Barth, 1969, 1993; T.H. Eriksen, 1993), and the state was a principal actor in its construction (Smith and Østerud, 1994). National political identities emerged in Europe as an explicit attempt to wipe out or weaken existing identities and social and political ties (Merkl, 1967; Bendix, 1968). In the process of building national identities, communities were imagined and history invented (Hobsbawm and Ranger, 1983). National solidarity associated with a political unit having a distinct territorial location and (usually) a distinct language became the dominant organizing principal of politics.

National solidarities are linked to other senses of belonging. In part, those linkages are competitive. Solidarity with the state competes with other solidarities. Loyalty to religion, class, family, gender, ethnic group, profession, or age group produces conflicts with loyalty to the state and threatens the dominance of the political order. Recently, loyalty to the nation-state has again been portrayed as in competition with loyalties not only to less inclusive but also to more inclusive solidarities (Habermas, 1992c; Nauta, 1992; Sbragia, 1992; Smith, 1991, 1992). In part, however, the various solidarities of social life are organized to be mutually supportive. The organization of units in a political or administrative system results in a nesting of solidarities that tends to reduce conflict. Family solidarity may sustain national solidarity through family traditions of service to the state and its institutions; religious solidarity may confirm national loyalties through a linking of religious symbolism and belief with national symbolism and patriotism.

Perhaps the most conspicuous modern example of the melding of one solidarity with another is the mobilization of class identification in the service of the state. Marxist-Leninist ideology was uncompromisingly international, portraying the class struggle as uniting workers across national boundaries. The ideology was implemented in the form of numerous international institutions organized to replace national loyalties with class loyalties. Nevertheless, Marxist-Leninist identifications seem generally to have been marshaled more effectively to serve the nation-state than to serve broader class interests (Szporluk, 1994).

The future of national belonging and identity as the base of the nation-state, along with the future of the nation-state as the basis of political organization, is being reexamined in Europe, renewing perennial questions about the nature of the political order and the legitimacy of national solidarity (Wittrock, 1992, pp. 299–300). Many governmental authorities of the European Union, the nation-state, and subnational units of the state are deeply involved in trying to reconstruct political solidarities. Their efforts are sometimes consistent, sometimes not, but they are likely to reshape the meaning of national solidarity. Some see the possibility of a gradual remaking of collective solidarities, a European citizenship. Others see a withering away of identities associated with the nation-state, to be replaced by smaller, more homogeneous loyalties linked in a European confederation that makes the nation-state irrelevant, at least for certain issues. Still others forecast a reinstatement of nation-state identities as the state resists the encroachments of European union on the one side and regional loyalties on the other. Although some of these sentiments reflect a tradition of an intellectual bias against nationalism, a bias that unites writers of quite different political sentiments (Greenfeld, 1992; Hobsbawm, 1992; Gellner, 1993; Kedourie, 1993), modern economic, demographic, technological, social, and environmental linkages among states seem not only to call for a reconsideration of the political place of nation-state solidarities but also to provide a set of institutions within which broader identities might evolve (Wendt, 1994).

SOLIDARITY AND CIVILITY

Democratic governance depends on solidarity, yet it faces many of its problems in managing it. Difficulties arise primarily from the unstable dynamics of multigroup solidarity. Solidarity thrives on conflict among groups. Collective solidarity is sustained by identifying opposing groups from which the collectivity can distinguish itself. Each group maintains itself by differentiating itself from others and claiming superiority. The required fine-tuning of group and intergroup solidarities is difficult to accomplish in the face of the tendency for any particular solidarity to escalate itself into a frenzy that stimulates other frenzies. Solidarity within one ethnic or religious group stimulates oppositional solidarity in another. Solidarity in family groups stimulates efforts to strengthen overriding national loyalties. Group solidarities create pressures for favoritism and inequality. National solidarities create pressures for international conflict. In each case, the short-run advantages to solidarity are likely to obscure the more distant disasters due to solidarity escalations.

Political institutions that provide a framework within which both social and cultural pluralism and a sense of collective solidarity can be sustained are vital, particularly in contemporary multiethnic and multicultural societies (Di Palma, 1990; Walzer, 1983; Leca, 1992; Mouffe, 1992). Part of the craft of democratic governance is developing institutions that simultaneously accommodate the ideals of political community, equality, and reason and the ideals of pluralism and diversity, institutions that are capable of maintaining trust and mutual affection within a polity while simultaneously accommodating enduringly inconsistent subgroup demands based on family ties, religion, ethnicity, language, or personal affinity. That craft involves strengthening identities based on broad and long-term conceptions of a community of citizens and a concern for others in that community, including future citizens and unborn generations, and developing institutions that encourage both solidarity and civility.

Civilized Identities

The construction of identities in a democracy involves three primary concerns. The first is an *instrumental* concern. Democracy is a set of procedures for making collective decisions. In order to function well, it requires civilized citizens and officials, individuals who act according to identities and rules consistent with democratic procedures. The second is a *moral* concern. Democracy is not only a system for making collective decisions, it is also a system of education and socialization in the service of human virtue, a collective faith and way of life. The institutions of democracy instill identities, ideals, beliefs, and codes of behavior consistent with high human aspirations. The third is a *transformative* concern. Democracy is an arena for self-reflection and redefinition of individuals, institutions, and communities. Even as it creates identities and acts to fulfill them, it stimulates constructive social and individual reconsideration of their nature. Neither self-interest nor identities are, or should be, immutable, nor is the common good (Herzog, 1989, pp. 16, 235).

The three concerns are interdependent, but they are not the same. Conceptions of democracy and Western conceptions of human morality have developed together, and they tend to be mutually supportive. For example, a capacity for independent moral judgment and action and a consciousness of responsibility to others are features of identities consistent with many conceptions of both virtue and democracy. Similarly, the institutions and practices of democracy provide opportunities for intelligent discourse and engagement that serve the self-reflective requirements of a transformative system of values and identities. The demands of morality, democracy, and change are, however, not necessarily consistent. For example, moral concerns with personal integrity may conflict with democratic demands for compromise, self-restraint, and acquiescence in collective decisions. And demands for effectiveness in executing democratic procedures and for recognition of moral imperatives may conflict with transformative requirements for experimentation, openness, and revolt.

THE CIVILIZED CITIZEN

Democratic requirements for a shared ethos and the fear that the development of such an ethos will lead to totalitarian indoctrination have occupied a central place in the debate on liberal democracy (Friedrich, 1939). Democracy requires a sense of community and a shared democratic commitment and culture, but it is undermined by the imposition of conformity of opinion, by the suppression of individuality and personal identity, and by setting narrow restrictions on deviance, opposition, and conflict. Democracy requires liberty, but it is undermined when the passions of freedom overcome collective reason. The free and responsible citizen is the democratic solution to the twin threats of atomization, alienation, and factionalism on the one hand, and regimentation on the other (Olsen, 1990, p. 31; Orlie, 1994).

Citizenship is an identity defined by a bundle of rights and duties and by an awareness of others in a similar position. Other democratic identities—like the popularly elected official, the expert, the bureaucrat, and the judge—are defined on the basis of their relations to a community of free and equal citizens. It is an identity that imposes obligations in the service of liberty. The idea of citizenship as a collection of shared rights, duties, and responsibilities may be contrasted with the idea of an autonomous individual pursuing self-defined preferences. A claim to citizenship is a tacit agreement to confirm and elaborate an ethos of civic virtue, duty, and obligation. Since the rights of citizenship adhere to the identity of citizen, they are conditional on being recognized as a proper citizen. In particular, they depend on accepting the responsibilities of citizenship. Those include the duty to participate in matters of public debate and elections, the duty to defend the polity, and the duty to obey the law or accept punishment specified for disobedience. Willingness to obey the law is, of course, monitored by a polity's system of justice, which holds citizens accountable for transgressions, but the democratic ideal is that law-abidingness is sustained less by fears of punishment than by a commitment to citizenship.

Being a citizen means having standing as a person of political significance, as someone who can claim the right to participate in the democratic process. It also means defending those rights. Citizens defend the right to vote (and to have a vote counted) and to participate in deliberations over public policy through free speech, free association, and free access to information. These rights are defended as aspects of citizenship rather than as personal prerogatives, and citizens are as zealous in protecting the rights of other citizens as in protecting their own. The rights of citizenship are also inalienable. They belong to the role, not to the individual. Through emigration, an individual can renounce a personal claim to citizenship, but a citizen who chooses to remain a citizen cannot exchange the rights of citizenship through autonomous voluntary act—for example, by selling the right to vote or speak.

THE CIVILIZED OFFICIAL

The actions of public officials are vital to democracy (Lundquist, 1988). If democracy is not to be impotent, it must delegate authority to officials (Bay, 1965, pp. 380–81; Dahl, 1989). Delegation is imperative, but it raises the specter of loss of control. Officials may act in ways that are inconsistent with the common interest or the collective will. As an important supplement to the governance of officials through the imposition of sanctions and rewards, institutional perspectives emphasize the socialization of public officials to an ethic of administrative duty and conformity to the law.

Officials are enjoined to act in a manner appropriate to their official responsibilities and duties rather than in accord with personal preferences, loyalties, or pressures from others (Friedrich, 1940; Finer, 1941; Lundquist, 1988). They can be trusted to do so, even in the face of considerable temptation to do something else. They are expected to see themselves as rule-abiding trustees for the polity, rather than as advocates or agents of particular interests. The obligations of public officials to serve as trustees for other citizens is an important part of political rhetoric and the rules of political propriety. Restrictions on bribery of officials, on contributions to political campaigns, on postpolitical employment, and on the awarding of gifts or preferment are all attempts to place frictions on the corruptions of officials; but the chief friction is provided by the definition of a proper public servant. Actions in the service of personal values or interests are viewed as contrary to good sense, justice, efficiency, and the elementary obligations of office.

The ideas are Weberian (Weber, 1978). Weber presumed that an official could, would, and should separate private sympathies and beliefs from public actions. The model Weberian bureaucrat was a person of integrity, basing action on the demands of an official role and eschewing both personal aggrandizement and the private entreaties of relatives, friends, or clients. Students of jurisprudence have long claimed and advocated similar behavior for judges. Judges and other officials are enjoined to act without regard to self or to the claims of other identities. Intrusions of personal considerations in the courts or the bureaucracy are viewed as inimical to a proper political system.

The watchword is public trust and professional integrity, and the appeal is to values that transcend self (Lægreid and Olsen, 1978; Thompson, 1980). Trust and integrity can be seen as stemming partly from organizational structures and procedures, including accountability arrangements, and partly from training in appropriate personal commitments that those structures provide (Friedrich, 1940; Finer, 1941). Indeed, many of the institutions of democracy are better portrayed as instruments of political socialization and training than as decision-making bodies. Participation is directed toward socializing citizens and officials into their responsibilities. The challenge, however, is not only to train or select selfless people of integrity. It is also to protect selflessness from the temptations of office. Authority and autonomy are essential accouterments of official positions, but they tend to undermine the qualities that are indispensable to their proper functioning. Power entices officials into misplaced beliefs in their own unique perspicacity and morality (O'Halpin, 1989). It tempts them to confuse arrogance with independence and to overestimate the clarity of their communications from God (MacArthur, 1964; Freud and Bullitt, 1966).

The complex way in which democracies construct officials is illustrated by the institutional, ritual, and interpretive elaboration of authorization and accountability. Authorization creates official actors, giving them the right to act on behalf of society and to commit collective resources. The scope of authority and the conditions of its use are subject to interpretation and disagreement. Conflicts over the elaboration of the meaning of any specific authority are mediated by trial-and-error political testing and through specific mediating institutions constituted for that purpose. The authority of the mediating institutions are, in turn, subject to interpretation and negotiation, leading to an interlocking set of understandings and procedures that provide both stability and opportunities for change.

The granting of authority provides the right to exercise discretion, but authority is controlled by accountability. Traditions of democracy require political officials to account for their actions; to report, explain, and justify any exercise of authority; and to submit to sanctions if necessary. Public officials are expected to act in anticipation of having to account for their actions (Pitkin, 1967). Authority is the right to exercise discretion, subject to being held accountable, but the system of discretionary authority combined with a postaudit accounting is eroded by the twin fears of the consequences of action and the ambiguities of accountability. The complications of historical causality confound efforts to establish (or claim) responsibility, thus making accountability for outcomes both essential and arbitrary. The relation between official actions and historical outcomes is cloudy. Officials insist on clarifications. Citizens insist on prior approval. Officials negotiate understandings with those to whom they are accountable, delaying action while they arrange prior approval through consultation.

The elaboration of procedures for prior consultation, however, tends to overload citizens and to eliminate the advantages of giving authority and discretion to independent officials, making public actions slow, indecisive, and uncreative. Assigning or taking responsibility tends to become a political ritual largely useful in sustaining a myth that the person at the top of an organization is in charge (Thompson, 1987, p. 44). As the consequences of these effects become conspicuous, there is a tendency to demand that authority be reinstated. The advantages of a postaudit of political action rather than a preaudit are rediscovered. And officials are enjoined to take leadership, to exercise discretion, and to do what is proper and just, rather than rely on prior consultation of constituents or "customers."

Civilized Conflict

The old observation that politics is warfare by other means is usually taken as an invitation to think about political relations in the same tactical terms as one might think about making war. The observation is, however, also a reminder that politics is different from warfare. Politics is premised on inconsistencies and conflicts, but the use of "other means" is critical to democracy. What democracy requires is not that conflict be eliminated but that it be civilized, that the encounters occurring among individual citizens exhibit empathy, generosity, and patience, and that political processes be based on reflection and discourse.

EMPATHY, GENEROSITY, AND PATIENCE

Civilized democratic politics can function in the face of distrust and callousness, but democratic civility achieves its primary claims by stimulating empathetic feelings in citizens, attitudes that allow for sympathetic consideration of the plights and possibilities of others, capacities for feeling sorrow and joy in concert with others. Civility in conflict is encouraged by encounters of understanding, generosity, and restraint. Consideration is given to the desires and feelings of others, and short-run advantages are forgone without firm assurances of longer-run returns. Current and local majorities accept (or are required to acknowledge) limits to their authority, implicitly recognizing their ephemeral and peripheral positions in a longer-run, broader process of civil accommodation and development. Opponents are disputed and co-opted, rather than arrested and shot. Justifications are expected and provided.

Democratic politics is a politics of patience. Although democratic polities are often born in revolutions and sometimes adapt relatively rapidly, particularly in the face of external threats, they are primarily slow-moving systems. They accommodate gradual changes of substantial character with considerable grace, but they normally frustrate champions of immediate, forceful transformations. This is true despite the fact that democracies often grant great formal power to simple electoral majorities. The intricacies of consent as they are elaborated through multiple legislative, judicial, and administrative agencies in the face of a free press and limitations of attention make precise, rapid change difficult within democratic institutions. The process of creating the welfare state took decades, as has the process of trying to dismantle it. Patience in action goes hand in hand, of course, with rhetorical proclamations of major new directions and reforms, and such rhetoric is a useful feature of civilized conflict. Victories are proclaimed more than they are gained, and words replace cannons.

The institutions and the socializations of democracy are particularly consistent, therefore, with situations in which slow change is tolerable. In contemporary terms, that means situations in which great, enduring disparities of wealth, resources, rights, or fundamental values are absent or so widely accepted as to provide no basis for political controversy. Democratic institutions and processes are strained by internal religious, ethnic, or racial intolerance; by economic adversity; and by extreme inequalities in the distribution of wealth. The historic concentration of democracies in overwhelmingly white, religiously fairly homogeneous societies with substantial middle classes is probably not an accident, nor is the concentration of modern democratic problems in situations of increasing diversity (or increasing intolerance for it) and increasing economic inequality.

TALK AND THE CIVILITIES OF DISCOURSE

Democratic institutions are temples of talk. They form communities of argumentation, informed debate, public deliberation, justification, and criticism. The central position of talk stems from democratic confidence in the capacity of human beings for reasoned discussion and constructive deliberation, even in ambiguous, uncertain, and conflictual situations. Democratic governance provides arenas in which citizens provide reasons for proposed actions, interpretations of history, explanations of beliefs, and justifications for failures. Those reasons, interpretations, explanations, and justifications are organized around the routines of making decisions, but their contribution to political life is much broader. They create frameworks for continuity of argument and interpretation of competing definitions of identities and loyalties. They encourage an informed matching of principles to situations by providing institutional contexts for discussing identities and their implications (MacIntyre, 1984, p. 222). What is appropriate behavior by a public official? By a citizen? How is an identity expressed in this situation? What does it mean to be a proper political person? Since these understandings are produced within the social context of political institutions, they are social meanings molded by the necessity of talking about them.

At the same time, institutions that encourage deliberation contribute to developing the climate of democracy. Since the process is built on the principle that disagreements are settled by reflection and open, competent discourse among equals, it can help create, maintain, and strengthen bonds of common citizenship. Civilized debate can promote respect, trust, affection, loyalty, and mutual obligations. It can stimulate tolerance for variation and deviation. It can make it easier to locate areas of substantive agreement and to develop genuine political communities.

Unfortunately, the democratic aspirations for talk sometimes exceed its effects. The demands of tolerance and reason are not easily met in any group, and they are particularly difficult to satisfy when strangers with manifest differences meet without incentives or obligations toward civility. A framework of shared values and substantial agreement about what is morally acceptable and cognitively plausible may be needed to keep political discourse from degenerating into pettiness, rancor, or violence (Reich, 1988, p. 146; Majone, 1988, p. 160). Without such a framework, talk is likely to accentuate differences rather than reduce them, escalate conflict rather than de-escalate it. Democratic governance creates conditions for civil discourse when it can and avoids discourse when the conditions cannot be created, for example by removing certain issues from the public agenda.

GOVERNING SOLIDARITIES

In the course of defining and redefining solidarity, history produces a continuous reconstruction of social integrations. Even demands for individual liberty frequently bring into being new associations (Dewey, 1927, pp. 193–94). Every individual or collective identity establishes itself through a set of differentiations, by creating, maintaining, and changing boundaries. Conflict with out-groups stimulates internal cohesion, identity, and loyalty, and in turn is stimulated by them (Coser, 1956; Schattschneider, 1960; Connolly, 1991). An important aspect of governance is influencing the processes by which these criteria for inclusion and exclusion are crafted and applied.

Creating Solidarities

Ordinary individuals in a social context come to make distinctions and draw boundaries between themselves and others and thereby create foundations for their political identities. What conditions lead people to be mobilized politically on the basis of citizenship, race, ethnicity and nationality, religion, age, territory, gender, or class? What processes help to sustain or reduce differences among separate groups of humans in a world that is contradictory, incoherent, and in flux (Barth, 1993)?

PROCESSES OF SOLIDARITY

National solidarity cannot be created arbitrarily. It involves a mix of territorial control, historical mythology, cultural awareness, and the sharing of formal rights, many features of which are beyond easy control. Nevertheless, nations can be built. Governments can help create national identities as well as reflect them (Eisenstadt and

Rokkan, 1973; Rokkan, 1975, 1987; Flora, 1983; Eisenstadt, 1987). Territories can be claimed, mythologies can be created and propagated, cultural traditions can be glorified, and rights can be granted and proclaimed. The idea of being a German, a Korean, or a Turk is molded by the state's political influence on education and cultural life. In their review of the processes by which national consciousness develops, Smith and Østerud (1994, p. 11) write:

> The *structural conditions* of national consciousness are formed by patterns of communication, mobility, and institutions. The *substance* is made from collective memories, recollections, recognizable myths and interpretations of tradition. The *foundation* is an inter-marriage of a cogent doctrine and an ethnic community, whether dominant or dependent. The *trigger* for nationalist doctrine or movements is generally constituted by more short-term conditions—crises composed of challenges to and options for national reassertion.

In dramatic circumstances—"the great mentality-shaping controversies" (Habermas, 1988, p. 12)—governance and politics may play a key role in identity formation. For instance, the ideology of citizenship in Jacobin thought was an attempt to establish citizenship as the dominant identity against alternative identities of religion, estate, family, and region (Walzer, 1989, p. 211). Likewise, the Declaration of Independence from England by the American colonies was an attempt to mobilize support for a definition of a new, shared identity. It was an attempt to inspire colonists to change their identities and so to forge "one people" (Farr, 1989, p. 27).

National solidarity is supported particularly by the development of external solidarities that can be portrayed as antagonistic to the nation. Solidarity in one group stimulates solidarity in another group that differentiates itself from the first. As a result, efforts to encourage national identity involve focusing differentiation processes and solidarity-matching at the national level, reducing the effects of such processes at either an international or a subnational level. That means doing such things as reducing regional or group competition and conflict, facilitating cross-boundary memberships within the nation while discouraging them across national boundaries, and inhibiting information that encourages or makes possible internal group comparisons while making information relevant to international comparisons readily available (Kramer, 1991).

SOLIDARITY AND THE STATE

Proclamations of the demise of the nation-state are almost certainly premature (Mann, 1993), but a system of political order based primarily on nation-states seems to be under stress. Modern accounts of democratic governance have been created primarily in the context of the nation-state with its emphasis on the organization of solidarity into mutually exclusive and exhaustive loyalties. Contemporary political life seems much less contained by such an organization, and the social and psychological processes for generating solidarity seem to have eluded national boundaries. The elaboration of international communication networks into dense systems for transmission of information and culture has stimulated efforts by nation-states to stem the internationalization of language, values, and knowledge, but with only modest success. The mobility of individuals across national boundaries has created large, fluid communities of strangers within national boundaries and greatly expanded cross-national contact.

Contemporary transformations in the character of political solidarity could be as important as the changes in character as democracy moved from the city-state to the nation-state (Dahl, 1989, pp. 312–19). Torn between internationalization and ethnic-based demands for autonomy within the nation-state, contemporary democracy requires a rethinking of the relevance of boundaries to political solidarity and to democratic justifications. The questions underlying such a rethinking are not easy ones: Within a democratic creed, what justifies national boundaries as a basis for allocating rights and obligations among individuals? What is the relation between the size of the polity and the quality of its institutions and governance (Dahl and Tufte, 1973)? What is the moral significance of state borders for international distributive justice (Føllesdal, 1991)? To what extent do democratic governance and accountability require new solidarities and institutions that are above the nation-states (Milward, 1992)?

Integration and Disintegration

The changing nature of political solidarities produces the phenomena of political integration and disintegration that have become central concerns of contemporary students of governance. Those concerns are reflected in the rhetoric of politics, a rhetoric crowded with the terminologies of diversity and unity. They are also prominent in theories of political development, particularly as those theories address issues of state creation, European unity, and religious and ethnic challenges to the primacy of the nation-state. Much of contemporary West European politics is organized around issues of European integration. Much of contemporary East European politics is organized around issues of Soviet disintegration. The issues are not new ones. The problems of combining divergent interests, perspectives, cultures, and talents into a reasonably coherent system while maintaining a human sense of individual and local autonomy are central to political philosophy and theories of social organization (Barnard, 1938; Gilje, 1988).

UNDERSTANDING POLITICAL INTEGRATION

Students of political institutions try to understand the conditions in which political systems increase and decrease consistency and coordination, the processes by which such changes are realized, and the long-run consequences of specific periods of integration and disintegration. The concerns are not new. Historians of political systems have explored the processes by which such countries as Germany, France, and Italy came to be constituted, the rise of the nation-state in Europe, and the durability of its institutions and practices. Historians of empire have explored the expansion and contraction of great imperial systems—for example, the Roman, Chinese, Ottoman, Spanish, French, and British empires—and their enduring consequences (Eisenstadt, 1987).

Research on integration and disintegration in these various contexts has generally focused on three broad questions: First, what are the conditions of convergence and integration. What are the circumstances under which things that were previously different and uncoordinated become similar and coordinated? Second, what are the conditions of divergence and disintegration. What are the circumstances under which things that were previously similar and coordinated become different and uncoordinated? Third, what traces does a history of integration and disintegration leave? To what extent and in what ways do the consequences of previous integration or disintegration endure into subsequent periods?

Similar concerns are typical of students of many different kinds of social systems. Historians of religion describe the development of great organized systems of religion in terms of theological and organizational pulses of integration and disintegration (Greeley, 1967). Historians of economic systems record the rise and fall of coordinated systems of trade, finance, and fashion (Viljoen, 1974). Historians of science picture the ways in which the development of knowledge is characterized by fluctuations in paradigm coherence (Kuhn, 1962). Historians of language trace the tensions between the centrifugal and centripetal forces of linguistic development and the long-term traces of those struggles in contemporary speech (Bailey, 1991). Historians of human development describe the historical/biological processes by which differentiated human attributes arise, are stabilized, and disappear (Campbell, 1985).

Stories of political development emphasize the significance of identities—national identities, ethnic identities, gender identities, etc.—to the evolution of political systems. The architects of the nation-state relied on the creation of a national identity. The architects of empire reconstructed political identities within their empires, drawing relatively arbitrary boundaries that have often survived decolonization. The development of European political unity is sometimes viewed as dependent on the creation of a European identity. Students of recent political disintegration have examined the involvement of religious, linguistic, and ethnic identities in the collapse of nations.

Empirical studies of social and political integration and disintegration have been framed by three alternative ways of thinking about historical development in social systems. The first is a systemic, functional frame. It sees a system (social, economic, etc.) as having certain functional requirements, perhaps enforced by a struggle for survival. Thus, for example, some students of the development of the multidivisional firm, like some students of the nation-state, portray the particular structures they observe as surviving because they match environmental conditions. The key idea is that historical processes make social structures consistent with environmental conditions. Different environments dictate different structures.

The second frame is an intentional, rational bargaining frame. It sees social structure as arising from negotiation among rational actors pursuing self-interest in a circumstance in which gains may accrue from coordinated action. The level of integration represents a "contract" negotiated among actors with conflicting interests and varying resources. Whether coordination is achieved, and the terms of coordination (for example, who adopts whose system), depend on the bargaining positions of the actors. In more complicated versions, the actors themselves are coalitions of rational actors, and the negotiation goes on at several different levels simultaneously.

The third frame is an imitative, mutual adaptive frame. It sees homogeneity or heterogeneity, integration or disintegration, as arising through contact and processes of mixing, diffusion, mutual learning, and imitation. The specific mixing/imitation processes may be as varied as sexual reproduction, behavioral or attitudinal modeling, or network communication. The basic idea is that contact between parts of the system results in some kind of modification. The modifications may be symmetric between the contacts, but they need not be. The modifications may lead to reducing differences, but they may also lead to increasing them.

The three frames can be illustrated by looking at one theme of considerable current importance in politics—the development of a common European political identity. Within the first (functional requirement) frame, political identity is an instrument of political mobilization and coordination and will evolve to match the survival requirements imposed by the environment. Shared or consistent identities facilitate coordinated action. They will develop as they contribute to competitive advantage to pan-European political institutions. Within the second (rational bargaining) frame, political identities are contracts among rational actors. The nature of a European identity and its acceptance is a bargain among self-interested sub-European actors. It will develop to the extent that it serves those individual and corporate political actors. Within the third (imitation) frame, political identities develop through contacts and spread like diseases or features of the gene pool. As different groups experience each other, they modify their own definitions of self, building new identities through imitation and contradiction. European identity will evolve (or not) as a result of the pattern of contacts and the rules of imitation.

The ways in which elements of integration endure are of particular interest. In studies of technology, these are normally examined under the heading of "lock-ins" or "network externalities." Technologies that tie a system together tend to continue, even after the conditions that initially gave rise to them have changed. Many similar stories are told in other research areas. The British and French empires created boundaries, imposed languages, and introduced numerous trappings of English and French culture and political institutions that have survived long past their imperial basis. Some elements of German traditions of scientific education, imitated in the United States and elsewhere, have endured. Some practices and institutions introduced by German conquerors in Norway and American conquerors in Japan have endured.

But integration often collapses, and students of political and social systems try to understand the conditions in which collapse takes place. Some explanations emphasize the bureaucratic and technical inefficiencies of coordination, centralization, and coherence. Other explanations emphasize the complexities of maintaining consistent integration along multiple (e.g., religious, linguistic, national) dimensions. Others emphasize the positive role of differentiation and contrast in creating meaning. And still others emphasize the contagion of experimentation and revolt.

THE CONTEMPORARY CONTEXT OF INTEGRATION AND DISINTEGRATION

Modern democracies often seem to be characterized by a tendency toward disintegration. The Weberian concept of the state as a unitary political organization with a monopoly of the means of coercion seems inadequate to grasp current realities that involve complex combinations of institutionalized principles and rules organized into "archeological layers" reflecting the context and the time of birth and other critical experiences of various institutions and their constituent identities (Stinchcombe, 1965; Østerud, 1979; Orren and Skowronek, 1994). For many observers, the recent history of the

West is a history of the erosion of consistent cultural traditions that helped to secure social integration, shared moral codes, and a meaningful, purposeful society. In this view, integrated societies have been replaced by uncivil conglomerates of disparate individuals lacking shared perceptions of a common good and shared ethical principles to constrain self-interested egocentrism (MacIntyre, 1984; Willke, 1989, p. 227). Such descriptions are in clear contrast to ideas of either a unitary state (Marin and Mayntz, 1991) or a polity based on a clear division of labor and power among institutions.

The symptoms of incoherence and disintegration are consistent with earlier descriptions of polities characterized by confusing, overlapping, and conflicting demands on individual allegiances, polities organized around emperors, kings, feudal lords, the church, chartered town, the guild, and the family. Like those earlier political systems, contemporary democratic polities seem to be collections of loosely coupled institutional spheres with different purposes, logics, principles, and dynamics. They involve relatively stable, self-organizing networks of interdependent but partly autonomous actors with resource bases and rule structures of their own (Walzer, 1983; Mayntz, 1989; Marin and Mayntz, 1991). Moreover, they are often embedded in divisions based on highly ideological and emotional factors of ethnicity, language, culture, religion, and nationality (Rawls, 1993, p. xviii).

These descriptions of social and political disintegration exist in parallel with descriptions that deplore the overintegration of social and political systems. Some observers have noted (and usually regretted) a decline of individualism. For them, modern societies regiment the thoughts and actions of individuals. They undermine individual autonomy in the process of preference and identity formation. They subvert individuality, independence, privacy, self-determination, and responsibility, creating subjects rather than citizens (Morley, 1958). Individuals may be oversocialized so that their personal aspirations are indistinguishable from those of public opinion, custom, or the state (Mill, 1956; Shklar, 1990). Many of the critiques of the welfare state during the 1980s and 1990s included a call for more diversity and individual variation (Olsen, 1990).

The contrast between descriptions of modern societies as oversocialized and descriptions of modern society as undersocialized and the fervor with which the alternative descriptions are defended may, however, overstate the mutual exclusivity of the two. Community and individual autonomy may decline simultaneously into a mass society, and a strong community and strong autonomous individuals may develop together. Demands for autonomy seem to increase with the development of interdependence, and increasing demands for freedom seem to be simultaneous with increasing demands for government (Lindsay, 1914, p. 131; Hinsley, 1986, p. 128). Modern society seems to make individuals more aware of their rights and obligations to be independent, at the same time as it makes them participants in large-scale coercive systems (Wolff, 1970, p. 17). Growth in state power (de Jouvenal, 1949) and bureaucratic control (Weber, 1978, ch. 11, pp. 1403–5) are sometimes seen both as destructive of a civil society and as inevitable, because the loss of organic solidarity requires the imposition of mechanical solidarity (Gretschman, 1986, p. 398).

THE DIALECTIC BETWEEN INTEGRATION AND DISINTEGRATION

A modern civil society is neither a harmoniously unified moral community nor a collection of free-floating individuals. Politics built exclusively on either (a) individual calculation of interest and business contracts, with no constitutive belonging, obligation, or fellow-feeling, or (b) a community of virtue and a shared identity, with a commitment to subordinate the individual to the common good, remove the contradiction between the capabilities for coherent, coordinated action found in a moral community and the capabilities for experimentation and heresy based in individualism (Yack, 1985). The historical development of democratic institutions reflects continuous attempts to reconcile political authority and individual autonomy and to locate an appropriate balance between community and individuality (Sabine, 1952).

Citizens have certain things in common, which lead them to align themselves with shared traditions and their fellows in the public realm (Miller, 1990, p. 17). At the same time, however, citizens differentiate themselves from others in order to live a private life characterized by a separate and distinct individuality (Friedrich, 1963, p. 139). Notions that equate effective governance with integration built on a unified conception of the good are counterposed to notions that emphasize the necessity of maintaining independence and diversity (Spragens, 1990; Morengo, 1993).

The democratic task is to construct identities that sustain a commitment to civic membership and the moral responsibility to act according to the obligations of one's citizenship and office, along with a simultaneous commitment on the part of both the individual citizen and the political authorities to individual autonomy and the moral responsibility to act according to the obligations of one's personal identity and to sustain the capabilities of others to do so. Such systems maintain an unresolved dialectic between conformity and revolt (Wrong, 1961), between the "bourgeois" calculating and taking care of his personal interests and the "citoyen" serving the common good. Ultimately, the systems work because of institutionalized limits and mutual trust. Institutional actors refuse to exploit opportunities for autonomous action that might compromise the system and are therefore granted a reasonable range of independence. Sustaining those limits and encouraging that trust are an essential part of institution-building (March and Olsen, 1989, p. 166).

GOVERNING IDENTITIES

The institutions of democracy seek to create democratic citizens even as they respond to them. A civilized citizen cannot be assumed. There is ample evidence that the burdens of democratic citizenship weigh heavily on some modern individuals, that genetics, education, socialization, and the structural demands of modern life do not reliably produce individuals who will defend and exercise the rights of citizenship or satisfy the responsibilities. In a society of conflicting interests, identities, values, and beliefs, citizenship rather easily becomes a minor identity rather than a dominant form of self-definition (Boström, 1988; Walzer, 1989, pp. 211–15). Whether an extensive program of civic education is possible and, if so, by whom it would be developed, who would be its proper recipients, and what exactly would be the messages it promulgated all become difficult to answer.

The Political Construction of Identities

Although it is built on a credo of individualism and freedom, and must sustain that credo, democracy is also a set of understandings and shared expectations. Democracy requires citizens and officials whose beliefs, commitments, and conceptions of self and society sustain processes of civilized democratic politics. Being a citizen or public official means accepting an identity and understanding its implications. Governance involves affecting how identities are formed and changed and how they are interpreted.

The dream of a political system regulated entirely through the fine calibration of consistent identities is, however, a fantasy (Berezin, 1991). If it were possible to imagine producing a society of "appropriate" citizens, it is a power that should be denied human agency. Such a nightmare is, however, spared us. There are limits to what can be accomplished by influencing identities within any polity, but particularly within a democracy. Those limits stem not so much from the intractable character of human beings as from their pliability and the difficulty of producing a world of such insularity and stability as to isolate citizens from a babel of identity peddlers.

SOURCES OF THE PREMISES OF ACTION

All institutional theories emphasize the importance of rule-following while recognizing that human action is a mixture of rule-following and preference-following. They differ, however, in their assumptions about how the premises of action arise. There are three main variations:

1. *Premises as given.* In the first variation, the premises of action are seen as given. Expectations, preferences, identities, and rules exist. The task is to determine actions, given those exogenous, prior conditions.
2. *Premises as taken from an actor's experience.* In the second variation, the premises of action are seen as learned from the experience of a political actor. Expectations, preferences, identities, and rules change as a result of learning. The task is to determine how experience leads to particular premises and thus to particular actions.

3. *Premises as taken from others.* In the third variation, the premises of action are seen as diffusing through a population of actors. Knowledge about expectations, preferences, identities, and rules is shared in an ecology of interacting actors. The task is to determine how the sharing and imitation of knowledge and premises leads to actions.

Early work on theories of institutions, whether it emphasized a logic of consequence or a logic of appropriateness, tended to take premises as given. More recent work has moved strongly to seeing premises as emerging over time on the basis of experience. Commitments to preferences, identities, rules, procedures, and forms have all been viewed as products of experiential development and learning. For the most part, this work has considered the ways in which premises of individual actors are shaped by the experiences of that individual, but it has also examined the ways in which premises of action spread among actors.

THE SOCIAL PSYCHOLOGY OF IDENTITY FORMATION

Social psychological studies of identity formation highlight the relation between identity and belonging. When individuals claim or accept identities as citizens of a political unit, members of an occupation or profession, or persons of a particular gender, ethnicity, or religion, they connect themselves to groups of others similarly identified. Group identity becomes a cognitive and motivational basis for the elaboration of beliefs and behavior.

From a cognitive perspective, identities are instruments of simplification. Identities accentuate distinctions, they permit editing of cognitions and framing of actions. They lead not only to stereotyping of others (Fiske and Taylor, 1984; Marcus and Zajonc, 1985) but also to self-definition and stereotyping of oneself (Turner *et al.*, 1987). Being defined as a public official, for example, encourages an individual to articulate a personal set of beliefs associated with that identity and to accept the behavioral demands of office as demands of self.

These cognitive effects depend on (and contribute to) the motivational force of group belongings, the ways in which individuals associate themselves with some groups and dissociate themselves from others (Hogg and Abrams, 1988). Individuals secure their identities and develop self-esteem through solidarity with groups of similar others (Oakes and Turner, 1980; Turner, 1985). They notice and glorify characteristics of their own groups that contrast with characteristics of groups to which they do not belong (Tajfel, 1972, 1978, 1981; Turner, 1975). They share identity simplifications with other individuals in their groups. Conceptions of self are derived from interpretations of actions of others in the groups around them.

Group belonging is often associated with feelings of interpersonal agreement, affection, and perceived similarity—as in balance theories (Heider, 1958)—with positive experience in interaction—as in reinforcement theories (Lott, 1961)—or with current task or resource interdependence—as in exchange theories (Homans, 1961). Group belonging may, however, develop without any of those. In the latter cases, belonging seems to be tied particularly to the distinctiveness of group values and practices relative to comparable groups, to group prestige, and to the salience of outgroups (Ashforth and Mael, 1989).

FORMING IDENTITIES THROUGH DEMOCRATIC PROCESSES

Understandings of self and community are both the basis of democratic politics and one of its products (McPherson, 1982; Sandel, 1982, 1984). Identities develop through debate, education, socialization, and practice within political institutions (Aristotle, 1980). Civic education, institutional training, and public discussion about exemplary identities and lives lead individuals to see themselves as belonging to a culture and to learn the standards by which their conduct is to be assessed. They learn the difference between what they want and what they ought to want in order to sustain a political community and a good life not only for themselves but also for generations to come (Morrisey, 1986; Goldwin, 1986). Democracies teach the canons of democratic citizenship, the importance of law abidingness, respect for the rights of others, and the need (at least sometimes) to give priority to the commonweal over private concerns. Without surrendering their standings as individuals, citizens learn to pursue a vision derived from a socially constructed identity.

In the democratic ideal, culture is accepted knowingly and modified or rejected thoughtfully (Finley, 1973, p. 94). Beliefs, morals, and institutions are neither imposed unilaterally nor transmitted from generation to generation automatically or unchanged. Identities are created through a critical and experimental process of reflection, interpretation, evaluation, discourse, and struggle, of discovery and creation (Tribe, 1972; West, 1988; Nussbaum, 1990, p. 222; Bellah *et al.*, 1991, p. 9), what Habermas calls a "self-activating, reflexive form of appropriating a tradition" (Habermas, 1988, p. 5). In this ideal, citizens reason and deliberate about what is good, who they are, who they want to be, and the kind of community in which they want to live. Attempts by authoritarian regimes as well as revolutionaries aimed explicitly at creating "new citizens" have usually ended in disappointment for the willful architects. Citizens are remarkably resistant to the preachings and teachings of governors when they do not trust their commitment to shared norms (Wolin, 1960, p. 90).

Democratic identities are developed through civic education, in particular for immigrants and children. Indeed, one of the primary ways in which the state's concern with the education of children is made legitimate is by noting their role as future citizens (Rawls, 1988, p. 268). Children learn what good citizens and officeholders are supposed to do, and what it means to perform roles with integrity and skill according to the standards and expectations of a political community. Public programs and public life also establish and exercise political identities. For instance, welfare states have created a large number of identities and conceptions of appropriate behavior via the creation of agencies and jobs, public loans, and welfare arrangements.

Participation in democratic deliberations and decision-making also helps develop democratic citizens and a democratic society (Mill, 1956, 1962; Pateman, 1970; Pitkin, 1981). Citizens react to reminders, public validations, and criticism. Such reminders are given regularly when citizens and officials exercise their obligations and rights, for instance in public elections, national holidays, and other ceremonial occasions. In more dramatic circumstances, officials or citizens are provided with reminders in the form of judicial or political rituals of accountability. Such rituals function both as ceremonies of sacrifice and as dramatic portrayals of exemplary or unacceptable identities and ways of life. Critical public debate, public insight, and legitimate pluralism, opposition, and conflict not only inform and activate citizens but also give them an occasion to develop capabilities to elaborate democratic institutions and identities (Roper, 1989, p. 117).

The Political Management of Identities

Political life is organized by conceptions of identities and appropriate behavior associated with them, and governance involves reminding officials and citizens of the obligations of their identities. Each individual, however, is a mixture of loosely linked identities, rather than a coherent self (Wrong, 1961; Gergen, 1968). Since the occasions on which specific identities are evoked and what they mean are often ambiguous, governance includes attending to what identities are considered and how they are interpreted. Evoking processes are particularly significant in modern, developed, multicultural societies, which provide a large pool of possible identities and where most individuals are not limited to one dominant identity.

Determining the implications of identities, principles, and laws and how they are to be applied in particular cases involves interpretation (Dworkin, 1986). It involves molding beliefs about what obligations, rights, and rules are relevant to a specific situation, which identities are relevant, and what actions follow from each identity in that situation. Studies of the evoking of identities and the rules associated with them suggest a few major mechanisms by which identities are brought to the foreground or pushed into the background (March, 1994b). Individuals learn to evoke identities and rules by experiencing positive consequences of having done so in the past. Individuals treat some aspects of themselves as more central to self than others and evoke those aspects more readily. Individuals conserve recently evoked identities in memory and evoke them more readily again. Individuals are sensitive to the social context, evoking socially acceptable or socially distinct elements of their own identities when the presence of an audience of others is made salient.

Those factors are not all amenable to easy control, but when individuals are seen as collections of coexisting, inconsistent identities, such things as "consciousness-raising" and identity-mobilization have increased relevance. Identities may be evoked or reinforced, for instance, by evoking or mobilizing emotions. A dormant sense of injustice may be aroused (Shklar, 1990, p. 87). For example, managing perceptions of external threats that allegedly endanger identities and forms of life is a way of mobilizing specific identities, political cleavages, and logics of action. A disaster may be used to remind the selfish of human solidarity (Dower, 1991, p. 273). Defining a situation as "normal," on the other hand, may evoke different identities and capabilities. Governance involves organizing experience to provide positive experience to key political identities, encouraging the centrality of the political self, exercising political identities frequently so that they are available in memory, and designing social contexts to elicit attention to the demands of citizenship (March, 1994b).

GOVERNING CONFLICT

The institutions of politics are institutions for dealing with inconsistencies among identities and preferences. Individuals and groups confront one another in elections, revolutions, bureaucracies, legislatures, street corners, essays, and speeches. Maintaining civility in such confrontations is a responsibility of governance. That responsibility is exercised through three main activities: (1) buffering inconsistencies, (2) shaping discourse, and (3) dealing with unacceptable preferences and identities.

Buffering Inconsistencies

Democracies buffer inconsistencies through specializing attention to the demands of different identities (Cyert and March, 1963). Deep conflicts among legitimate concerns are concealed by restricting each to particular times and places using different logics and principles (Walzer, 1983, 1984). For example, taking care of one's self-interest is more legitimate in some institutional spheres (the market) than in others (public bureaucracies). It is more legitimate for some roles (defendants) than for others (judges) within the same institutional sphere (courts of law).

Buffers to attention restrict participation in any particular decision arena and thereby reduce the realization of potential conflict. Coalitions and communities that would be threatened by explicit conflict if attention were not limited are sustained. The variations in attention lead to spatial and temporal inconsistencies that support democratic ideals more than would the alternatives of unresolvable confrontation or value homogenization. This buffering of potential tensions and contradictions is made easier by the existence of slack resources, one of the reasons, perhaps, why democratic political institutions seem to suffer during extended periods of severe resource constraints.

Modern democracies build barriers to conflict by specializing access to institutional spheres so that many individuals and groups are excluded from many spheres, while retaining an interpenetrated and diffuse network of popular control. Hierarchical organization, departmentalization, division of labor, specialization, and the division of responsibility are standard ways in which attention is specialized. They build cognitive and procedural buffers between groups and activities. The flow of attention from one part of a system to another part is restricted. Autonomy, decentralization, delegation, and federation insulate the politics of one set of activities from the politics of another. They localize attention and conflicts and reduce pressure on processes of democratic consensus (Herzog, 1989, p. 173). A judge can define something as legally irrelevant and thus outside the province of the court, and researchers can define something as scientifically irrelevant and thus outside the province of science, in spite of the fact that the same things may be viewed as highly relevant in the province of politics and public opinion.

Such specialization of attention obscures conflicts. Political institutions channel a decentralized flow of capabilities, interests, problems, identities, and solutions through rules of access that mandate, permit, or prohibit attention. The right to participate in particular decisions may be limited to particular people or roles. For example, many kinds of political domains are restricted to citizens; access is denied to noncitizens. The occasions for evoking identities are organized to limit the simultaneous evocation of inconsistent demands in the same place. Only certain problems, solutions, and arguments may have legitimate access to certain decision arenas. For example, constitutional guarantees of freedoms of speech and religion exclude certain forms of policy with respect to religion.

In addition to arranging spatial buffers of attention, politics arranges temporal buffers. Democracies go through periods when the need for community, unity, and shared identities is emphasized, as well as periods when priority is given to the need for diversity, variation and separate identities. Constitutional rules that delay decisions to a later election period may be seen as attempts to provide temporal buffers against short-term waves of feelings and demands for immediate action. Those buffers are essential to sustaining democracy. They allow a democratic polity of disparate voices to function without necessarily reconciling all conflicts (which would be difficult) or eliminating them (which would be deleterious).

More generally, competing demands are accommodated sequentially, rather than simultaneously. As attention shifts, policies shift. For example, consider the cycles of institutional autonomy and politicization in the governance of social welfare. After World War II, there was a tendency throughout the Western democracies to isolate new state agencies of social welfare, protecting them from traditional political processes (Ashford, 1990). Built to insulate their policy processes from traditional governance, these procedures proved less and less workable as welfare states grew and imposed unprecedented demands on governmental budgets. After three decades of substantial autonomy, social policy bureaucracies were forced into closer political ties. New forms of participation required professionalized agencies to organize and cultivate constituents. The political neutralization of the professionalized welfare state gradually dissolved. As the politicization of social welfare grew, so also did the backlog of pressure for a return to professionalization, a pressure that presumably will someday turn the cycle back again. The persistence of such cycles makes it tempting to imagine a procedure for dampening their amplitude, or even for achieving a stable balance. Such dreams have proved to be romantic. There are elements of political genius in a system that buffers the concerns of some groups from those of others so that they are confronted through their sequential effects on each other rather than simultaneously.

Stimulating and Shaping Discourse

Democracy presupposes free opinion-formation, expression, and discussion. A democratic polity is a collection of arenas for discourse. It provides institutions for the formulation and expression of informed sentiments and for the collective consideration of information and options (Bay, 1965, p. 6; Næss, 1968, pp. 111–15). In the ideal democracy, practical reasoning and reasoned compromise determine the course of action (Habermas, 1981, 1992b). Practical reasoning is the judgement of citizens informed by thoughtful discussions and debate. It reflects awareness of the political context, of the natures and desires of other citizens, of physical and social realities, of moral and ethical imperatives, and of historical circumstances (Nussbaum, 1990). Reasoned compromise is the mutually sensitive accommodation of unresolved conflicts through the articulation and exploration of sentiments and the empathic balancing of diverse concerns. Providing an institutional context for practical reasoning and reasoned compromise is not easy. It requires providing institutions that generate relevant and valid information and providing institutions for informed and civilized argument.

INSTITUTIONS OF INFORMATION

Democratic discourse implies relevant and valid information. The classical political problems with information are (a) that knowledge is never neutral, so ignorance may be seen as serving the interests of some political actors, and (b) that experts may not be neutral and may manipulate political actors by misrepresenting knowledge. Political institutions cannot avoid these problems. They cope with them by some combination of a division of labor, a cobweb of overlaps, and public competition. The division of labor is celebrated in virtually every treatment of expertise and politics: Experts attend to issues of knowledge (means); citizens and politicians attend to issues of political values (ends). The overlaps are reflected in the internal organization of the community of experts and the community of politicians: Some politicians become quasi-experts; some experts become quasi-politicians; thus they monitor the others (and are co-opted by them). The public competition is played out in political contests and competition of contending experts and politicians: Experts solicit political confrontations to further the interests of their expert groups; politicians solicit expert confrontations to further the interests of their political groups.

In pure form, there are two rather different procedures for the democratic organization of expertise. The first depends on the idea of "expert opinion" as the refined reflection of the collective voice of a community of experts. One concrete institutional manifestation of this procedure is found in requests from governmental agencies or the U.S. Congress to the U.S. National Academy of Sciences for reports that reflect the scientific community's best judgment on the scientific facts associated with particular problems. These reports purport to assess the evidence, mediate among contending opinions, and render a set of judgments. They may report disagreements, but their main thrust is to allow scientific expertise to speak with a single, carefully considered voice.

A second pure procedure for organizing democratic expertise relies on public confrontations among contending experts, possibly speaking as representatives of particular political groups, possibly speaking simply as experts with conflicting views. In this case, there is expert opinion but no attempt to certify a common assessment by the community of experts. An institutional manifestation of such a procedure is found in testimony of contending experts before committees of the U.S. Congress.

In practice, democratic institutions rely on a mixture of the two procedures, honoring the first particularly in situations where political lines are not sharply drawn and the expert establishment is relatively unified, and honoring the second particularly in situations where political and expert opinion is more sharply and publicly divided. The practical problem is simultaneously to develop, refine, and communicate a shared picture of the world and to explore possible alternative pictures. The balance between establishing an understanding of a temporary "truth" and keeping the system open for consideration of alternative "truths" is continually threatened by the short-run advantages of stabilizing belief into a reliable, socially certified truth (March, Sproull, and Tamuz, 1991).

To accomplish this, a democratic polity requires a rich mélange of information and suffers when there is monopolistic control over information or when an expert community is monolithic in belief or organization. Improving democratic information involves tolerating, even encouraging, a critical stance toward political and expert authorities, cherished truths, and shared beliefs (Thigpen and Downing, 1987, p. 645; Shklar, 1990, p. 116). Discourse profits from engaging deviant opinions and conceptions of identities. It profits both by the exercise of exposing them and by the opportunity to learn from them (Bobbio, 1990, p. 22).

Much of the information on which a democratic polity acts is gathered, analyzed, and communicated by government agencies, and the way in which that information is generated and disseminated by and within the government affects the quality of democratic discourse. The tensions among technical experts, their government masters, and their masters' political opponents are legendary with respect to government-collected information about population characteristics, national economic product and productivity, employment and unemployment, cost of living, population changes, trade balances, crime rates, pollution, literacy, income distribution, tax avoidance, safety records, and a host of other topics. Negotiating such information involves delicate attention to the twin dangers of technical error and political suicide. The objective of governance is not to eliminate either the technical or the political concerns in information negotiation but to assure that the tortured results of a melding of those concerns can be used as a credible basis for intelligent political discourse.

The print and electronic media are similarly crucial to organizing information in a democracy. Democratic theory celebrates a free press as an instrument of improving public information. The celebration is continually compromised by the disparity between the ideal of a free press communicating to an intelligent and concerned citizenry and the reality of the media and the patterns of readership, listenership, or viewership that exist. Media information inadequacies are matched by inadequacies (from the standpoint of democratic discourse) in the demand for information by media customers. The governance problem is to imagine ways of managing a system of news that is free and also contributes to intelligent discourse.

INSTITUTIONS OF ARGUMENTATION

Democracies make decisions by means of discussion and deliberation, and a key democratic objective is to form a community of reasoned debate for such collective decision-making. Actions are to be
based on judgments informed by civilized argument among citizens
and officials (Rawls, 1971, 1985; Habermas, 1981; Yack, 1985;
Manin, 1987; Dryzek, 1990; Spragens, 1990; E.O. Eriksen, 1993).
Citizens and officials need to congregate, confront, and educate each
other (Crick, 1983, p. 33; Habermas, 1981; Dryzek, 1990). They
need to deliberate about what the rules for living together are, which
rules are relevant in specific situations, and what changes in rules are
required as circumstances vary.

Political discourse is not simply a matter of applying intelligent
debate to the difficulties of the polity, resolving conflicts, and solving problems. Democratic politics is also a process by which citizens
construct interpretations of collective difficulties, their causes, and
their remediation, and by which they achieve reasoned discussion
of purposes, ends, and identities (Yack, 1985; Hanson, 1985; Spragens, 1990; Dryzek, 1990). The dream of democratic argumentation is integrative. Clashes among private interests may be
transformed by deliberation into a question of what is good for the
community and acceptable in it. Insofar as they are induced to support their arguments by relating them to general rather than particular interest, speakers in public deliberations become united by a
common enterprise and bound by obligations to, and understandings of, others.

As new arguments and information are introduced to political discussion, citizens are led to revise not only their choices but also their
perceptions of themselves, other citizens, and their situation (Gilje,
1988). They come to understand what counts as good or bad arguments or interpretations within democratic practice (Dworkin,
1986, p. 14). They come to conceptions of individual and common
purpose, a tolerance of differences, and an acceptance of obedience
to democratic decisions as a necessary condition of civilized social
existence (Finley, 1973, pp. 13–14). The core idea is neither to eliminate conflict nor to be indifferent to it. Citizens remain distinct persons who retain their own integrity and honor the autonomy of

others (Spragens, 1990), but they maintain the contradiction between individual desires and the common good that typifies the democratic experience (Yack, 1985).

The elaborate rules of parliamentary procedure found in democratic legislatures have evolved in such a spirit. Although they are frequently violated in practice, the intent of the principles of such rules
is clear. It is to express the mean spirits of interpersonal and intergroup conflict in the form of cooperative, collective problem-solving. Political enemies address each other with elaborate forms of
politeness; the rules of debate assure that a variety of voices will (at
least in principle) be heard and that even the most obvious appeals
to prejudice and self-interest will be expressed in terms of service to
the commonweal. Public standards of fairness make citizens observe
constraints on the public agenda and their behavior. Attention is directed away from issues that may be destructive for the polity and
public discussion is protected from dangerous confrontations
(Rawls, 1980, 1987, 1988).

Democratic procedures of discourse seek systematically to subordinate authenticity in the expression of personal feelings, intentions,
and motives to a ritualized politeness that mimics a community of
shared commitments, values, and affection. The hypocrisy is not a
flaw but a gamble that sentiments can be shaped by conventions of
expression. It is a gamble that is, of course, not always won, nor
should it be. The practice of hypocrisy protects the self at the same
time as it transforms it. And politeness and rules of argument are
rarely politically neutral. Moreover, the civility that makes communication possible and tolerable may sometimes allow unexpressed
feelings to fester. Sentiments that are inappropriate to express may
nonetheless exist, and the contradiction between individual autonomy and the common good may be confounded with the contradiction between what is felt and what should be said. Nevertheless, the
civilizing of democratic conflict through procedural and linguistic
constraints on discourse is an essential element of governance. Exclusion from discourse of issues such as those involving religion, language, or nationality are manifestations of democratic tolerance.
They are also practical procedures for removing divisive argument
from the political arena.

Dealing with Unacceptable Preferences and Identities

The basic presumption of democracy is that the political system will be responsive to the wishes of citizens. Many of the more important features of democratic politics are designed to assure such responsiveness, and probably the most common political diagnosis of social ills is a breakdown in responsiveness. Such a diagnosis cannot be assumed, however. To attribute all defects of democracy to defects in representation requires the unconditional granting of legitimacy to existing identities and preferences. Sometimes a democratic system is functioning well in the sense of reflecting the wishes (preferences, interests) of citizens, but the wishes are defective in the manner of their creation or the nature of their content. As a result, theories of democratic governance have to attend to two kinds of defects in identities and preferences: defects reflecting false consciousness and defects reflecting the existence of evil.

It is a responsibility of substantial delicacy. Definitions of unacceptability in wishes have often been used historically to exclude potential political actors whose main perversion was disagreement with established authority. A democratic polity is a pluralist association of separate, distinctive, and unconditionally valuable individuals (Wolff, 1970; Gutman, 1985). Nevertheless, pluralism does not require equal responsiveness to all identities and desires (Selznick, 1992, p. 91). It is neither possible nor just to allow all conceptions of the good to be pursued. There must be bases for defining the limits of acceptability and procedures for determining whether they are exceeded in a particular case (Rawls, 1988). Governance involves being unresponsive to identities and preferences that are conspicuously inauthentic or evil.

THE PROBLEM OF FALSE CONSCIOUSNESS

False consciousness is a dangerous concept, and imputing unconscious desires to a free individual is a pernicious habit that should, in general, be resisted. In modern polities, the idea of false consciousness and its associated therapeutic devices have, in fact, been major contributors to loss of authenticity. "Consciousness raising" is often used as a label for techniques that subordinate individual, autonomous creation and realization of a self to a sloganized, standardized caricature. Democracy assumes that most of the time the best judge of a person's needs is that person and that efforts to reinterpret the self should be protected from manipulation.

The presumption that individuals have privileged access to their own identities and purposes seems a natural and desirable premise of democracy, but the privilege is not absolute. Individuals can be misled or mislead themselves. Authenticity is supported by dialogue, reasons, and reflection that confirm the autonomous basis of individual claims on the polity, and good democratic governance includes the possibility of rejecting the authenticity of claims that are inadequately based (Perry, 1988, pp. 20, 151–53). Identities and preferences lose authenticity when their bases are corrupted by false information, frames, emotions, or conclusions—in short, by false consciousness. Democratic governance involves assessing the authenticity of beliefs and responding to them in ways that reduce the dependence of political action on wishes that misrepresent the individuals who hold them (Meyers, 1989).

If the cure is not to be worse than the disease, however, governors must act to ensure an open process in which beliefs are created and confirmed (Sunstein, 1990, pp. 47, 58). Attention should be focused on the social and political conditions that facilitate rather than impede the exercise of self-critical rationality and an undistorted vision of possibilities. Preferences and identities need to be criticized, tested, transformed, or rejected through public (moral) discourse, rather than through the unilateral imposition of governmental dictates. Political processes should seek to be thoughtfully responsive to those identities and preferences a citizen might have developed with full awareness of available opportunities, with all available information, and without illegitimate or excessive constraints on self-determination, including social pressure and governmental demands (McPherson, 1982, p. 267; MacIntyre, 1984, p. 52; Selznick, 1992, p. 29).

Autonomous, thoughtful, farsighted, sensitive selves command consideration. Manipulated, unreasoned, myopic, insensitive selves do not. In particular, the preferences and identities to which the polity should respond are those that allow individual citizens to flourish as free human beings. For example, identities may be deformed by monotonous tasks, long hours, and lack of control over work activities. Circumstances may confine imaginations, awareness of alternatives, and actual possibilities so that individuals "learn" to endure injustice. Individuals learn to keep their wants consistent with their achievements. They adjust preferences to possibilities and identities to experience, and thus adapt themselves to injustice. The hopelessly deprived learn to desire little, not because deprivation is a just fate but because unfulfilled desire is an unbearable pain. People come to believe that they should be in an inferior position (Elster, 1983; Perry, 1988; Nussbaum, 1990; Sunstein, 1990, 1991).

As Amartya Sen observes (1992, pp. 6–7):

> In situations of persistent adversity and deprivation, the victims do not go on grieving and grumbling all the time, and may even lack the motivation to desire a radical change of circumstances. Indeed, in terms of a strategy for living, it may make a lot of sense to come to terms with an ineradicable adversity, to try to appreciate small breaks, and to resist pining for the impossible or the improbable. . . . The extent of a person's deprivation may be substantially muffled in the utility metric, despite the fact that he or she may lack the opportunity even to be adequately nourished, decently clothed, minimally educated, or properly sheltered. The misleading nature of utility metrics may be particularly important in the context of stable differentiation of class, gender, caste, or community.

Satisfying such inauthentic preferences or fulfilling such inauthentic identities makes a polity less democratic rather than more and frequently succeeds only in supporting the status quo.

THE PROBLEM OF EVIL

Authenticity is a necessary, but not sufficient, condition for democratic responsiveness. Among the varieties of human desires and identities that are produced by authentic processes, some are evil. They are unacceptable, inconsistent with the polity or culture. At various times democracies have placed certain preferences or behavior beyond democratic negotiation, including such things as certain kinds of marital and family relations, certain modes of dispensing justice, and certain practices based on interpretations of religious or philosophical doctrines. Modern democratic governance, for example, would not be expected to respond to desires, however widespread, to be or possess a slave.

Like the concept of authenticity, the concept of evil is a dangerous one for democratic theory. Democracy has often been destroyed in the name of combating evil, and the capacity of a democratic system to transform, rather than banish, the absolutism of true believers, fundamentalists, moralists, bigots, and the sin police into healthy hypocrisy is one of its most precious capacities. Sustaining democracy involves recognizing clearly the reality of evil but confirming any particular manifestation slowly and with great care and wisdom.

Chapter Four

DEVELOPING
POLITICAL CAPABILITIES

Developing appropriate identities and acting in accordance with them require resources and capabilities. The rules of a political order distribute capabilities among rulers and ruled, among individuals and communities, and among various institutions and corporate bodies. Political institutions establish, protect, and control education, the media, politics, social mobility, markets, systems of private property, the legal system, the family system, technology, and research. They manage the development of knowledge, access to it, and the distribution of skills for exploiting it. They maintain social norms and constitutions, and preside over their change. They develop and support organizations through which political energy can be applied to political problems. They provide a structure of laws and sanctions for not obeying them. In this chapter we examine these political capabilities, their dynamics and their links to political identities, how capabilities are diffused, how they are mobilized, and how they are matched to democratic hopes. The tending of capabilities—creating, sustaining, mobilizing, and regulating them—is a task of governance (Sen, 1992). Without such a structure of capabilities, little in the way of individual or collective purpose can be accomplished.

BUILDING CAPABILITIES

Government can contribute to the creation of rights, the allocation of resources, the development of competence. Capabilities can be built. Many of the capabilities used in politics are nominally developed outside the political system. Wealth, knowledge, physical energy, and organizational capacity are products of an economic and social system. That system cannot be controlled precisely by political action, but it can be influenced.

Varieties of Capabilities

Among the many capabilities created, distributed, and maintained by democratic polities, we can distinguish four broad types particularly relevant to governance: rights and authorities, political resources, political competencies, and organizing capacity. *Rights and authorities* empower citizens and officials. They provide discretion over resources and actions. Officials need legitimate authority, and citizens need autonomy. Authority to levy taxes is granted to a legislature. Authority to make certain decisions and allocations, to take certain actions, is granted to an official. By exercising valid authority and having that exercise certified by political institutions and culture, officials establish their existence as officials. The right to vote, the right to engage in free speech, and the right to hold property are granted to a citizen. By making valid claims of rights and having those claims confirmed by political institutions and culture, citizens establish their existence as citizens.

Rights and authorities are capabilities easily enshrined in formal rules but more difficult to maintain in day-to-day political life. The modern terrain of political regimes is populated by impressive legal arrays of rights for citizens and authorities for officials, but many regimes with comprehensive systems of legal protections are models of tyranny in which citizens are routinely mistreated and officials routinely bullied. Rights and authorities are protected, interpreted, and enforced by a structure of norms and institutions that depend almost entirely on public support for their ability to function. Any protection can be ignored and, being ignored, does not exist. Support by any one citizen depends on expectations of support from others, expectations that depend on the perception of those rights and authorities as meeting shared standards of appropriateness. Both the strength and the occasional fragility of rights and authorities stem from this reflective property of legitimacy. And while the process maintains the norms and institutions that assure stability, it also provides arenas in which rights and authorities are continually being negotiated and renegotiated, interpreted and reinterpreted. Controversies over and discussions about legitimate rights and authorities constitute an important part of the democratic political process.

The second type of capability includes the *resources* available to individuals and institutions. By resources we mean the assets that make it possible for individuals to do (or be) things or to make others do (or be) things. Those assets include money, property, health, time, raw materials, information, facilities, and equipment. They also include such individual attributes as social standing, location, physical size and energy, ethnicity, gender, and age. They include such institutional attributes as size and location. Individuals and institutions vary in their wealth, in their access to other material goods, and in the time they have for (or choose to spend in) politics. They vary in their access to information. Hospitals without bandages cannot function as proper hospitals. Libraries without books cannot function as proper libraries.

Although modern enthusiasms for competitive markets tend to remove normative constraints on the exchange of assets across institutional sectors, democratic polities have traditionally tried to make assets institution-specific. Much of democratic governance involves building and protecting barriers to trade or formulating conversion rules across the borders of institutional spheres. Physical strength cannot legitimately be used to threaten political representatives, bureaucrats, judges, or fellow citizens, but it can be used to work long hours. Money cannot legitimately be used to buy a desired court decision directly, but it can be used to buy the best legal expertise available. Money cannot legitimately be used to have a desired public policy adopted, but it can (within some constraints) be used to support political parties and candidates, professions, or newspapers who work for that outcome. There are few direct rules against spending time in politics, and usually the complaint is that many citizens attend too little, but systems of representation and various access rules tend to constrain the political value of free time and energy. Likewise, inalienable rights and autonomous institutions tend to limit the political value of being a majority.

The third type of capability includes the *competencies* and *knowledge* possessed by individuals, professions, and institutions. Individuals have competencies gained from education, training, and experience that affect their effectiveness in political settings. They know things. To act appropriately as a translator from Arabic to English requires knowledge of both languages. To act appropriately as a police officer requires knowledge of police procedure. Citizens without resources of education cannot function as proper citizens; they have difficulty resisting the sloganized election appeals purchased by campaign spending (Kenny and McBurnett, 1994). Institutions encode knowledge in traditions and rules. They sustain those capabilities through socialization and systems of knowledge retention and retrieval. They have educational systems, libraries, archives, and traditions.

Knowledge is a foundation for political capabilities in most democratic polities (Crozier, 1964; Weber, 1978), but the value of specific knowledge depends on such things as changing political agendas, changing beliefs in political means, and changing competition from groups with alternative knowledge and experiences. For instance, the development of the welfare state increased the political relevance of some professional groups. Medical doctors, nurses, teachers, and their associations became more valued participants. Shifts in professional beliefs also change the political relevance of professional competencies. In many countries during the 1970s and 1980s, Keynesian economists had to surrender political positions to monetarists and supply-side economists. Likewise, one profession may face competition from another. When government by rules is replaced by government by objectives, lawyers and other experts on rules tend to lose positions to economists and other means-end experts.

The political capabilities generated by knowledge are contingent rather than absolute. Democratic grants of authority to experts are constrained by fears of meritocracy. Politicians know that they depend on bureaucrats but try to avoid bureaucratic dominance. In a similar way, the political capabilities of institutions of knowledge, such as the university, vary over time. The ebbs and flows are tied to changing assessments of the risks of ignorance and dependence and are orchestrated by accounts arguing for the self-governance of universities or for their control by political authorities and market forces.

The fourth type of capability is the *organizing capacity* that allows effective utilization of formal rights and authority, resources, and competencies. Democratic political thought has long focused on the dangers of organized factions (Hamilton, Jay, and Madison, 1964) and well-organized military or police forces; such concerns have been echoed in more recent discussions of the organizing rights of antidemocratic parties or movements and of the democratic contributions and threats stemming from corporative representation in democratic politics (Schmitter and Lehmbruch, 1979; Lehmbruch, 1984; Rothstein, 1992). Nevertheless, an important part of the development of democratic polities has been the granting of rights and capacities of organization to deviant groups (Dahl, 1966). Without organizational talents, experience, and understanding, the other capabilities of democracy are likely to be lost in problems of coordination and control, logistics, scheduling, allocation and mobilization of effort, division of labor and specialization, motivation, planning, and the mundane world of meeting deadlines, budgets, and collective expectations. Attention must be focused; activities must be meshed to produce combined effects; people must be consulted and involved; resources must be conserved and expended in a timely fashion.

Capabilities for organizing are partly created by the polity. Legal rights to constitute an organization and to exercise its privileges are typically granted, protected, and regulated by the state. Organizing capabilities in modern democracies are, however, less dependent on political regulations and constraints than on the availability of other political resources and competencies, such as money and knowledge. Although democratic history shows that strong mass organizations have sometimes been developed on a basis of sparse formal knowledge, modest practical organizational experience, and little money, organizational capacities often feed upon and contribute to other political resources and competencies.

The Dynamics of Capabilities

Capabilities can often be created by deliberate action. Wealth can be redistributed. Education can be made available. Rights to participate in political processes can be granted. Organizational capabilities can be created. The welfare state is an experiment in creating, regulating, and reallocating capabilities in a democratic context. But capabilities have a dynamic of their own. Some capabilities are depleted by use; others are augmented by use.

CAPABILITIES THAT ARE DEPLETED BY USE

Many capabilities are expendable. Capabilities that are used at one time or in one place are unavailable for use at another time or place. Many kinds of financial or physical resources fit this description. Spending money or extracting oil leaves less money to spend or oil to extract. Resources devoted to one project are not available for another. Expending energy or political power leaves less energy or political power to expend. Energy used to execute one set of rules is not available for another.

One of the more common complaints about political systems is that legislators fail to consider those opportunity costs. They overload implementing agencies, imposing new obligations without providing resources adequate to fulfill them (Bardach, 1977). They waste their material and political resources on unimportant projects, leaving fewer resources for more important ones. In particular, they devote resources to coping with current crises rather than to reducing the likelihood of future crises. The current political generation taxes future generations by borrowing for current consumption.

Certain kinds of power, rights, and authority also are depleted through exercise. The claim of a right or authority may make its future exercise less feasible because of the sense of imposition that it makes on those responding to the claim. Rights and authorities sometimes draw on a "credit" of tolerance and can exhaust that credit when used repetitively. Similarly, rules of reciprocity are based implicitly on notions of capability depletion. Relationships of friendship, trust, or alliance provide political capabilities. If they assume reciprocity, however, use of the political capabilities provided by the relationship reduces the amount of political capability available for future use (in the absence of reciprocal favors).

CAPABILITIES THAT ARE AUGMENTED BY USE

Some capabilities are augmented by use. Many kinds of technical and organizational skills fit this description, as do some forms of political power. The more frequently a task is performed, the more competently it is done. The more often an organizations faces a problem, the more effectively it deals with it. The more often power is exerted, authority is claimed, or rights are asserted, the more they are conceded to exist. The more claims that are made on (nonreciprocal) friendships, the greater the friendship and the possibility of further claims.

The "learning-by-doing" characteristic of some kinds of capabilities has consequences for governance. On the one hand, it suggests that political capabilities profit from exercise. Even if early experience with a program demanding new competencies or rights results in failure, subsequent experience may be more favorable. The returns from new projects or legitimacies are likely to be disappointing at first, more satisfying later. Insofar as democratic institutions respond to immediate pressures, there is a tendency to abandon activities, rights, or authority before competence is gained, thus a tendency to abandon potentially good initiatives prematurely.

On the other hand, "learning-by-doing" also leads political institutions to become overcommitted to what they have done and are doing. Since current performance depends on both the potential return from an activity and present competence at it, performance shows increasing returns to experience (Arthur, 1984). Each increase in competence at an activity increases the likelihood of rewards for engaging in that activity, thereby further increasing the competence and the likelihood (Argyris and Schön, 1978; David, 1985). It is quite possible for competence in an activity to become great enough to make activities with greater potential unattractive in the short run (Herriott, Levinthal, and March, 1985; Levinthal and March, 1993). The argument extends beyond technical competencies to experience with the rules of a political institution. Experience with a particular combination of rules, rights and authorities tends to develop competence within existing frameworks and makes experimentation with other combinations less likely.

The argument has been used to explain some of the stability in political systems. Proponents of a British parliamentary–cabinet government system in the United States or of an American separation of powers systems in the United Kingdom recognize that the accumulated experience of each country with its own institutions makes a change unlikely. The accumulation of competence is one reason for the difficulty of moving to a democratic political system after an extended period of centralized authority. It is also one possible partial explanation for the persistence of welfare policies in states where there has been extensive experience with the welfare state and the persistence of market-based policies in states where there has been extensive experience with markets. The technical and political skills required by either system are so developed and refined by experience with them that shifting to another technology of economic and social policy and rights leads (at least for an extended period of time) to a substantial decrease in performance.

Just as political competence is augmented by experience in using it, it atrophies through disuse. When societies do well, settling political issues without effort, or when they are buffered from problems by slack resources, those political capabilities that are susceptible to augmentation through use tend to wither. For example, the political skills involved in forming coalitions, negotiating compromises and deals, and adapting to a changing world may wither when one group or party has an extended period of unchallenged power or when broadly shared values or abundant resources reduce experience with conflict and its effective resolution. When the world is forced to adapt to a dominant actor over an extended period, the capabilities of that actor for adapting to the world are degraded—a traditional problem of dominant cultures, technologies, firms, nations, and religions (Deutsch, 1966; Levinthal and March, 1993).

Nearsightedness in Building Capabilities

Some political capabilities are particularly difficult to build and nurture in a democracy. The difficulties stem from the nearsighted nature of democratic political processes. Democracy has difficulty seeing costs and benefits that are distant, either in time or in space, from the locus of political action. It responds to current and local pressures more easily than to future or distant ones.

NURTURING FUTURE CAPABILITIES

Some capabilities require investments of time and other resources that are well prior to the realization of their benefits. The demands of current problems exhaust current capabilities, leaving nothing to invest in extending capabilities. The political necessities of immediate problems overwhelm the capabilities of political institutions to sustain a longer-term perspective. This is a direct consequence of the temporal distance, uncertainty, and diffuseness of the returns on investment in capability development. Much of the infrastructure of a polity fits such a description. Returns are diffuse and in the future; costs are immediate and focused.

Since long-run survival depends on sustaining and augmenting capabilities, those tendencies to increase the utilization of current capabilities and reduce investment in capabilities that might be needed in the future make democratic political processes potentially self-destructive. It invites some kinds of governance of intertemporal exchanges. A democratic political system based on bargaining and exchange among self-interested citizens is poorly equipped to deal with those problems. In particular, it is poorly equipped to deal with exchanges between current citizens and future citizens. The problem is not a problem of responsiveness, but a problem of representation. In practice, democracy represents the living better than the unborn. A competitive democratic political system makes the long-run interests of future generations vulnerable to the short-run interests of the current generation of political actors.

In order to deal with those problems, the democratic imperative is to develop some way in which future citizens obtain political representation. The political voice of future citizens must be found by enhancing the political capabilities of those current citizens who might speak for them. To some extent, of course, a political system can commission an explicit spokesperson for future citizens. It can create an agency with responsibility for defending the rights of the unborn. It can also create a climate of concern, guilt, or shame—the traditional way in which the weak have mobilized the strong in their defense.

The main mechanism for strengthening the political position of the unborn, however, is the institutionalization of political action. By the institutionalization of political action, we mean two things. We mean (1) that there are key social institutions that are viewed as existing over time, enduring through generations of individuals, and accumulating a collection of practices and rules that reflect generations of social and political experience. And we mean (2) that individuals act within the political system as trustees of those institutions, rather than as autonomous individuals. When a farmer sacrifices current crops to maintain the water table for future generations of his family, he acts as a trustee of his family. When a political official refuses to increase the public debt even though it would ameliorate immediate problems of unemployment, inequity, or injustice, he acts as trustee of the future community. The erosion of institutionalized responsibility through the breakdown of institutions of intergenerational continuity, such as the family, and through the ideological glorification of the individual self have weakened the representation of the unborn and have made democratic politics systematically less attentive to the problems of nurturing future capabilities.

NURTURING DIVERSITY IN CAPABILITIES

Political myopia across time is matched by myopia across distance. Democracy tends not only to be unduly attentive to the pressures of the moment. It also tends to be unduly attentive to pressures exerted at the locus of decision. Some institutions and the capabilities associated with them are more valuable than they are powerful. They have to be nurtured by the self-restraint of a political system. We shall mention briefly two specific forms of distance myopia in democracy: The first is the case of institutions whose value to the political system arises from their removal from politics. The second is the case of institutions whose value to the political system lies in their deviance and variety.

Eunuchs, judges, and scientists. Eunuchs are particularly valued in a seraglio because they pose no threat to the sexual order. At the same time, they are vulnerable because they have no basis for protecting their position within that order. Eunuchs who try to protect themselves by seeking autonomous position in the sexual order of the sultanate will probably fail and will compromise the irrelevance that is vital to their being tolerated. If they are successful, they will become sexually significant, but the significance itself makes them socially less useful.

In a similar way, democracy depends on the removal of certain institutions from an active role in politics—the courts, universities, and civil service. Their value is augmented by their disengagement from politics. They defend political institutions and rules, thus are important parts of the political process, but they are separated from party politics and partisanship. That disengagement, however, makes them vulnerable. Judges, teachers, scientists, and civil servants often are tempted to try to protect themselves by improving their capabilities for affecting politics. Whether they succeed or fail, the effort itself compromises their capabilities for serving the political community.

On the other hand, as long as institutions like the courts, universities, and civil service are not present in the political process, they are dependent on self-restraint on the part of others in political arenas. Self-restraint is not always characteristic of political actors. Recent history, in particular, suggests that local political exigencies easily overcome traditions of political support for the eunuch institutions of democracy. The community of science is a case in point. This community can be imagined to be an association of autonomous, independent scientists, autonomous servants of an international conglomeration of political democracies. Professional standards provide the basis of authority. Scientific opinion is formed in overlapping networks of critical judgment (Polanyi, 1962). Scientific advice is provided to political participants as a basis for policy actions. Such a vision of eunuchry is rather distant from the realities of contemporary science. Political institutions are often mired in unsuccessful attempts to control the processes, directions, and conclusions of science. Governments have often tried to strengthen or control science or the networks of science to further social and political policies (Sörlin, 1994), but the hopes of political authorities to shape science have generally been no more satisfied than have the hopes of scientists to do so.

At the same time, science is often deeply compromised by involvement in politics. Scientists exaggerate their knowledge to secure political support. They twist scientific results to justify further appropriations for their institutes and for political programs they like. They confound their science with their ideologies. They seek public approbation and use their scientific reputations as instruments of political pressure (March, 1980). Those perversions are not accidents. They stem from the underlying instabilities of the eunuch role. The authority, the autonomy, and the innocence of the eunuch are unstable. An effective partnership between eunuchs and their masters is vulnerable to the short-run local advantages either can gain by exploiting the relation. As a result, it is also vulnerable to the consciousness on the part of each of the threat that the other will act exploitatively. The required mutual self-restraint is difficult to sustain.

Requisite variety. Political pressures are Janus-faced with respect to coherence. On the one hand, they tend to be practical. They are directed toward solving immediate problems, particularly problems in maintaining political coalitions. They are more likely to invest in answers than in questions, more likely to adopt reliable procedures than experimental ones. Their horizon is local and current. At the same time, however, they tend to be decentralized. They focus on problems in the near neighborhood of the political arena, and each arena looks at a different set of problems. They respond to the concerns of people who are present more than to those of people who are absent, and the participation patterns change over time and over place.

The result is a continual struggle between centripetal and centrifugal forces in politics. The multiplicity of political arenas, the many semi-autonomous institutions, and the difficulties of coherent political mobilization of interests all conspire to produce a cacophony of policies, actions, and pressures. Those forces are, however, counterbalanced by political, administrative, and mimetic tendencies toward consistency. The ideas of a state, of systematic political programs, and of legal consistency all work against inconsistency. The social construction of legitimacy and the imitative processes by which practices, forms, and rhetorics diffuse through a society lead formally autonomous processes to converge (March and Olsen, 1983).

As we shall note in Chapter 6, where we discuss some of these issues further, determining the optimal level of diversity is itself an exercise in balancing conflicts across time and space, and it is possible that the balance resulting from political struggles may indeed often be fairly sensible. That result, however, would be mostly a happy accident. In addition, the struggle over variety is complicated by strategic exploitation of it. An old principle of organization theory is that each manager wants decentralization (diversity) down to his or her level and centralization (unity) up to it. As one would expect from such a principle, high-level authorities tend to see the short-run advantages of coherence more clearly than the long-run advantages of experimentation, though they may, in the face of adversity, pursue a policy of decentralized autonomy in order to spread responsibility for poor outcomes. Subordinate authorities, on the other hand, seem able to see somewhat more clearly the social advantages to inconsistency, heterogeneity, and variety.

Thus, although many would applaud the variation advantages of pluralism and decentralization, those advantages are often reduced by self-serving exploitation of the resulting independence from control and coordination. Developing semi-autonomous institutional frameworks, for instance, can become not so much a device for protecting variety as a technique for protecting agencies against parliamentary review and influence. And an institutional structure that protects variety runs the danger of fragmenting society into powerful veto groups, representatives of partial interests that use claims of diversity to justify their pursuit of self-interest and prevent a policy directed more to the common good (Willke, 1989, p. 229).

Links Between Capabilities and Identities

The ordinary requirements of survival tend to match identities to the capabilities necessary to sustain them. We can imagine capabilities and identities to arise autonomously and to come together in a match. Inconsistent combinations tend not to endure. Inconsistencies between the two can be seen as failures of a diffuse matching process. Sometimes, however, the links between capabilities and identities are more direct. Capabilities create identities, and identities create capabilities.

IDENTITIES CREATE CAPABILITIES

Most discussions of democracy, appropriately, emphasize the distribution of political capabilities as a factor in the distribution of power. However, capabilities are not independent of identities. The ability of a political actor to fulfill his or her identity depends significantly on the distribution of those identities and preferences in a society and on the institutional rules for making the democratic system respond to those distributions. Consider, first, a vision of politics as a system of voluntary exchange, a search for Pareto-improving accommodations to prior wishes. Such a political system thrives on a certain kind of heterogeneity. In order for voluntary exchange to take place, each trading partner must believe that the exchange increases the fulfillment of his or her preferences or identity. Trading advantage comes from two things: The first is possession of capabilities useful to others; the second is desiring things that others do not. In an exchange system, political power is furthered by demand irrelevance, and political equality is furthered by mutual indifference.

Some of the buffers that produce mutual indifference are excess social resources, ignorance of opportunities, heterogeneity in cultural traditions, physical and social distance, and ideologies of cooperation and affiliation. For the most part, modernism, the rise of nationalism and internationalism, rapid changes in the ease of communication and travel, the development of modern weapons of trade and war, and ideological emphases on domination and subordination all reduce such buffers and make widespread mutual indifference a less characteristic feature of national political systems. From this point of view, many of the social, economic, and ideological changes of the past century have made a democratic process based on voluntary exchange and the discovery of mutually beneficial trades less, rather than more, feasible. That has occurred at the same time as the ideology of exchange has become dominant and a basis for elaborate international political and economic institutions (e.g., GATT, the World Bank, European Union, NAFTA).

Consider, second, a vision of politics as the pooling of prior wishes with respect to collective action. In this vision, politics is a process that produces a collective choice as the weighted average of individual desires, where the weight assigned to each individual desire is some measure of that individual's resources or power. In the politics of pooling, heterogeneity in identities seems less favorable for political equality. Citizens with identities that lead them to want something far from the center of gravity of wishes in the society will be systematically less successful in pooling processes than will be citizens who are less deviant. Just as indifference to the wishes of others provides an advantage in a system of voluntary exchange, agreement with the pooled wishes of others provides an advantage in pooling. In a pooling system, identity or preference heterogeneity in a society places some citizens at a palpable political disadvantage.

Since the political capability of any one citizen is affected by the distribution of preferences and identities among citizens, political institutions for discovering, comprehending, and shaping the preferences and identities of citizens are vital to the democratic principles of political equality. In a pooling political process, the most obvious routes to identities and preferences that make power widely shared rather than concentrated involve institutions that foster shared preferences and consistent identities. The difficulty lies in designing political institutions that promote such identities and preferences, but at the same time sustain the individuality and heterogeneity desired on other grounds.

One idea is to develop an ecology of preferences and identities and a process of political competition and coalition formation that prevent any group from being permanently disadvantaged (Miller, 1983). It is possible, for example, to imagine developing heterogeneous identities and preferences whose policy implications vary independently on different policy issues, so that the positions of individuals similarly vary across different issues. This would produce disparities in power in any one policy domain, but a tendency to equalize power on the average.

It is also possible to sustain political equality through fluctuations in political mobilization and with institutions that partition society into internally homogeneous subgroups. Institutional and regional partitioning may produce serious problems in reconciling the various claims of different subgroups, of course, but systems vulnerable to variations in political activation, and systems of local autonomy, including local governments and political parties, allow many individuals to experience power without requiring that the demands of their preferences and identities be consistent with those of the rest of society. The main point is not that a political system should necessarily embrace federalism or other kinds of partitioning, but that some attention to the distribution of identities and preferences in a society is essential to building a democratic political ecology (March and Olsen, 1989, ch. 8).

CAPABILITIES CREATE IDENTITIES

Capabilities also create identities. Institutional capabilities are solutions in search of problems, competencies in search of purposes and identities. The basic proposition is that capability demands exercise. Legal departments lead to identities for which litigation is appropriate. Hospitals lead to identities that find medical problems. An institute for research on children leads to identities that find research problems associated with children. If a business firm has an office in a national capital, it discovers reasons for involvement in politics (Martin, 1994).

Consider, for example, the relation between the state and professional identities. Programs of the state augment the capabilities of professions associated with those programs and encourage the elaboration of professional identities. Those identities, in turn, stimulate the discovery of reasons for expansion of the programs. The development of the welfare state created new capabilities for social welfare professions, which in turn led to elaborated social welfare identities and professionalization and encouraged the discovery of new social welfare problems and social welfare approaches to old problems. The development of a legalistic state created new capabilities for legal professions, which in turn led to elaborated legal identities and encouraged the discovery of new legal problems and new legal approaches to old problems.

The provision of resources, the definition of rights, the transmission of competencies, and the creation of organization structures all stimulate the development of political identities. On the one hand, those identities are sets of rules associated with having and exercising the capabilities. They bring order to power. At the same time, those identities come to define political actors and through them the political process. People of power in politics see a greater role for governmental action than do people without power, not only because power permits them to accomplish their private goals through governmental action but also because governmental power leads them to define identities that make governmental action seem natural.

DIFFUSING CAPABILITIES

In an ecology of political institutions, the capabilities of any one institution depend on the capabilities of others. Through networks of contact and comprehension, technologies, policies, information, structures, and competencies are diffused. The role of governance is to make it feasible for a system of political institutions to identify, use, and build upon relevant capabilities. A primary problem is how to manage education and the diffusion of knowledge. The objective is not so much to strengthen any particular institution as to make it possible for the collection of institutions that constitute a polity to gain and use knowledge.

Networks of Contacts

Capturing the knowledge of others requires access to them. As polities seek to extend trade; protect political, cultural, and scientific positions; and monitor world events, they develop communication and transportation linkages and regulate their use (Knoke, 1990). Modern technologies have enormously increased the possibilities. The frequency and range of contacts among institutions have multiplied many times over the past few decades. Political institutions routinely maintain contact with other institutions within the same country and internationally. Bilateral and multilateral contacts among political institutions are an ordinary part of international economic, cultural, scientific, and political exchange. Letters, telephone calls, visits, and resources are exchanged. Individuals, committees, task forces, and delegations establish contacts with counterparts elsewhere. They trade information, gain knowledge, and create mutual awareness and the conditions for reciprocity. They establish and maintain networks of association (Håkansson, 1992; Powell and Smith-Doerr, 1994). These networks lead to the spread of political practices (McKeown, 1994). Involvement in rich international contacts are particularly characteristic of small, well-developed countries, and less characteristic of large, less-developed countries.

The structure of contacts is heavily influenced by three standard factors in the development of networks. The first is the tendency for contacts with higher status or more knowledgeable individuals or institutions to be sought by those of lower status or less knowledge. Institutions seek contacts when they expect to profit from them, either by gaining status or by gaining knowledge. For example, more foreign scientists seek to visit Cambridge University than seek to visit a lesser-ranked university. More military officers from small, underdeveloped countries seek training in developed countries than the other way around. The practical complication in translating such desires into actual contacts is establishing a basis for exchange. While the lower-status institution stands to gain both concrete information and political and social standing by the contact, it is less clear why higher-status institutions would facilitate such contacts, except insofar as the receipt of delegations confirms their own higher standing. In fact, high-status institutions often transform such contacts into rituals that reaffirm their own status, grant reflected standing to the visitors, and fulfill collegial identities, but that do not result in serious information or material exchange.

The second factor is the tendency for contacts to maintain consistency with existing norms and relationships. Many contacts between institutions are driven less by calculations of self-interest than by senses of appropriateness connected to definitions of what it means to be a proper scientific institute, military unit, or university. Obligations of appropriate behavior dictate various forms of contacts that are unrewarding in an immediate self-interested way but confirm important identities. Individuals in one country who see themselves as fulfilling a particular identity or belonging to a particular profession are likely to make contact with individuals with the same identity or profession in another country. Two institutions, each of which maintains contact with a third, are likely to establish direct contact with each other. If some institutions of a polity have contact with parallel institutions in another polity, other parallel institutions in the two polities are likely to establish contact.

The third factor is the tendency for contact patterns to be reinforced by immediate favorable experience with them and extinguished by immediate unfavorable experience. Contacts that are comfortable and immediately beneficial tend to be repeated, others tend not to be. Immediate favorable experience with interinstitutional contacts is most obviously connected to their linguistic and cultural ease. When French was the language of international discourse, contact with French culture and institutions was endemic among elites. When German was the language of chemistry, contact with Germanic culture and institutions was endemic among chemists. The extensive contacts among countries formerly part of the British colonial empire are partly a consequence of shared history and resulting parallelism in institutions and partly a consequence of a long history of contact facilitated by a common language and (in many cases) cultural similarity. The durability of such contacts, as well as their elaboration even after they have lost much of their functional imperative, is testimony to the role of past experience in shaping current contact networks. Differences among former British colonies in their linkages with the United Kingdom and each other are traceable to differences in the ways in which the imperial experience was interpreted. Similarly, patterns of contacts between Spain and the former colonies of the Spanish empire in the Americas and between Russia and the former East European client states of the Soviet Union reflect the way those contacts developed in a history of immediate positive and negative experiences.

Contacts are institutionalized through numerous *ad hoc* and continuing associations. Virtually every known collection of identities and professions has networks of international connections, as do many individual institutions. Universities, museums, medical facilities, legal systems, communication and transportation systems, and construction firms maintain ties with their counterparts elsewhere. Private, semipublic, and public international agencies cover most of the world with cobwebs of organized networks, many of them connected to such multipurpose international agencies as the World Bank, OECD, the European Union, or any number of divisions of the United Nations. Efforts to construct international systems of rules, for example in the European movement toward integration, have produced an explosion of rule-devising and rule-confirming networks.

Transferring Capabilities

Exchanges of capabilities, like other exchanges, are sources of collective intelligence (Håkansson, 1987; Kogut, Shan, and Walker, 1993). As institutions in different settings share their individual knowledge, each of them can improve. The benign story of joint progress through transferring capabilities is, however, not the only story of diffusion through networks of contacts, and such transfers are not always viewed favorably. There are occasions on which either side of a capabilities exchange might plausibly discourage it. There are three interrelated threats: (1) the threat that the capabilities and beliefs of one polity will be corrupted by knowing those of another; (2) the threat that the capabilities and beliefs of one polity will be diminished in value by being known to another; and (3) the threat that the capabilities of any one polity will be lost through the turnover of regimes.

THREATS TO NATIONAL IDENTITY AND CULTURE

Ever since the earliest use of resident agents—diplomats, colonial officials, or overseas managers—to establish contacts with other countries, both receiving and sending countries have been concerned about the risk to national identity and culture that such contact entails. It is common for either the receiving or the sending country to impose constraints on contacts between resident agents and local individuals or institutions. Those constraints, when they are effective, limit the transference of capabilities or beliefs.

Sending countries are concerned about the possibility that their agents will go "native," identifying more with the countries to which they are sent than with the countries sending them. Such concerns are accentuated by a consciousness that a certain amount of identification with local residents increases the usefulness of the agent. The concerns are manifested in rules regulating contacts and by efforts to ensure that agents are rotated home frequently enough to renew their allegiances. The latter efforts, of course, face the possibility that returning agents become, in effect, agents of the countries from which they return. Returning agents may infect their home countries with alien ideas and practices, possibly corrupting them into activities that undermine national identities and cultures.

Those threats are not limited to contact between official foreign agents and the citizens and institutions of the country to which they are assigned, nor are they products of espionage and counterespionage plots. The threats are general ones of foreign contact, celebrated by the efforts of many cultures and regimes to restrict the frequency and form of contact between their own nationals and foreign individuals and institutions. It is the problem of candy, drugs, music, television programs, and books—things known to be attractive in the short run but also known to have particularly deleterious long-run consequences for the culture, regime, and institutions of a nation not previously exposed to them. Japan and China were closed to Europeans for many years. The Soviet Union severely restricted contact with Western countries. Many contemporary countries, working with international organizations like UNESCO, have attempted to create a New World Information and Communication Order to counteract what they see as cultural "invasions" from other countries, particularly the United States (Schlesinger, 1991).

That contact among individuals and institutions leads to the diffusion of beliefs and capabilities seems beyond question. The process of homogenization, however, is not quite as smooth as might appear. Knowledge of another person or culture produces divergence as well as convergence, distaste as well as attraction. Returning travelers may well come home with renewed affirmation of allegiances rather than with a new loyalty. Returning technicians may well come home with renewed confidence in their own methods rather than with a new technology. Returning political officials may well return home with renewed faith in their own practices and ideologies rather than with enthusiasm for a new political system. Returning missionaries may well be reconfirmed in their faith rather than converted.

THREATS TO NATIONAL CAPABILITIES

The diffusion of knowledge and capabilities often serves the interests of the source of the diffusion, for example where the value of an idea or practice is a positive function of the number of institutions or individuals knowing or using it. This is the situation most commonly considered in sociological discussions of the diffusion and normalization of organizational practices (DiMaggio and Powell, 1983; Scott and

Meyer, 1994) and in economic discussions of network externalities (Arthur, 1989). A standard example is knowledge about a new managerial practice or a new theoretical idea. Since part of the point is to gain validation of one's own knowledge through its acceptance by others, both parties benefit from the spread of knowledge. Similarly, where norms of proper behavior dictate sharing knowledge, transfer is easier. When politics is defined in terms of collective problem-solving rather than as confrontation of conflicting interests, a norm of cooperative sharing in knowledge is common.

Often, however, diffusion of capabilities and knowledge decreases their value to the original source. That is so in cases involving military or organizational secrets (Sitkin, 1986) and technological transfer, where knowledge provides a competitive advantage (Mansfield, 1985). It is also the case when politics is defined as conflict among contending private interests. Where the spread of knowledge does not benefit the original holder of it, or where norms of proper behavior define knowledge as personal property, transfer is made difficult. Some of the more interesting cases involve situations where there is a conflict of interest between an organization and its members, for example in the case of professionals who gain reputations by sharing knowledge with professionals in other organizations, even as that sharing reduces the value of the knowledge to their own organization (von Hippel, 1988; Schrader, 1991).

Contemporary students of knowledge transfer are particularly interested in the problem of appropriability, the ease with which knowledge developed in one place can be transferred to another (Cohen and Levinthal, 1989; DeBressen and Amesse, 1991). Knowledge is a scarce good, a strategic resource, and a normatively charged possession. As a result, knowledge exchange is regulated by incentives and norms, particularly by incentives and norms that inveigh for or against sharing. As the problem of appropriability is usually framed in economics, it is one of balancing the ease of transferring knowledge with the motivation to generate it. The standard argument is that the social usefulness of knowledge depends on its transferability, but that easy transferability of knowledge (appropriation of knowledge) makes it difficult for a self-interested creator of knowledge to realize rents from it, thus reduces incentives to create it.

From that standpoint, a distinctive feature of the norms of traditional scholarship is an emphasis on the appropriation of ideas as a goal to be pursued, rather than a theft to be prevented. Formal education, for example, involves a massive transfer and appropriation of knowledge. The experience and learning of Newton is transferred to new students so that they gain the knowledge without having to go through the experiences. Since the ones who appropriate the knowledge ordinarily provide little or no compensation to the ones who developed it, educational institutions can be seen as gigantic dealers in stolen goods, modern Robin Hoods, as it were. To be sure, the "theft" of knowledge does not deprive the "victims" of their knowledge, but it does deprive them of whatever value is associated with its exclusivity. The emphasis placed by traditional norms of scholarship and education on the importance of knowledge as a shared public good is in stark contrast to the emphasis placed by some contemporary theories of intellectual "property" on the privatization of knowledge.

The incentive formulation of the knowledge diffusion problem emphasizes the necessity of assuring that those who generate knowledge are rewarded by those who use it. This is, of course, the logic of patents and copyrights. The incentive analysis of appropriability questions may, however, underestimate the role of norms and the institutionalization of exploration. Political institutions and identities contain rules of appropriate behavior that dictate occasions of exploration. Nations must have universities and research in order to be proper nations. Scientists do research and exchange knowledge because that is what scientists do. All of these features of knowledge and its uses have implications for governance. For example, questions about the social management of "property rights" in accounts, ideas, and rules are inextricably entangled with questions about the diffusion of knowledge. Questions about the development of a sense of community and commitment to the commonweal are inextricably entangled with questions about normative structures for knowledge generation and sharing.

In many modern settings, the capability to understand and use new knowledge depends on prior knowledge (Mowery and Rosenberg, 1989). Suppose, for example, that scholarship not only generates new knowledge but also enhances the ability to absorb new knowledge generated by others (Cohen and Levinthal, 1989). Then there are two forms of returns to scholarship: The direct discoveries generated (minus the losses incurred by the ability of others to appropriate the discoveries), and the gains from increased ability to appropriate the discoveries of others. The returns from increased capabilities for using the discoveries of others are likely to be substantially greater than the direct returns from a polity's own discoveries, but those returns depend on the willingness of others to engage in scholarship.

As a result, there may be two quite different stable equilibria in such a system. In one equilibrium, all political systems connected by contact networks devote substantial resources to scholarship. Most of the returns to scholarship for each individual polity come from building capacity to absorb the occasional discovery, ordinarily by others. No individual polity has incentive to decrease commitment to scholarship. That is true even though the direct returns to one's own scholarship are less than the costs. Political systems that allow themselves to fall behind in competence will find it difficult to appropriate the knowledge of others, even if they have access to it (Romer, 1986). The equilibrium is sustained by the advantages of diffusion and the inability to separate the processes that build capacity for exploiting the discoveries of others from the processes that underlie discovery. The second stable equilibrium occurs if no individual polity invests in scholarship. Since the returns to scholarship are primarily returns from using ideas generated elsewhere, those returns are insignificant if no other country is engaging in scholarship. As long as no other country is engaging in scholarship, there is inadequate incentive for any individual one to do so. The governance problem is to nudge the system in the direction of one of these two equilibria or the other. In modern visions, the first equilibrium is usually seen as preferable to the second.

Inventories of Competencies

The changing nature and importance of knowledge both make investment in knowledge bases critical to a polity and pose problems for investing intelligently. Since the acquisition of knowledge requires time and the relevance of possible knowledge is often difficult to know long in advance of when it is needed, political systems cannot ordinarily delay decisions about knowledge accumulation until they know what will be required. They must invest in knowledge inventories (Feldman, 1989). A good knowledge inventory policy, however, is difficult to specify and implement. Education and training build capabilities, but in the short run their costs are more conspicuous than their benefits. Developing databases, generalized expertise, and policy alternatives for domains of possible public interest requires investments in time and mastering many forms of knowledge that will prove to be unnecessary. Political systems that require crises to focus attention on problems and to mobilize support for solutions, as well as political systems that are particularly eager to avoid developing competencies that are subsequently not used, will be disadvantaged in accumulating knowledge inventories.

In practice, democracies have developed knowledge inventories through the efforts of interlocking policy constituencies that include government offices, political parties, business and trade associations, policy consultants, universities, professional associations and journals, and autonomous and semi-autonomous policy research institutes. Those efforts have traditionally been coordinated, if at all, by swings in public and private enthusiasms and by occasional more massive efforts to stimulate work. Most of the time, however, they have continued in relative political obscurity, laying the groundwork for future issues of governance but incubated relatively far from the political process itself. They are part of the "slack" of political and social life.

The importance of governing knowledge inventories suggests that democratic systems of the future may well need to consider more consciously how an adequate inventory of knowledge can be assured in a political system. It is a question tied closely to more general social concerns about the organization and utilization of knowledge in a knowledge-based world. At least on the surface, the idea of knowledge inventories seems to indicate that the organization of governance might be improved by becoming somewhat more similar to computer networks, journals, and libraries than it now is. It is a thought, however, that suffers from assuming that the practice of governors is determined by functional demands. That may be true, but it is also determined by mythology, imitation, and symbolism (Benavot *et al.*, 1991; Hook and Weiner, 1992). Since the symbolism of "political leader as librarian" flies in the face of deep sentiments about the gender of politics and the rhetoric of power, such a change in governmental ideology or practice may well not occur even if warranted.

MOBILIZING CAPABILITIES

Capabilities are necessary for effective action, but they are not sufficient. Action also requires activation and attention. Since attention is a scarce resource, political systems are responsive not only to the distribution of resources, competencies, rights, and authorities, but also to their mobilization. As a consequence, the management of attention is a major activity of governance.

The Organization of Attention

Research on both the private and public sectors has emphasized the allocation of attention and the organization of time as essential to understanding management (Carlsson, 1951; Mintzberg, 1973; Cohen and March, 1986; Hannaway, 1989). Time and attention are scarce resources in decision-making (March, 1988a). Each individual faces more claims on attention than can be satisfied. The various demands of life intrude upon each other (Cohen, March, and Olsen, 1972). An increase in attention to one thing reduces attention to others. The claims of attention from employment and family intrude upon those from citizenship. The claims of attention from constituents intrude upon those of colleagues. The claims of attention from one crisis intrude upon those of other crises. Attention to problems of crime are limited by attention to problems of economic health and international security. Attending more to energy policy means attending less to tax policy. The distribution of attention in a political system is an aggregation of individual allocations. The attention given to any particular political issue, therefore, depends not only on attributes of the issue but also on the distribution of alternative claims on attention.

The idea of attention scarcity requires some emendation that recognizes the extent to which it is possible to attend to more than one thing at a time and the extent to which the attention of any one individual may be augmented through purchase, barter, representation, or threat, but it is a central feature of modern political life. Since not everyone can attend to everything all the time, capabilities mobilized at one time in one place are likely to lead to actions that are inconsistent with those produced by capabilities activated at another time or place. Policies created in the context of one pattern of attention are implemented in the context of another. One pattern of attention results in outcomes that stimulate mobilization of a new set of capabilities. Problems are solved at one time or in one part of a political system in ways that create problems at another time or in another part, which in turn are solved in ways that create problems in yet another time or part.

Garbage can models of temporal sorting illustrate the effects of those constraints on attention (March and Olsen, 1986a). In theories of temporal sorting, problems are defined by the demands of activated actors. Solutions are linked to problems by virtue of their simultaneous evocation (rather than their causal connection). Choices are made by participants who are present. Choices are implemented by actors mobilized at the time and place of implementation, attending to interpretations and issues evoked in that context. The issues, options, decisions, and interpretations are all dependent on patterns of attention. When access of problems and participants to choice opportunities is specialized, or when choices, problems, and participants are each arranged in hierarchical order, the effectiveness of the process in bringing problems to the attention of political actors or in resolving problems is affected (Cohen, March, and Olsen, 1972; Anderson and Fischer, 1986). Empirical observations of garbage can processes also confirm that structural constraints on attention make a difference (March and Olsen, 1976; Powell, 1978; Levitt and Nass, 1989).

Attention scarcity underlies some of the mysteries and opportunities of power. In political competition, attention is a resource that can be used to compensate for disadvantages in the other resources of political power. If less powerful people have narrower concerns than more powerful people, the "weak" can mobilize their capabilities in their own domains and exploit the scarce time and more diffuse interests of the "strong" (March and Romelaer, 1976). This possibility has led to frequent proposals for increasing the political activation of citizens whose position is otherwise disadvantaged by limitations in the other resources of political competition. The strategy is effective, and there is a substantial tradeoff between activation and power, but the effectiveness of the strategy is constrained by the possibility that increasing one group's activation may stimulate the activation of another group sufficiently to result in a net decrement in influence for the first.

Those flows of attention affect not only the mobilization of capabilities but also their development. Attention leads to experience, and experience leads to learning. Skills for dealing with activities or concerns that do not attract attention tend to be lost. When political life goes, well, citizens attend to their private concerns and political skills are degraded. When most problems are solved within the legal system, other systems atrophy.

Perversities of Attention

It is fairly easy for individual attention allocation decisions to result in aggregate patterns of attention and uses of capabilities that are collectively perverse. Individuals, problems, and solutions are found in choice arenas that are (from a collective point of view) less than optimal. Problems and solutions are overlooked because they do not have access to choice situations in which they might become salient, or because their timing is poor. Individuals with talents and values particularly relevant to one set of problems find themselves busy with another set. We mention here two important perversities in the allocation of attention.

GRESHAM'S LAW OF PLANNING

It is frequently observed in both individual and organizational studies of decision-making that search and change are stimulated by failure. In political arenas, it is not hard to observe situations in which economic, social, or military reversals produce demands that are translated into political change. Those observations have led to a number of "demand" theories of individual, social, and political change. Such theories are useful, but they require considerable qualification. Performance crises are neither necessary nor sufficient for change. Failure is subjective, and adaptive aspiration levels make it difficult to predict reactions to particular levels of performance without knowing the history of previous experience. Change is often driven not by demand but by supply, by the existence of an alternative that attracts attention and support and thereby stimulates a perception of a problem to which it is a possible solution (Cyert and March, 1963; March, 1981a, 1994b).

The problems of mobilization are a further complication. If, on average, the ease of mobilization of capabilities were positively correlated with the magnitude of the problem, there would be only some more or less random errors in fitting attention to problems. But the ease of mobilization seems to depend rather heavily on some factors that are actually negatively correlated with the magnitude or difficulty of the problem. Simple problems require less organizational capability than more complex ones. Familiar problems require less organizational capability than novel ones. The easier the problem, the easier it is to organize to deal with it. In general, the likelihood of attending to a problem depends on the time pressure, the clarity of goals, the familiarity of procedures associated with the problem, and the ease of solving it (March and Simon, 1958, p. 185). Deadlines and alarms direct attention to some problems and thereby divert attention from others. Problems that have clear goals and are approached through well-defined programs attract more attention than those for which an approach is poorly specified and the objectives unclear.

There is no particular reason to expect that decisions associated with long time horizons and ill-defined goals and procedures are systematically less important than those with short deadlines and clear performance programs, but the latter clearly divert attention from the latter. This tendency, sometimes called "Gresham's Law of Planning," makes the mobilization of attention surprisingly independent of the importance or magnitude of the performance problems faced. Political systems are continuously exposed to dissatisfaction and desires for reform. Response to those desires depends on the capability to mobilize attention. That capability, in turn, depends not only on the reality of the problem but also on the existence of organizational capabilities for giving meaning and direction to the reforms, mobilizing resources, and creating public support. This allocation of attention makes a certain kind of sense. It focuses effort on things that are known to be achievable. Such a focus, however, is likely to lead politics away from large problems toward solvable ones, away from new problems toward familiar ones.

WRONG PEOPLE, PROBLEMS, AND SOLUTIONS

A second source of possible perversity in the allocation of time and capabilities is a variation on problems that are usually called "externalities" in the social welfare literature of economics. The local allocation decisions of individuals are presumably driven by local calculation of preferences and consequences or local determinations of appropriateness. The aggregate consequences of attention allocation, however, may give these local decisions much more global consequences. The social advantages to having a particular individual, problem, or solution attached to a particular choice situation may not be in line with local incentives and conceptions of identity. From the standpoint of the overall system, a process involving decentralized attention allocation may result in bringing the wrong individuals, problems, or solutions to the decision arena.

A common complaint in this vein is one that points out that those people, problems, and solutions with time to spare are likely to be the people, problems, and solution for which there is relatively little demand. And those people who are most desired are likely to be least available (Olsen, 1976). Busy people are busy, in part, because they have talents and values that put them in high demand. Available people are available, in part, because they do not. Available problems are available, in part, because they represent problems without solutions. Available solutions are available, in part, because they represent solutions that do not solve problems. The result can be perverse. For example, one study of school desegregation in a large U.S. city showed that a relatively sudden increase in official desire to have ethnic minority leader representation on all (rather than a few) public committees resulted in such a load on ethnic minority leaders that their participation in each committee became ephemeral (Weiner, 1976). It is unreasonable to expect that a socially useful allocation of attention will automatically arise from a system in which individuals, problems, and solutions make decentralized attention decisions. In particular, it is likely that the tradeoff between attention relevance and attention availability will be made in a way that is socially undesirable.

The natural market solution to the allocation problem is the introduction of prices, and some kinds of price systems function in some parts of government—for example in the employment of consultants. The natural rule solution to the problem is a system of rights and duties of participation, and such systems are common in government, indeed are the bases of most modern political orders. People with particular useful talents or values are obligated to participate in civic activities for which their talents make them appropriate.

MATCHING CAPABILITIES TO DEMOCRATIC HOPES

Democratic theory presumes that capabilities follow obligations, that the distribution of rights and resources is constructed around, and is designed to serve, the structure of identities. Inconsistencies between rules of appropriateness and capabilities for political action are notable features of contemporary political life. The distributions of political and economic capabilities are often inconsistent with the distributions of rights and authorities. A political system can suffer from assigning too many resources to a particular individual, group, or institution or from assigning too few. It can suffer from having some individuals with too much competence, as well as from having some with too little. Capability corrupts as well as empowers. As a result, societies not only create institutional capacities for action, they also create constraints on the use of those capacities. They specify the time and occasion for the legitimate use of political capability. They restrict the use of physical strength, military capability, economic resources, expertise, and organization. Moderation in using individual, group, and institutional capabilities is a part of the political culture of a democratic, well-ordered civil society.

Capabilities and Democracy

Organized capabilities are a necessity for democracy, and also a threat to it (Dahl, 1989). The contributions of officials to democratic aspirations depend on their capabilities, that is, the degree to which citizens are willing to authorize their use of resources such as coercive power, bureaucratic time and talent, and public funds while linking those capabilities to the will of the people (Schumpeter, 1942, p. 269). Similarly, the contributions of citizens depend on their capabilities, on their ability to control officials, to make them responsible, to hold them accountable, and to keep their authority revocable. Democratic ideals describe how political capabilities, based on rights, authority, power, and other resources, should be constituted, used, regulated, and transferred. Both citizens and officials are supposed to have rights, resources, and capabilities adequate for acting appropriately according to their identities and roles. Individuals and private groups are supposed to have resources adequate to resist illegitimate use of public power, but they are not supposed to be strong enough to disregard or pervert democratic processes.

THE GEOGRAPHY AND GENEALOGY OF CAPABILITY

Political systems grant formal power to adult individuals by virtue of their citizenship. Citizenship is defined, for the most part, in a geographic and genealogical way, linking the capability to function within a polity primarily to residence and parentage. As a result, for the most part the citizenship mapping of individuals onto states is a one-to-one mapping. Each individual is a citizen of precisely one state. Civic rights and freedoms are community and boundary specific and do not extend beyond the polity. The capabilities of citizens are derived from the capabilities of the state, which in legal theory at least are derived from the sovereignty of the state.

A simple threefold division of the domains of governance is implicit or explicit in the idea of a sovereign nation-state. The first domain could be called the domain of administration. It involves the implementation of rules, principles, and policies adopted by a sovereign state. It is a domain of expertise and problem-solving in which there are problems of incomplete information but not of conflict of interest. The second domain could be called the domain of politics. It involves establishing the rules, principles, and policies of a sovereign state. It is a domain of constitutional procedures by which diverse interests and beliefs are translated into rules, principles, and policies that are binding within the state. The third domain could be called the domain of international relations. It involves dealings among sovereign states. It is a domain of war, competition, voluntary cooperation, and negotiation among sovereign states pursuing their own rules, principles, and policies.

Since the capabilities conferred on individuals through citizenship depend on the ability of the nation to enact its claim of sovereignty, democratic theory is compromised by any disparity between the legal fiction of national sovereignty and the realities of political conditions. Such a disparity clearly exists in the contemporary world. The realities of governance seem to escape the boundaries of the nation-state. Modern nation-states are neither all-powerful internally nor autonomous externally; the domains of administration, politics, and international relations are intertwined in ways that considerably complicate their description and effective governance within them. Strong functional interdependencies among states undermine any idea of a congruence between national political capabilities and national political desires (Held, 1991). Crucial decisions have escaped the control of the nation-state as currently constituted. National sovereignty and autonomy have been eroded. Many political units have the legal status of sovereignty without adequate capabilities to give the legal fiction any substantive significance (Jackson, 1990), and even powerful nation-based polities have only modest ability to control several things that are of great concern to their citizens: employment, peace, financial markets, health, environmental quality.

Modern democracy probably requires a conception of political rights, resources, and capabilities that is less dominated by ideas of state sovereignty and the linking of capabilities to geography and genealogy. It cannot be taken for granted that the nation-state is the exclusive framework for democracy, that the fate of a national political community lies in its own hands, and that democracy can be understood in relation to actors and forces within national borders (Held, 1991; Rogowski, 1993, p. 435). This suggests a return to older concerns with how the interaction of interstate and intrastate relations affects political capabilities and political success (Hintze, 1968). It also suggests that students of democratic governance might attend to both the development of capabilities for action in democratic political institutions that are not co-terminus with the nation-state and the development of capabilities for holding such institutions accountable. Such students might, in particular, consider ways of describing and improving the democratic qualities of the global and regional institutions and cooperative arrangements that have developed since World War II (Held, 1991; Wendt, 1994).

To imagine leaping from the current international system to a totally new one in easy steps is undoubtedly romantic. Even modest steps in such a direction face several conspicuous problems: First, geography and genealogy are not only traditional bases of citizenship, they are also deeply embedded bases of feelings of solidarity. Those feelings of solidarity are important elements of effective democratic governance, and it is not clear that democracy is viable without them. Second, every extension of democratic capabilities and rights across national boundaries has to confront the twin reality that the spirit of political equality is clearly redistributive and the current locale of democracy is in relatively rich, economically well developed countries (Burkhart and Lewis-Beck, 1994). The history of expansion of democratic rights suggests that the moral force of equality is typically balanced by the reluctance of the favored few to surrender advantages needlessly. Third, modern networks of international connections are complicated, overlapping, and incomplete. Although most contemporary democracies have some experience (some considerably more than others) with political organization in which different constituencies exist for different purposes and at different times, traditional democratic procedures seem ill-designed for *ad hoc* "virtual" communities.

POLITICAL EQUALITY AND POPULAR SOVEREIGNTY

The dominant conception of legitimate political capability in modern political thought is one based on political equality and popular sovereignty. A necessary condition for democracy in a modern society is the election of governors on the basis of free and equal voting by citizens. Indeed, the history of democracy can be written in terms of the gradual granting of participation and voting rights to an ever more inclusive set of individuals (Bendix and Rokkan, 1964; Rokkan, 1970). In most Western democracies, that process has reached a stage in which almost all adult citizens have a right to vote.

The principal political actors without formal voting rights are resident noncitizens, nonresidents who are substantially affected by the decisions of the polity, children, and the unborn. Contemporary struggles over the rights of resident noncitizens (immigrants or guest workers), the responsibilities of democratic states to nonresidents who are affected by the actions of the state (and vice versa), the political and legal rights of children, and the representation of future generations suggest that the process of extending the franchise has not yet reached its conclusion.

Voting rights are not enough, however. Differences in such resources as wealth and competence translate routinely into political advantages and disadvantages and make equality in formal voting rights inadequate by itself to satisfy democratic ideals (Dahl, 1985; 1986; Held, 1987, p. 290). If the distributions of informational, intellectual, social, and economic resources allow the well-informed, educated, high-status, well-organized, and rich to oppress the uninformed, uneducated, low-status, unorganized, and poor, formal political equality is a sham (Moore, 1966, pp. 498, 501). Political philosophers from Aristotle to Marx have seen political equality as depending not only on an equal distribution of the formal right to vote but also on the equal distribution and effective regulation of economic and social resources.

Democratic traditions make it a responsibility of government to detect and counteract distributions and uses of economic and organizational resources, knowledge and skills, and organizational capabilities that move society away from democratic ideals. Through social policies of taxation, education, and welfare, all democratic societies have tried (some with more vigor and success than others) to moderate differences in the rights, resources, and competencies of different citizens. Complementing formal rules of political equality with a distribution of economic resources that supports them, however, has proved difficult (Dahl, 1985). In the contemporary world, democracies typically have a more equal distribution of nonpolitical resources than do other political systems, but they nevertheless exhibit very substantial differences among individual citizens and groups. The fact that in many contemporary democracies poor people are a minority, rather than the majority that is implicitly assumed in some democratic theories, makes significant redistribution of economic resources to them, rather than to the middle classes, an improbable result of democratic competition for voters.

A constitutional democracy is a form of government that is ultimately rooted in popular sovereignty and majority rule, but democratic ideals call for a community bound together by constitutive rules and roles, identities, shared accounts, and laws (Elster and Slagstad, 1988). Resources, rights, and discretion over their use are embedded in institutions and rules. Those instruments define how agents of authority and power (including citizens) are to be constituted, regulated, controlled, and made accountable and responsible. Constitutional and institutional rules organize political competition. They set out the ends, purposes, and responsibilities of the organs of government, how they originate, their mutual relations, and the relations between governors and citizens.

Constitutive rules specify procedures for making collective decisions and rules for transcending and transforming those procedures in an orderly way. They civilize policy-making and political transformations, minimizing the risk of destructive conflicts. They make certain transformations of resources across institutional spheres illegitimate, thus creating deliberate barriers to free trade in resources. For example, the right to vote is ordinarily made inalienable; it cannot be sold. Rules define spheres of privacy and autonomy from public authorities. Majority rule is tempered by constitutional protections of life, liberty, and property. Attempts have been made to extend the privileged position of civic and political rights to social and economic rights (Marshall, 1950), and regimes that define "democracy" to include constitutionally protected social and economic as well as political rights are common in Northern Europe (Allardt *et al.*, 1981; Olsen, 1990).

Rules turn rulers into officeholders by replacing authority based on power with authority based on office legitimately obtained (Skinner, 1989). They define how authority is created, exercised, transferred, and made responsible. They limit power and authority by the law (Wolin, 1989). They define the proper jurisdictions, procedures, and performance criteria for institutions and institutional roles, for

example what it means to function as a proper parliamentarian, bureaucrat, or judge. The pursuit of personal or group advantage, of
justice, and of practical solutions to the practical problems of community life are all framed within procedural rules that are taken for
granted and not subject in the short run to discretionary political
processes. Special majorities are required for special actions.

Even beyond specific rules, democracy presumes an ethic of voluntary self-restraint on the part of legitimate authority, a residual
rule of democratic humility. It presumes self-imposed limitations on
the arbitrary exercise of power, including legitimate political power,
in the name of freedom, privacy, and a vigorous civil society. Majorities voluntarily yield to minorities in some circumstances. Not all
possible political advantages within the rules are supposed to be
taken, or are actually taken. Political authorities moderate the demands of their contemporaneous interests with an awareness of their
roles as trustees for the community. Normally included in this requirement is the understanding that individuals, minorities, and the
disfranchised—including the unborn—shall be protected against actions that make it impossible for them to act effectively as citizens in
the future. The future is protected against the imperium of the present. The weak are protected against the imperium of the strong.
Strangers are protected against the imperium of the self.

THE TENSION BETWEEN RULES AND POPULAR SOVEREIGNTY

As numerous writers on democracy have observed, democratic ideals
with respect to political capabilities are clearly contradictory. The
contradictions are reflected in the way philosophical treatises on political capabilities mix an emphasis on individual liberty and rights
with an emphasis on the rights of majorities and governors. Locke
(1690), among others, insisted that the personal rights and property
of individuals were prior to all social and political organization and
therefore inviolable. The role of the state was to protect the personal
rights and property bases of the capabilities of individuals. For that
purpose, the state and its officials needed certain capabilities. But the
legitimacy of the government depended on its ability and willingness
to respect and protect individual rights.

Such a perspective, built exclusively on a conception of inherent individual rights, became less dominant during the long period of state- and nation-building, particularly during the development of welfare states with comprehensive agendas for redistribution of resources and significant institutionalized capacities. This view of the state as justified primarily as a defender of individual civil and political rights and property has nonetheless received renewed support in many Western countries in recent decades (Hayek, 1960; Friedman, 1962; Nozick, 1974). Even in states where welfare state ideology has had a firm hold, individual-centered, as opposed to collective- or society-centered, arguments are familiar and legitimate (Olsen, 1990).

For most of the history of democratic thought, however, the democratic ambivalence between liberty and constitutionalism has been maintained by imagining the achievement of various balances of power. Majorities are to rule, but they are to be subject to restraint. Officials are to be provided with adequate freedom and resources to act efficiently, and yet they are not to be made so strong that an accountable and popularly responsible government is threatened. Individuals should have the freedom and resources that allow them to flourish and exercise their rights, yet the exercise of those rights should not be allowed to endanger the democratic process or the rights of others. Autonomous and resourceful voluntary organizations are to be sustained as a precondition for a democratic society, yet they are not to be allowed to become a threat to democracy (Mill, 1956; Hamilton, Jay, and Madison, 1964; Berg, 1965; Dahl, 1982).

Achieving this democratic ideal of balanced power is difficult, particularly in the face of two fundamental facts of democratic life: (1) The same political capabilities that are used to protect against tyranny can often also be used to establish it, and (2) most individuals judge the encroachments by others on their own liberty more negatively than they do comparable encroachments by themselves on others. Thus, the classical conundrums of democracy are how to achieve majority rule in a way that is consistent with the maintenance of a community of free citizens that protects and elaborates differences and endures over time, and how inconsistencies among subjective judgments of collective and individual needs can be reconciled in a way that offends neither the demands for community coherence nor the demands for individual liberty.

As we have seen, the democratic reaction to such facts and their associated conundrums is to distribute power as nearly equally as possible, and at the same time to create a consistent bias toward maintaining the status quo, toward requiring more political power to achieve change than to prevent it, toward attending more to claims of individual hurt than to claims of needs to hurt. The distribution of power is implemented through the allocation of equal voting rights and through the redistribution of political and economic resources. The bias against change is implemented by a set of relatively inviolate constitutive norms and rules that secure liberties for all members of the political community and that constrain and protect citizens as well as governors.

Every rule is a constraint and its acceptance an act of faith. There are frequent occasions on which individuals or majorities are frustrated by the rules. In order for democratic constitutions to thwart individual and majoritarian instincts of greed, they must also become the bane of individual and majoritarian visions of virtue. The tension between the capabilities defined by political equality and the authority of the majority, on the one hand, and the capabilities defined by constitutive rules, on the other, is a central tension of modern democratic governance. Democracy presumes that some vital rules are taken for granted. They are not subject to continuous calculative considerations of self-interest. Significant opportunities to secure advantage by violating or changing the rules are forgone. And though all contemporary democratic systems have experienced occasions on which fundamental rules have been violated, democratic aspirations require that those occasions must be few and those few must be sources of subsequent shame.

Problems of Capabilities

Democracy presumes political capability. It cannot succeed without it. In particular, it cannot succeed unless citizens are capable of being citizens and officials are capable of being officials. At the same time, however, political capabilities pose problems. The capabilities of political actors and institutions that are precious to effective governance are, at the same time, a threat to democratic political control.

INEFFICIENCY AND TYRANNY

Individuals want freedom to acquire resources and to enjoy the benefits of their resources. They want to be free from government and rules (often including those they impose on themselves). At the same time they want protection against the adverse consequences of the use of resources by others and to enjoy the predictability that follows from stable rules and expertise. Citizens look to governors and experts for solutions to individual and collective problems. At the same time they fear the power of governors and experts and seek to limit their power (Cerny, 1990, p. 143). Elected representatives want the knowledge that comes from staff expertise, but they fear the loss of control when their staffs become too large or too important (Olsen, 1983). In short, effective political actors and institutions are characteristic of enduring democracies; yet efficient political institutions are potential threats to democracy. Democratic governance requires delicate balances between public power and individual power, between majority power and minority rights, between central guidance and institutional autonomy. Avoiding tyranny while pursuing capability and developing capability while preventing tyranny are central problems (Dahl and Lindblom, 1953).

It is a part of democratic traditions to be willing to err on the side of inefficiency in government in order to protect politics from the powerful. Intentions to bring efficiency to government are invariably supported as a matter of rhetoric but often resisted as a matter of practice. Insistence that capabilities should follow obligations is a canon of organizational and democratic rhetoric, but it is routinely ignored in practice. Resistance to tyranny lies at the heart of democratic resistance to new technologies for information gathering and sharing by governmental agencies, monitoring of the activities of individuals and groups, observation of conformity to laws and regulations, adjudication of disputes, consideration of proposed legislation, and implementation of enacted rules. The benefits of efficacy stimulate the creation of powerful authorities and rights. Fears of tyranny lead to providing less than commensurate capabilities.

To protect against the dangers of political capabilities, most democracies try to counterbalance one organized capacity with another. They encourage competitions among political agencies and offices and among political jurisdictions. Armies confront navies; treasuries confront welfare agencies; ministries of education confront ministries of trade; journalists of television confront journalists of newspapers; regional authorities confront central authorities. To the extent to which well-endowed individuals and groups compete with each other for political control, the effects of the endowments of each tend to be controlled by the endowments of the others.

The conditions for effectiveness of competition in controlling the political capabilities of private endowments are so restrictive, however, that few democracies imagine that it is adequate by itself. At various times and places, the well-endowed have been educated (taught the principles of democracy), bribed (provided with incentives), and coerced (threatened with incarceration) into not using their full resource capabilities. Since none of those efforts has ever entirely succeeded, nor seems likely to, the struggle to regulate political capabilities derived from inequalities in wealth and other endowments is a constant feature of democracy (Walzer, 1983, p. 10). Political rules are enacted to regulate the pursuit, delegation, exercise, justification, criticism, and transfer of authority and power. Procedural aspects of democracy are emphasized, particularly those regulating encroachment on rights (Gutman, 1985, p. 315). Citizens look for a stable political structure and process, for rights and rules, and for legal guarantees against others and the state (Roper, 1989, p. 216).

The balance between individual freedom and governmental action has been strained by rapid expansions of demands for each (Hinsley, 1986, p. 128). The modern citizen and modern instruments of opinion formation seem to complain with equal fervor about the misuse of authority and about the failure to exercise it. On the one hand, democratic citizens increasingly ask that power be dispersed and limited in order to avoid excessive interference in their lives. They seek to constrain the capabilities of the state and of central authorities out of concern that those capabilities will restrict individual autonomy and effective participation in collective choices (Gould, 1988). They see the potential for tyranny that lies in governmental capabilities.

For instance, after a long period during which the public sector grew in response to demands for welfare services, a reaction gained strength during the 1980s. Although it has been argued that the turnaround in public policy may not always have reflected a change in public opinion (Bennett and Bennett, 1990; Steinmo, 1993), elections were won on the basis of programs calling for shortening the public agenda, reducing the power of public agencies, and relying more on competitive markets and private property. Definitions of appropriate capabilities changed. Concerns about constraining governmental capabilities became much more conspicuous in theories of governance than concern over creating adequate governmental capabilities. Such definitions and concerns could change again if the public mood were to find the threats of market competition and private concentrations of power more serious than the threats of public power, or if fundamentalist religious movements placed the maintenance of religious orthodoxy on the public agenda.

On the other hand, impatience with the ungovernability and inefficiency of democratic regimes leads citizens to demand more potent governance, less dispersion of power, and more concentration of authority (Bobbio, 1990, p. 88). They demand central intervention when institutional autonomy makes popular control difficult or impossible (March and Olsen, 1989, p. 166). They complain that society is fragmented into powerful veto groups that prevent a consistent, positive policy for the society as a whole (Willke, 1989, p. 229). They ask that the separate interests of a society take into account the needs of the whole society (Fürst, 1989, p. 221), restrict their own personal opportunities in order to benefit the society (Willke, 1989, p. 243), and exhibit a "new ethic of responsibility" (Henke and Fürst, 1989, p. 537). The escalation of pressures has accentuated the dilemmas of political capability, making democratic authority at the same time more circumscribed and more in demand.

The balance between inefficiency and tyranny is made particularly unstable by the tendency for the issues to be seen through personal glasses. Individuals and groups often seem to see the dangers of tyranny more clearly when they are out of power than when they are in power, seem to see the dangers of inefficiency more clearly when they are in power than when they are out of power. Majorities seem to find limitations on government and minority rights much less compelling than minorities do. These self-interested biases in assessments are only part of the story of instability, however. Individuals do not reliably see the world in terms of calculated tradeoffs. They are inclined to see their desires as absolutes rather than as goods subject to marginal rates of substitution. Rather than exhibit some kind of steady exchange rate, their attention to inefficiency and tyranny oscillates as their focus of attention does. Cycles from an emphasis on granting authority to an emphasis on enforcing accountability seem endemic to democracy, although established democracies seem to exhibit somewhat shorter and less dramatic cycles than do societies in which democratic experience is more limited.

The difficulties of striking a good balance are accentuated by the economic context of modern political life. The demands of democracy seem to conflict with the demands of international financial markets. The rules of law and equity seem to conflict with the rules of supply and demand. The capabilities of political actors to fulfill expectations of their political identities seem to restrict the capabilities of economic actors to fulfill theirs. The legitimation of multiple cultural identities within a single nation-state weakens the link between national identities and the state. Such conflicts are of long standing, but the stakes have grown larger. The European Union and the efforts of Western democratic polities to define relations within the former Soviet Union are modern experiments in developing and utilizing political capabilities.

As the stakes increase, so also do the dangers. Building political capabilities increases the risks of political action. Capabilities make the effects of action greater and more variable. Such risks are conspicuous in the technology of warfare and genetic engineering and in the application of rationality to decision-making, but they are observable throughout modern governance. For example, democratic institutions have traditionally been sustained by mechanisms that assure that most citizens experience domains and periods of being in power as well as domains and periods of being out of power. Rotation in power and specialization in power facilitate an appreciation of both sides of the inefficiency/tyranny dilemma. Sequential bouts of experience with the exercise of power and with powerlessness discourage citizens from embracing unconditionally the beauties of either efficiency or inefficiency in governance. It is essential to such a system, however, that experiments with capabilities be modest enough in scope not to destroy the rotation in power. As governments develop competence to defend themselves militarily, they risk internal pressure from the military or the military–industrial complex. As governments develop competence to understand and respond to public opinion, they risk becoming competent to manipulate it. As governments develop competence to record and interpret information flows in a society, they risk becoming competent to destroy privacy. Each of these gains in competence places a system of power rotation at risk.

IRRESPONSIBILITIES OF CAPABILITY

The management of capabilities is partly a matter of balancing the risks of inefficiency and tyranny, but it is also a matter of dealing with the ways in which the organization of capability affects democratic control. Both political weakness and political competition can contribute to making democracy function irresponsibly.

Irresponsibilities of political incapacity. Institutional and personal identities cannot be fulfilled when capability is lacking, yet inconsistencies between identities and capabilities, between obligations and actions, seem to be characteristic features of democratic governance (Baier, March, and Sætren, 1986). That is one of the chief lessons to be learned from efforts at administrative reform in the 1980s (Olsen and Peters, 1995a). Officials are asked to take action, to provide services, and to lead, but the demands on them are frequently beyond the capabilities of their offices. When what is appropriate is not feasible, democracy suffers from a problem of incapacity.

Some individuals and institutions are incapable of doing what is appropriate because of moral or ethical weaknesses, a lack of personal integrity. Their incapacities stem from corruptions of the soul. Our focus here, however, is on incapacities of a more mundane sort: institutional and personal incapacities stemming from inadequate resources, skills, knowledge, and organization. Officials need authority, resources, competencies, and organizational capabilities in order to be effective. They need to be protected from pressures to deviate from the expectations and duties of their official roles. While being held accountable for appropriate action, they often need to be buffered from immediate political or constituency pressures by protection against removal from office (Keech, 1992, p. 261). A democracy seems often to mandate public services without providing the resources necessary to implement them, to mandate equal treatment of citizens while encouraging those with extra resources or superior political credentials to demand special favors, to expect public officials to be responsive to public opinion without providing procedures for molding and clarifying disparate voices into a public opinion.

Individuals are also likely to face inconsistencies between their identities as citizens and the capabilities necessary to those identities. The democratic ideal of political equality requires that every citizen have the capability of participating equally in decisions about how the community should be governed. In order for a citizen to act as an independent, equal citizen, he or she must be able to obtain relevant information, join freely in discussion and coalition formation, and possess resources that make him or her attractive as a political partner. Variations among democratic systems in their approximations to these conditions and the persistent failure of techniques for providing adequate capabilities for ordinary citizens are part of the history of democracy.

The inconsistencies produced by political incapacity not only undermine the effectiveness of political actors but also encourage moral rigidity. The moral purity of the weak is legendary in interpersonal conflict, national politics, and international relations. A consistent inability to act in a manner appropriate to one's identity weakens commitment to the proposition that values and action should be connected. Weak links between actions and standards of appropriateness, mismatches between proper behavior and capabilities, encourage a political system to avoid responsibility for its values, to confirm identities that are fantastical. Virtuous beliefs are sustained by the manifest impossibility of acting on them (Brunsson, 1989).

The irresponsibility of weakness is both a blessing and a curse of political institutions. It is a blessing in the way it supports identities unsullied by their inconsistencies and impossibilities, and in the way it creates separate political arenas for talk and action. Proclamations of the obligations of a role can substitute for providing the capabilities necessary for its fulfillment. It is a curse in the way it removes political action from the control of political discourse about proper behavior. Identities maintained and purified by their incapacities are simultaneously threatened by their irrelevance. A frustrated imperative to behave appropriately can easily produce sentiments of anger, cynicism, and loss of efficacy, which undermine a normative system of identities and a social structure that depends on them to shape action.

Irresponsibilities of political competition. It is a presumption of many theories of democracy that political competition for power yields political leaders who can govern effectively in the name of the people. The presumption has often been questioned. Competitive processes pit political actors against each other in pursuit of scarce resources and opportunities. Business firms compete for governmental subsidies; political agencies compete for budgets; nations compete for economic advantage; and bureaucrats compete for hierarchical promotion. In these competitions, political actors, whether driven by a logic of consequence or by a logic of appropriateness, seek to enhance their capabilities for political effectiveness.

It is not self-evident that electoral political competition will necessarily produce leaders who represent the interests of the people well or who are competent to govern. There is considerable ambiguity in what it means to "represent the interests of the people," and electoral competition has been faulted for producing a caricature of such interests, reducing decisions on governors to popularity contests in which name recognition and politically irrelevant factors seem to be pervasive. Such criticisms are made suspect by the fact that they seem to reflect the sentiments of the more richly endowed members of democratic society more clearly than the less well-endowed. They may underestimate the capabilities of competitive political advertising and campaigns for informing the public. Nevertheless, the issue is critical: Political competition can easily produce democratic irresponsibility.

Neither is it self-evident that the capabilities needed to succeed in political competition are the same as the capabilities needed to govern. The problem is a familiar one to students of organizations who note the potential inconsistency between the qualities required to be promoted in a hierarchy and the qualities needed to perform well at higher levels. Indeed, political systems recognize the problem explicitly by providing different routes to power for different governance roles. The political competition by which judges are chosen is often different from the political competition by which legislators or bureaucrats are chosen. The matching of competitive capabilities with job capabilities is quite rough, however, and numerous examples can be cited of people whose abilities at being chosen to govern do not match their capabilities at governing.

Finally, it is not self-evident that political competition yields winners who are reliably the best, even in terms of their competitive capabilities. As an example, consider a political candidate engaged in electoral competition with other candidates, with victory going to the candidate running the most effective campaign. We can think of the effectiveness of any particular campaign as represented by a probability distribution over the candidates' capabilities. Better candidates have higher average effectiveness than poorer ones, but there is some random variation due to complications in implementation or the inherent riskiness of the campaign strategies chosen. The outcomes in any one election are determined by a comparison of the realized effectiveness of the various candidates in that particular campaign.

In such a competition, the best candidate (the one with the highest average effectiveness) faces the good chance of losing in a particular election to someone who is less able but combines large variability with good luck. High-variance, low-mean candidates will, on average, do poorly, but when the number of competitors is large, the winner in a a competition to be first among many is very likely to be one of the high-variance candidates instead of the one who is best on average. If finishing near the top in a competition among many matters a great deal, those actors with effectiveness distributions characterized by comparatively low means will be willing to sacrifice average effectiveness in order to augment the right-hand tails of their effectiveness distributions. That is, they will be willing to pursue high-variance campaign strategies. As the weaker candidates do this, they improve the chance that one of their number will win, thus force their more capable competitors to pursue high-variance strategies likewise, and thereby convert political competition into a right-hand-tail race in which average effectiveness (due to capability and mobilization) becomes largely irrelevant.

Those dynamics comprise reminders of a serious source of instability and ineffectiveness in political systems. Stable, established political regimes, characterized by relatively high political competence, thus (in the present terms) by relatively high means and relatively low variances in their effectiveness distributions, are vulnerable to successful challenges by one among many low-mean, high-variance competitors—who is subsequently vulnerable to others. The process yields a series of victories by competitors who are likely to have relatively low average capabilities, thus likely to serve the polity relatively poorly. As a result, democratic governance involves managing political competition to minimize situations in which many competitors compete directly for only a few positions. The traditional procedure of using party organization and tournaments of bilateral competitions that filter out high-variance, low-mean political performers has been considerably compromised by modern political contests in some democracies.

The Social Basis of Capabilities

Rights, resources, competencies, and organizational capacities are developed and regulated within a social order. The social order within which they reside, however, is not a social order based on undifferentiated, comprehensive, and direct political capabilities of citizens. The contemporary state is a single political community in some respects, but it is a collection of separate communities in others. Conceptions of popular sovereignty, like earlier conceptions of royal sovereignty, have been modified to accommodate the realities of a more elaborated political world in which the state is neither independent from external pressures nor all-powerful internally (Hinsley, 1986).

Political capabilities are socially constructed within a society that is a federation of semi-autonomous institutions and groups, with overlapping resources and political power. Individuals and groups exercise their abilities to achieve their political identities in the context of other individuals and groups pursuing conflicting identities and seeking instruments for personal effectiveness. Wealth is distributed, competence is shared, and access is provided to institutional capacities for organized action through processes that are negotiated, changed, and preserved in a history of political and social life. The definition of capabilities, the terms of their acquisition, and the conditions of their use are elaborated as part of a set of cultural understandings. As a result, democratic capabilities depend on being embedded in a political culture that sustains them (Dewey, 1927, p. 151; Inglehart, 1990; Offe and Preuss, 1991; Dunn, 1990, p. 204).

Cultural understandings of political norms coevolve with the creation, distribution, and use of political capabilities (Muller and Seligson, 1994). The fact that such cultural understandings are capable of change is obvious in history and to any modern student of international cultural diffusion, but they are entwined with the culture and not easily or arbitrarily changed. Because they may erode without attention and can sometimes be transformed by persistent effort over many years, they must be a part of an agenda for maintaining political institutions; but they are not amenable to fine-grained, willful political control.

Chapter Five

DEVELOPING
POLITICAL ACCOUNTS

The events of history are frequently ambiguous. Human accounts of those events characteristically are not. Accounts provide interpretations and explanations of experience (Scott and Lyman, 1968; Meyer, 1986). They make actions imaginable and consequences interpretable. They mold assessments of history and the roles of individuals in it. Ambiguities about the definition of a situation, about the relevance of particular identities and rules, and about the actions they imply are made less obscure (Hannerz, 1992). An account explaining why one party won an election and another party lost is developed and accepted. An account explaining why unemployment is high rather than low is developed and accepted. Accounts explaining why a war was begun and why it was lost become social facts. Such accounts facilitate political life. They provide elaborations of identities and preferences, thus are important parts of a system based on conceptions either of appropriate action or of consequential choice. They affirm that history is subject to meaningful control (March and Olsen, 1989).

Formal systems of accounting used in economic, social, and political institutions are accounts of political reality. The budget represents expected expenditures. Gross national product, unemployment rates, life expectancy, political popularity, and the test performance of students represent outcomes in a political reality. The stories of newspaper reporters, gossips, participants, biographers, and historians create explanations of outcomes, fitting them into cultural and political myths. What happens in politics depends on the reality that is represented by those accounts. Democratic political intelligence depends on the development of institutions capable of generating and using accounts that lead to wise collective actions. We focus here on the role of accounts in supporting democratic accountability. The role of accounts in supporting democratic adaptiveness is considered in Chapter 6.

ACCOUNTS AS A BASIS FOR ACCOUNTABILITY

The concept of political accountability links two traditions of thinking about the relation between the outcomes of history and human agency. Each tradition uses accounts to relate action to individual will, power, and autonomy. The first tradition establishes conditions for and principles of personal responsibility for *individual* action. Conventions of legitimate explanations shape the stories and justifications found in literature, journalism, autobiography, legislatures, meeting rooms, and courtrooms. Individuals are (or are not) held accountable for their actions and the consequences of those actions. The second tradition establishes conditions for and principles of personal responsibility for *collective* action, or for action in the role of an *official*. It is exhibited in systems of law, accounting, and management that surround formal organizations. Individuals are (or are not) held accountable for the actions taken by their organizations, the actions they take as officials, and the consequences of each.

Justification and Action

The use of accounts to explain, justify, and excuse action is a fundamental feature of civilized discourse. Behavior is not accepted simply on its own terms as behavior. Human action is to be interpreted as comprehensible, evaluated, fitted into a framework of normal expectations, and judged as proper. Beliefs that order and rationality can be imposed on social and political life through planning and intervention (Myrdal, 1967, pp. 9, 17–20) make questions of responsibility and accountability significant. Much of the apparatus of civilized life is directed to developing explanations of history that allow such understandings and judgments.

Studies of the effects of accountability on human judgment, decision, and justification have generally found that being held responsible for one's own actions makes a difference both to behavior and to the way individuals justify their behavior (Tetlock, 1992). Identities are defined and defended; justifications and decisions are created in a context of expectations. Norms of appropriate behavior are enforced through expectations of having to justify one's actions as appropriate to a situation.

These studies present a fairly consistent picture: First, accountability tends to accentuate deliberateness in decision making. It increases the amount of information considered and the care with which it is analyzed. That is particularly likely to be true when accountability is made clear before public commitments are made and when the views of the audience for accountability are unknown, not set, or in conflict. The effects of accountability on deliberateness in decision-making are illustrated by four clusters of results:

1. *The "fundamental attribution error."* Human subjects have been observed to see events as caused by the intentions and dispositions of individuals rather than by situational factors (Ross, 1977; Jones, 1979). This tendency has been reduced by making subjects personally accountable for their judgments (Tetlock, 1985). Accountable subjects seemed to be more thoughtful about their responses.
2. *Primacy effects.* There is considerable evidence that individuals form judgments on the basis of early information and are slow to revise those judgments in the face of subsequent disconfirming evidence (Nisbett and Ross, 1980). Being held accountable for judgments reduces this primacy effect (Rozelle and Baxter, 1981; Tetlock, 1983b).
3. *Confidence.* Individuals tend to have greater confidence in the correctness of their own judgments and predictions about the future than is warranted (Fischhoff, 1982). Being held accountable

(in advance) seems to moderate this tendency toward overconfidence (Tetlock and Kim, 1987).

4. *Dilution effects.* Human subjects frequently appear to pay attention to extraneous, decision-irrelevant facts, thereby reducing the importance of factors that are obviously decision-relevant (Nisbett, Zukier, and Lemley, 1981). This tendency to expand the number of factors considered appears to be accentuated when a decision-maker is made accountable (Tetlock and Boettger, 1989).

It should be observed that the first three of these effects are normally described as "positive" and the fourth as "negative," but the prescriptive status is not quite that straightforward (Tetlock, 1992). Accountability appears to make decision-makers more carefully thoughtful, but this may lead them to struggle too hard to find the relevance of irrelevant considerations and may lead them to lose the (false) confidence that facilitates action.

Second, accountability tends to increase caution about change and to reduce risk-taking. Accountability seems to make out-of-pocket costs more salient than opportunity costs, potential losses more salient than potential gains. That is particularly true when the views of the audience for accountability are well known and when decisions are seen as having substantial consequences for that audience. For example:

1. *Favored position of the status quo.* Individuals are more likely to choose an alternative if it is framed as maintaining the status quo than if it is framed as a change from the status quo (Samuelson and Zeckhauser, 1987). Being held accountable increases the favored position for the status quo (Tetlock and Boettger, 1994).

2. *Ambiguity and risk aversion.* In many circumstances, human subjects prefer alternatives with clearly anticipated consequences over those with less clearly anticipated outcomes (Curley, Yates, and Abrams, 1986). This effect is accentuated by being made accountable (Tetlock and Boettger, 1994).

3. *Social conformity.* Human subjects tend to adopt positions that they expect to be acceptable to others (Sherif and Cantril, 1947). Accountability to others with known rules of appropriateness accentuates this effect. However, accountability to unknown others with unknown norms leads to explicit attention to a wider range

of considerations (Tetlock, 1983a; Tetlock, Skitka, and Boettger, 1989).

4. *Uncooperativeness*. Individuals balance the potential gains from cooperative collaboration within a group and the potential losses from being individually associated with any failures that may result. Personal accountability focuses attention on the latter and reduces the willingness to gamble on gains from cooperativeness (Adelberg and Batson, 1978).

Caution in decision-making is neither unconditionally bad nor unconditionally good. The emphasis on accountability in political institutions, however, may account for the frequent observation that political decision-makers tend to have biases favoring reliability over high variance and maintenance of the status quo over change.

Third, accountability tends to increase rigidity and accentuate defensiveness. That is, it reduces flexibility with respect to reconsidering choices once made and leads to a focus on gathering information in support of a decision. Those effects are particularly notable when accountability is established after a commitment that is seen as irreversible has been made. For example:

1. *Rationalization and self-confirmation*. Individuals organize their experience and their justifications to confirm the correctness of their own previous decisions (Kiesler, 1971). Individuals tend to claim responsibility for positive outcomes and to deny responsibility for negative outcomes. If they are forced to accept responsibility for negative results, they tend to deny their negative quality (Greenwald, 1980).

2. *Escalating commitment*. Individuals generate justifications for prior positions and increase their commitment to them (Staw, 1976; Staw, Sandelands, and Dutton, 1981; Schlenker, 1982). Those effects are accentuated by being held accountable (Fox and Staw, 1979; Tetlock and Boettger, 1989), for example when international confrontation takes place before a domestic political audience (Fearon, 1994).

Once again, rigidity and defensiveness are not necessarily either good or bad, but they have implications for behavior in institutions that emphasize personal accountability.

In general, these results confirm the commonsense notion that accountability is a two-edged motivational and cognitive sword in decision-making. On the one hand, it sharpens social control and makes political actors more responsive to social pressure and to standards of appropriate behavior that they (and others) associate with their roles. It induces more careful consideration in defining a situation and in determining appropriate responses to it. On the other hand, accountability can also lead to procrastination and excessive consideration of possibilities, reduce risk-taking, make decision-makers cautious about change and about risking mistakes that might become public, and dispose them to persistence in courses of action that appear to have failed.

Accountability and responsibility are instruments of social control. At the same time, however, they often are associated with a sense of personal freedom (Johansson, 1993). To be held responsible for one's actions and their consequences is to be certified as a significant human being. People who are not held responsible (for example, infants, insane people) are less than complete individuals. Being held accountable creates a presumption of capability and a presumption of choice, thus of freedom to act. The possibility of achieving this subtle combination of control and freedom underlies the attraction of decentralized administration in management theory and the importance of the role of citizen in democratic theory.

JUSTIFICATION IN A DEMOCRACY

The democratic polity is both a community of good practice and a community of justification, and governance is organized by a tension between the two. On the one hand, democratic communities seek to take practical, intelligent action, to get the job done right. The task is to make performance reliable according to collective norms and the best available methods. On the other hand, democracy is a self-reflecting community, critically reexamining both means and ends, reasoning and deliberating about its experience, methods, technologies, strategies, values, and purposes (Anderson, 1990). It seeks to achieve interpretations of history that justify or condemn actions and establish responsibility for them. Justifications and condemnations tie action to a shared system of causal and normative beliefs in a political culture.

The construction of justifications in a context of large-scale, complex, differentiated, and rapidly changing environments is a considerable task. Optimistic hopes for democracy are linked to confidence that, at some meaningful level, a link can be made between the explanations communicated and understood among citizens and the fundamentals of a complex reality. Such optimism is persistently dampened by observations of inadequacies in public understandings and of the ways in which the demands of public justification—which lead to relatively simple, sloganized interpretive models—conflict with the demands of adequacy, which call for relatively subtle models. The most commonly shared ideological system in modern democratic societies is a commitment to rationality, the belief that action is appropriately justified by anticipation and evaluation of its consequences; but justification can be connected to a variety of normative systems, including traditional systems embedded in custom, tradition, and passion (Weber, 1978, I: 30). The end of the twentieth century has witnessed a resurgence of justifications based on the passions of religious fervor and deeply felt loyalties to national, ethnic, and gender groups. Demagogues, television, patriotism, and group loyalties have all been cast as democratic villains, with citizens normally seen as victims.

The pervasive presence of unenlightened citizens, perverted accounts, and misinformed public opinion are old observations. They encourage a portrayal of the process of justification as distorted, betrayed, or deformed, thus undermining confidence in democracy. The primary democratic defense against perversions in justifications is an institutionalized openness (*Öffentlichkeit*) to discourse, deliberations, and associations among free and equal citizens, a community of argumentation in which political actors engage in political debate and discussions of possible actions (Yack, 1985). The apparatus of democratic account-giving simultaneously reasserts the glories of socially accepted ideologies, legitimizes and institutionalizes competing justifications and accounts, articulates the identities on which actions are based, and provides an interpretation that makes actions and justifications consistent. Institutionalized openness protects the exchange of information and prejudices across differences in feelings and expertise. Action can be defended and criticized openly, and shared understandings can develop (Calhoun, 1992; Cohen and Arato, 1992; Habermas, 1992b).

Institutionalized openness is the primary defense against perversions, but it can also become perverse. Openness presumes a search for accounts that most participants can believe in, even if they have reservations and view "public truth" as temporary (Gambling, 1977, p. 142). But any openness is necessarily based on a set of rules that preclude some things, and democratic openness is always at risk of endorsing shared conceptions of propriety that glorify tolerance over a narrow range of justifications while excluding many.

BALANCING JUSTIFICATION AND ACTION

Justification is, however, only one side of the tension of governance. The other side is action. Democratic processes are threatened by the temptations of endless talk and search for justification. They are notorious for their delays and recurring reluctance to take action—"gridlock" in contemporary parlance. A key problem is reconciling discourse and the testing of justifications with effective government and administration. Democracies require procedures for acting even in the face of incomplete or inadequate justification. For instance, modern legislatures have supplemented previous concerns, dominated by the need to guard individual representatives against the usurpations of the Crown and the majority, with concerns about protecting the legislature against individuals and minorities who use the privilege of free speech to prevent decision and action. They have developed doctrines specifying when debate can legitimately be ended. The doctrines have led to procedures for setting legislative deadlines and establishing restrictions on debate (Friedrich, 1950, pp. 327–30).

The conviction that adequate action is timely action shows itself in a variety of forms of organization and governance. In situations of crisis, effective action is usually given precedence over deliberation, a priority enacted in the organization of fire departments and rescue teams. More generally, hierarchy and the right to command reflect a perception that rapid and effective action may sometimes be more important than a thorough debate. In much of the conventional democratic view, the legislature is seen as an instrument of public speech and deliberation more than one of action. The public bureaucracy, on the other hand, is seen as an instrument of action and implementation more than one of public justification. A traditional democratic problem is to develop a political order that balances the two. From this point of view, the democratic propensity to abide by majority decisions can be interpreted not only as a reflection of political equality but also as a practical device for "squaring a formation of opinion that seeks truth and is as discursive as circumstances permit with the temporal constraints to which the formation of will is subject" (Habermas, 1992a, p. 449).

Accountability in Politics

Accounts of politics are stories that bring order to the obscurities of political causality. Since both the outcomes of politics and the processes by which those outcomes have occurred are ambiguous, political actors and their monitors have to build a socially valid story explaining events. They experiment with alternative interpretations, seek social acceptance of one interpretation or another, and test the credibility of alternative stories. The construction of such accounts occurs within a set of norms and institutional arrangements that constrain both the process of storytelling and its outcome. The outcome must fit a recognizable story line, thus is bound by conventions of explanation. The process normally follows a course of some confusion leading to greater social clarity, even consensus. Stories are never secure from conflict and reconstruction, however, and political history records numerous cycles of interpretation.

Accounts define political reality, and the reality they define can attribute events to a variety of causes, including acts of fate, incomprehensible external forces, malevolent enemies, or beneficent gods. In particular, causes of adversity are often found in forces external to the polity. In modern times, in most nation-states, convenient scapegoats for political or economic woes are commonly found in the actions of outsiders, particularly the actions of superpowers, traditional enemies, or stigmatized groups. Individuals easily come to believe and repeat some version or other of a conspiracy fable dominated by attributions of consistent ill will on the part of anonymous members of an out-group. Political accounts in modern democracies also relate events to the actions of specific political actors within the polity. They present a story of human intention and agency that involves public officials and politicians and seeks to make those individuals accountable.

THE IDEA OF ACCOUNTABILITY

In democratic theory, responsibility refers to being answerable to somebody else and having to account for one's actions or inactions and their consequences. Responsibility also refers to acting rationally and honestly in accordance with the relevant facts and the best technical reasoning available (Friedrich, 1940; Pennock, 1979). And responsibility refers to a relation between formal authority and the results of history. Day and Klein describe accountability as being "all about the construction of an agreed language or currency of discourse about conduct and performance, and the criteria that should be used in assessing them" (Day and Klein, 1987, p. 2). The stories of political events construct accountability by assessing the match between political behavior and codes of proper behavior, by evaluating outcomes in terms of their social and political attractiveness, and by attributing those outcomes to the actions of particular individuals and institutions.

This idea of accountability builds on more general ideas of social order, ideas about the links between agents and principals, professionals and clients, subordinates and superiors, individuals and their gods. But it becomes especially germane through the democratic emphasis on informed consent as the basis of governmental authority. Informed consent is implemented through the development of accounts and the enforcement of accountability. Those who act on behalf of the political community by virtue of holding an office, and on the basis of authority and resources derived from that community, are accountable to the judgments of ordinary citizens informed by such accounts (Pitkin, 1967). They are accountable for the results achieved and for the means used, for single decisions as well as for the institutional conditions under which policies are made. Democratic political order is implemented through political recourse against those judged responsible for undesired actions or outcomes and political rewards for those judged responsible for desired ones (Thompson, 1987).

Popular sovereignty requires that rulers be answerable to the people, that power be conditional on satisfying popular demands. Two clear complications in such a requirement, however, are the uneven distribution of political actions and consequences over time and the changing nature of popular sentiment. If accountability and political competition require that political actions be appropriate and beneficial continuously over time, actions that are inappropriate or costly in the short run but appropriate and beneficial in the long run are hard to sustain. The fundamental accountability dilemma is found in the way efforts to achieve accountability seem inexorably to reduce the capabilities of political systems to maintain a long-run perspective. As a result, accountability enforced by monitoring and political competition is vital to democracy and simultaneously a potential threat to it.

Democratic political mechanisms for maintaining a long-run horizon include creating popular awareness of the necessities of short-run sacrifices, but they depend particularly on structural arrangements that make accountability primarily periodic and posterior, rather than continuous and prior. The democratic ideal of political accountability of rulers to an informed, forward-looking, and wise citizenry is achieved by providing periods of political power subject to periodic review and by making rules subject to occasional, rather than continuous, reconsideration. Time is accorded to rulers and rules to secure longer-run gains and to educate citizens, provided they submit to review and electoral competition at regular intervals.

The longer the intervals between elections and the greater the stability of rules, the greater the capability of the political system to maintain long-run horizons. Rules endure long enough to provide clear indications of their advantages and disadvantages. Rulers can risk short-run popular disapproval because they know that they do not face immediate threats of being held politically accountable. Both rules and rulers can shape the sentiments of citizens. Those ad-

vantages are obtained, however, at the risk of delay in correcting political mistakes and of corruption in popular tastes by prolonged
control over the government by a particular set of rulers. In practice,
as a result, democratic systems have usually augmented periodic
electoral accountability by some forms of continuous monitoring, by
making rules somewhat susceptible to short-run change, and by attempts to maintain popular control over rulers in the periods between elections.

The trade-offs between short-run accountability and long-run accountability have long been a focus of attention for students of democratic government (Burke, 1965), and the dilemma is not
susceptible to routine solution. Contemporary democracies seem,
however, to be more prone to risk the losses due to inadequate attention to the long run than the losses due to inadequate short-run
accountability. Changes in the technological and cultural premises of
political observation and behavior have strengthened the capabilities
of organized political interests and individual citizens to enforce
continuous political competition and accountability on both rules
and rulers. At the limit, each step in governance becomes subject to
popular oversight. This considerably strengthens the capability of
the political system to maintain control in the short run and considerably weakens the capability to experiment with longer-run perspectives or investments.

VARIETIES OF ACCOUNTABLE ACTORS

The ability of citizens to hold policy-makers accountable and the
ability of policy-makers to hold bureaucrats accountable are standard premises of democracy. In a modern democracy, however, the
problems of maintaining accountability extend beyond the control
of bureaucrats by public officials and the control of officials by citizens. The more general principle is that anyone who has power
within a democratic state should ultimately be accountable to the
people for the exercise of that power. The greater the power, the
greater the need to establish accountability. For example, as organized interests became major political actors, democratic political
systems struggled to enforce accountability on them (Schmitter,
1988).

Similar struggles have occurred with other groups as they have become organized to exercise power. Professional and occupational groups, producer groups, consumer groups, ethnic and gender groups, environmental groups, and single-issue pressure groups have all developed outside the formal system of governance and outside of political procedures for democratic accountability, as have actors in financial and other markets. The press and other media, publishers, and professors are conspicuous contributors to the political scene, but their public accountability is often unclear. The principle that power necessitates accountability has not been implemented consistently with respect to such groups, and even less consistently with respect to actors outside the nation-state.

For example, three important classes of participants in the development of modern public opinion are leading television personalities, leading journalists, and leading college professors. They shape beliefs and organize interpretations of history. In a country like the United States, a major television personality has more effective access to the public than any public official or party politician. The procedures for maintaining accountability of these political actors are haphazard. For example, the rules regulating the acceptance of lecture fees or other employment from interest groups, as well as the conditions for contact with such groups, are much more elaborately developed for legislators and public officials than for television performers, journalists, and college professors.

Most contemporary discussions of accountability also overlook democratic requirements for the accountability of citizens. Citizens have tended, ever since they replaced gods and monarchs as the final source of political authority, to claim a sovereign's right to be accountable to no one. They have generally assigned responsibility for public order to representatives and at the same time have alienated themselves from accountability for the election of those representatives (Collins, 1989, p. 168). Their own complicity in the failures and successes of democracy has been denied. The effective pursuit of democratic accountability probably requires challenging these pretenses of immunity from accountability. A prolonged combination of citizen power with citizen exemption from accountability introduces intolerable elements of irresponsibility into a democratic polity (Tussman, 1960, p. 108). Democratic citizens have an obligation to participate in civic and political life and to be concerned with the welfare of the political community. Citizens are accountable for how they use voting rights and the freedoms of speech and association, as well as their social and economic rights. Governance involves assessing how alternative institutional settings affect the exercise of those rights and the capabilities of citizens to fulfill their obligations.

DESIRABLE OUTCOMES AND PROPER BEHAVIOR

Many of the complications surrounding the accountability of political actors stem from an interweaving of the two standard logics of human action—a logic of consequence and a logic of appropriateness. A logic-of-consequence frame for accountability leads to demands that political actors be accountable for the consequences of their actions. In a world where human choices and actions are viewed as decisive to the course of history, being held accountable for the consequences of one's actions leads naturally to being held accountable for historical outcomes. Public officials are held accountable for changes in political, economic, and social health. They are evaluated in terms of whether the gross national product has increased or decreased, whether wars have been won or lost, whether social justice has been achieved.

A logic-of-appropriateness frame for accountability leads to demands that political actors be accountable for the appropriateness of their actions. Behavior is assessed as proper less because of its consequences than because of its consistency with cultural and political norms and rules. For example, democratic traditions demand conformity to the rules of coercion-free persuasion through the offering of good reasons, arguments, and moral appeals, and the evoking of shared cultural standards and rules of law. Citizens may agree that their self-governance should be based on accepting each other as free and equal citizens with the same political rights and obligations, without any agreement on outcomes and a definition of the good life. This regulation of the forms of interaction between competing factional interests enforces a style of accountability attached to conceptions of proper processes rather than results.

Such a spirit animates standard Weberian bureaucracies and the culture of the Rechtsstaat. Bureaucrats are responsible for following rules with regard to their office. They can be held accountable for not following the rules. But they are responsible neither to their masters nor to themselves for adverse consequences stemming from the execution of appropriate rules in proper ways (Löwith, 1982, p. 57). Political actors are held accountable for the legality, morality, political correctness, and professional justification of the policies they espouse; the tactics they follow; the decisions they make; and the attitudes they express. They are evaluated in terms of whether they perform the duties of their roles with dedication, integrity, and conformity to proper procedure.

Compared to the Rechtsstaat, with its traditions and rhetorics tied to a logic of appropriateness, twentieth-century democracies (particularly the welfare states of Europe) have embraced practices and rhetorics that are much more tied to logics of consequences. Effectiveness, efficiency, and substantive results have been emphasized more than the principles and procedures to be followed. Governance has come to assume a community of shared objectives rather than a community of shared principles and procedures. The key professions of the welfare state (e.g., medicine, economics, social work) embraced a much more consequence-oriented rhetoric than did the professions (e.g., law, public administration) that they replaced. The reforms in postwelfare states have continued that trend. Governments in the 1980s generally tried to change concepts of bureaucratic accountability even more toward emphasis upon results and away from emphasis on the procedures and rules that guide official behavior (Olsen, 1992a; Olsen and Peters, 1995a). Complaints of bureaucratic inefficiency increased relative to complaints of bureaucratic malfeasance or arbitrariness.

In practice, political actors may be held accountable for both the consequences and the appropriateness of their actions. The dilemma is that proper behavior sometimes is associated with bad consequences and improper behavior sometimes is associated with good consequences. From time to time, even democratic actors will get "dirty hands," that is, they may feel it necessary to achieve desirable outcomes through methods that they recognize as inappropriate (Thompson, 1987, p. 11). At other times, they will feel it necessary to maintain professional integrity at the cost of producing outcomes they recognize to be undesirable. Officials and their audiences struggle with this dilemma, exhibiting in the course of the struggle the ambivalence of accountability concerns. The stories they tell are woven with four story threads that are important parts of cultural lore but do not easily reduce to a simple, consistent tale.

1. *No conflict*. According to this thread, there is no conflict between proper behavior and outcomes, because one is subordinated, by definition, to the other. Either the propriety of behavior is defined in terms of its consequences (and therefore whatever has good consequences is by definition proper), or the desirability of an outcome is defined in terms of appropriateness (and therefore whatever is appropriate leads by definition to good consequences).

2. *No free lunch*. According to this thread, an individual can value both the consequences of action and its appropriateness but cannot expect to have everything. The values have to be compared. It is unfortunate, but (as is reflected in the raison d'état literature) achieving desirable outcomes sometimes requires doing something inappropriate. Or, put alternatively, sometimes acting appropriately requires accepting lesser outcomes. A political actor has to be willing to specify the trade-offs between them.

3. *Virtue is rewarded in the long run*. According to this thread, the rules of proper behavior have evolved in such a way that, in the long run, acting appropriately leads to the best outcomes. Any current appearance to the contrary is due to faulty analysis or a too-limited time perspective. Social norms of behavior reflect functional solutions to complicated problems of achieving optimal outcomes. Even if outcomes are the primary concern, confusions of causality make using outcomes as a basis for accountability unreliable and unjust. Appropriate action is assumed to lead, over the long run, to good outcomes.

4. *No virtue without temptation*. According to this thread, acting appropriately and achieving success are definitionally and morally inconsistent. In one tradition, appropriate action has virtue *only* if it leads to pain. Being rewarded for acting properly robs the action of its claim to standing as human action. For example, the soldier who receives a medal for bravery is thereby transformed from a hero to a tradesman. The politician who opposes the apparent wishes of the electorate but nevertheless wins reelection thereby loses a claim to

personal integrity. Similarly, successful outcomes attain the status of virtue *only* if they are associated with inappropriate behavior. Winning properly is not really winning. For instance, winning fairly in a card game of chance earns no honor among card cheats. Selling a candidate who would win on the merits earns no standing among political advertisers.

These threads are used to weave stories of political events into complex fabrics of accountability. Since each of the threads is familiar and normatively recognizable, each can become the frame for an acceptable tale.

THE AMBIGUITIES OF PERSONAL RESPONSIBILITY

A central concern of the telling of political history, the language of accountability, and the giving of democratic consent is the establishment of individual responsibility for history. As naturally as though it were obvious, accounts create human agents with personal responsibility for the course of history. If things go poorly, someone is blamed and portrayed as having bad intentions or poor judgment (Shklar, 1990, p. 54). If things go well, someone is praised and credited with virtue and intelligence. Responsible human agents are identified. The more important an event, the more important it is to establish personal responsibility. Politics seems to require an "adequately blameworthy agent" (Shklar, 1990, p. 62).

Despite its centrality to thinking about democracy and institutional control, political accountability is filled with ambiguity, ambivalence, and contradiction. The development of accounts is presumed to result in clear descriptions of outcomes and allocations of responsibility, but assigning blame and credit in a polity is not easy. Accounts are complicated by three conspicuous features of contemporary political life:

1. There are *multiple actors*. The number and variety of political actors, as well as the complexity of their interrelations, have increased substantially in the last two hundred years. Policies are made in complex networks of actors acting on the basis of mandates and commitments made by others, and within structures they have not chosen. Because many participants contribute in

many different ways, it is difficult even in principle to identify who is responsible for political outcomes and thus to establish political accountability. In particular, limiting accountability to officials seems myopic in modern political systems. Political outcomes are the product of "many hands" (Thompson, 1987, p. 40).

2. Outcomes reflect considerable *causal complexity*. It is difficult to establish clear causal explanations of events or to assign clear individual responsibility for them. The contribution of human agency is difficult to untangle from other historical factors. We have moved into "a new and disturbing universe of experience" and "cannot seize history and bend it readily to our collective purposes" (Giddens, 1991, pp. 53, 153). The ambiguities of influence in complex polities create ambiguities of accountability (Romzek and Dubnick, 1987; Thompson, 1987; Weaver and Rockman, 1993, pp. 1–2).

3. Outcomes are evaluated by *obscure standards*. Not only is personal control over performance ambiguous, so also are both the outcome criteria and the standards of appropriateness that are to be used to establish whether a role has been performed well or poorly. It is often unclear whether political actors are accountable for desirable outcomes or acting in appropriate ways. In either case, the criteria are likely to be ambiguous. Political mandates, rights, objectives, and rules require interpretation. Historical arguments about political leaders are less arguments over the facts of a particular regime than over the meaning of those facts in evaluative terms.

As a result, the assignment of accountability for historical events often seems largely arbitrary (MacIntyre, 1984, p. 74; March, 1984; Brunsson, 1985, 1989). Consider, for example, the process of establishing personal accountability for the performance of social welfare institutions. Accountability presumes an interpretation of events, determining how social welfare interventions, practices, or policies have affected social conditions. There is no well-established body of theory or empirical knowledge systematically linking variations in social welfare policies, procedures, or actions to variations in performance. It is difficult to determine the degree to which failures are to be blamed on, or successes credited to, particular policy or administrative decisions, or even broad policy directions. Effects are often indirect and contingent rather than uniform, direct, and unidirectional (Weaver and Rockman, 1993, p. 39). Moreover, the value of consequences is often ambiguous. How social welfare performance is to be measured or what the criteria for success and failure are may be quite unclear (Thompson, 1967).

The ambiguities of responsibility tend to make the extent, content, and forms of political accountability political issues of their own. When political actors are held accountable to poorly specified and changing standards, they seek to negotiate an interpretation that converts villainy into cleverness and ignorance into cunning. The negotiation turns account formation into an arena of political conflict and struggle for control. Political participants redefine objectives and identities more or less continuously, trying to interpret political aspirations in ways that fit, and simultaneously shape, the mundane activities of politics.

Ambiguity about standards can be used as a deliberate tactic of governors to reduce the effectiveness of the manipulation of information by those being held accountable. Clear standards and rules of accounting are invitations for officials to control accounts rather than the histories of which they are representations. Political leaders manage the measurement of unemployment instead of unemployment itself; they negotiate the measurement of the deficit rather than the deficit. Managers manage the measurement of performance instead of performance. Elements of ambiguity in accounting requirements and criteria make such manipulation more difficult and (perhaps) focus attention on achieving a goal, even one that is not precisely measured (March, 1987). Moreover, evocative ambiguity with respect to standards stimulates a continuing renegotiation and elaboration of standards.

Partly as a result of the ambiguities of responsibility, the idea of accountability has sometimes been transformed into an idea of co-accountability. Organized interests are accountable to policy-makers, even as policy-makers are accountable to organized interests. Policy-makers are accountable to bureaucrats, even as bureaucrats are accountable to policy-makers. Ideas of co-accountability reflect a desire to preserve individual responsibility and accountability (albeit in a reduced form) in an age of large-scale, complex systems in which simple causal orders rarely represent political and social reality (MacIntyre, 1984; Thompson, 1987).

In many respects, however, making someone accountable, or co-accountable, is an act of injustice. History unfolds in a complicated way that makes the search for pure causes, first causes, or even primary causes endlessly frustrating. Experience is not always generous with evidence. Historical events do not repeat themselves reliably. Their causes are often obscure. Events are produced by complicated combinations of interacting forces. Observations and interpretations of events are muddied by the inadequacies of human inference. What happened in history is unclear. Why it happened is unclear. Who caused it is unclear. How we should feel about it and what can be done are unclear. To attribute a specific historical event or set of events exclusively to the actions of a specific individual or group of individuals is, consequently, an exercise in fantasy. When a political leader is defeated in election because of events that have occurred during his or her time in office, or when a business leader is awarded a large bonus because of events that have occurred during his or her time in office, the chance that he or she has produced the attributed events is remote.

ACCOUNTABILITY WITHOUT RESPONSIBILITY

It is a hallowed doctrine of social organization that "authority must be commensurate with responsibility." From this perspective, officials can be held accountable only for outcomes they can control, and doubts about the importance of intentional actions by individual political actors in the flow of history would appear to require doubts about the meaningfulness of accountability. One interpretation of the persistence of concepts of individual responsibility and accountability in the face of such doubts emphasizes the way stories of history must fit culturally standardized scripts. As long as the structure of ordinary discourse is organized by scripts that exalt individual choice and individual control over destiny, accounts of history will be framed by those scripts. Villains and heroes will inhabit the stories of people who understand fully that there are really no villains and no heroes in the sense of the standard story lines. The story line is applied to people at a distance and replaced with a more complicated view when dealing with people in person. In this interpretation, understandings of the complexity of history can be sustained indefinitely without affecting the concrete frames of stories. Assertions of accountability are a kind of mythology that allows acknowledgment of the faith, roughly equivalent to parental tales about Santa Claus.

An alternative interpretation of the persistence of concepts of personal responsibility in history stems from expectations of adverse behavioral consequences from an explicit recognition of the complexities of history. In this view, there may be very little prospect of establishing accountability in the sense of causal responsibility. The things that happen may well be outside the control of individual human agents. Nevertheless, a strict application of arbitrary political accountability may be useful in motivating political actors to try to do what might be possible. If the complexity of history is treated as legitimate justification for inaction, a too-easy excuse is provided for not attempting to discover what is possible (Waligorski, 1990; Shklar, 1990). Indeed, many such excuses have been used to avoid personal responsibility. Causal complexity, lack of control, and lack of autonomy all have been accepted as legitimate reasons for absolving individuals of responsibility in politics. Such acceptance may be motivationally and socially perverse, even though it is intellectually defensible.

Those pragmatic interpretations of the persistence of concepts of accountability in the face of the ambiguities of history may, however, obscure a central reality of governance. Accountability is a more demanding concept than causality. Although modern ideas that hold individual responsibility to be bounded by individual control have affected concepts of accountability, the accountability of a monarch for the health of the realm does not depend entirely on royal control over the course of events. Democratic political systems have generally insisted on an allocation of personal accountability for political outcomes that most modern students of political history would consider descriptively implausible. Responsibility is a social convention and construction by which political actors affirm the preeminence of intentional human control over history. It is a myth, and an important one. When an intelligent administrator or politician says "the buck stops here" and accepts responsibility for things over which he or she has little control, the edifice of human myths is sustained. And those myths are central to a good life not only for the official but for a community of citizens.

Providing the Bases for Accountability

The proposition that democracy requires accountability of citizens and officials is a universal tenet of democratic theory. There is less agreement as to how this objective is to be accomplished (Pennock, 1979, p. 268). Efforts to produce accountability sometimes are ineffective and sometimes achieve effectiveness at too heavy a cost in terms of reductions in the capabilities of governmental action. As a result, it is less clear what specific forms accountability should take and what institutional arrangements should be used to make government more accountable. Almost without exception, however, democratic theories emphasize mechanisms for providing information and imposing sanctions.

INFORMATION AS A BASIS FOR ACCOUNTABILITY

Students of accountability in democracy consistently note both the necessity and the difficulty of assuring that citizens know what officials are doing. Governors can be held accountable by the governed only when publicity, transparency, and critical scrutiny provide a basis for an informed citizenry. There has never been agreement, however, on exactly what information is to be made freely available, what information is to be shared only with some agents of the public who thereby accept responsibility for assuring accountability, and what information may legitimately be concealed (at least until the inevitable memoirs of participants are invented).

Democratic politics and governance are worlds of competition, opposition, and conflict. They are worlds of coalitions and deals. They are worlds in which programs that are revealed prematurely become programs that cannot be achieved. They are worlds in which the free exchange of opinion and exploration of possibilities often require a willingness to express and defend unpopular opinions and to entertain deviant theories. They are worlds in which the fates of ordinary individuals, the innocent as well as the not-so-innocent, are decided as by-products of the resolution of the public's business. Consequently, politics and governance are worlds in which effectiveness often profits from discretion, secrecy, and the management of information.

Those gains in the effectiveness of the polity are difficult to accomplish innocently, because they are confounded by concomitant evasions of accountability. Decisions about what documents in the conduct of foreign affairs are properly kept secret are clearly affected by the desires of ministers and bureaucrats to conceal mistakes and villainy. Decisions about what discussions to report (and how to report them) are clearly affected by the desires of political officials to limit embarrassment and indictment.

Democracies have never developed a stable solution to the problems involved in balancing the information requirements of effective accountability with the confidentiality requirements of effective action. A traditional, imprecise compromise grants officials the right to keep matters secret or even to deceive under some circumstances but treats the license to do so as temporary and revocable (Thompson, 1987, p. 26). In practice, democratic systems differ significantly in their norms of disclosure, but all are continually renegotiating those norms as they conform to (and evade) them. Periods of political malaise lead to loss of public trust and to increased calls for exposing information previously imagined to be properly protected. Periods of political confidence lead to increased tolerance of secrecy. Fashions in exposure change over time, drifting from an emphasis on exposing the private corruptions and personal immoralities of officials to an emphasis on exposing the political premises for major public policies.

Since a large part of the information about the operation of government falls in the category of being neither routinely publicly available nor completely restricted, democratic accountability depends on an institutional structure by which the effectiveness of various independent auditors is secured. Historically, the emergence of legislatures, a free press, and the public sphere represented structural innovations providing institutionalized public spheres for forming and disseminating accounts. Legislators became public agents with special rights of access to information about the actions of the government and with responsibility for monitoring those actions. The

Burkean expectation is that a legislature can make an independent judgment on behalf of citizens. Legislative judgments are informed by information that may not be appropriately available to all citizens. Similarly, the voices of a free press act as agents of the public, able to use their rights of special access to information. Like legislators, journalists are not expected to report everything they know, but they are expected to make intelligent, independent, and responsible judgments about what can be legitimately concealed. When a government appeals to a free press to exercise restraint in exposure, it recognizes the rights of an independent judgment about information dissemination.

The basic story of auditing is everywhere the same. Auditors are agents of others who cannot be as well informed. They are always vulnerable both to co-optation by the audited and to pretensions of autonomous importance. In the case of democracy, legislators and journalists play a vital intermediary role in the information structure of accountability, but they have difficulty maintaining independence from the agencies they monitor. Special legislative committees to audit intelligence services come to see the information world from the point of view of the services. Journalists become dependent on sources, thus dependent on maintaining their good favor. At the same time, each is subject to temptations to trivialize the information function by reducing it to slogans and simplifications that secure attention and fit into a twenty-second segment of television news or provide short-run political advantage.

The political auditing function is organized by the structure and role of political parties and the media. As a result, it differs from one democratic system to another. Where—as in the United States in the 1980s and 1990s—individual legislators and journalists (or television personalities) compete as individuals for the approval of individual citizens, the competition for attention reduces the risks of individual co-optation but requires confidence in the capabilities of individual actors to make discriminating judgments on the basis of incomplete knowledge. Where—as in Norway between 1950 and 1980—legislators are organized into parties and journalists into clusters, co-optation is a greater danger, but the intermediary groups are more likely to shape political discourse in a meaningful way.

When large-scale, well-financed organizations dominate the electronic mass media, newspapers, and book production, competition loses some of its democratic force and publicity some of its innocence (Habermas, 1992a, p. 437), but without some structure to the shaping of opinion from information, democracy also suffers. There is a gap between public opinion as a construct of normative theories of democracy and constitutional law, on the one hand, and public opinion, as described by empirical research, on the other (Habermas, 1992a, pp. 439–40). Those disabilities make it impossible to specify a procedure for sharing information without simultaneously specifying a procedure for democratic discourse among citizens.

A presumption of accountability is that unfavorable information leads to the imposition of sanctions on political actors. Calling officials to account by associating sanctions with inappropriate behavior or outcomes, however, is not always easy. Since political actors expect that unfavorable information will lead to sanctions against them, they not only seek to behave properly but also seek to restrict the flow of information that might reveal they have not done so. At the same time, accountability can rather easily become a political ritual, where governors "accept" responsibility, while anticipating that acceptance will have no negative implications for themselves (Thompson, 1987, p. 43).

Concerns about the capability of citizens to impose effective sanctions on governors have long been voiced. Radical critics question the idea that real democratic accountability is possible as long as inequalities in social and economic resources exist (Frazer, 1992, p. 121). A broader version of the same critique came from a different political direction during the 1980s. The argument was that enforcing political accountability was impossible, not so much because of resource inequalities among citizens as because of the size and complexity of the public sector. The solution was to limit the political agenda rather than to strengthen control over it. Because political actors could not be held accountable, the size and responsibilities of government had to be reduced (Olsen and Peters, 1995a).

Democratic systems have traditionally relied on two sources of sanctions. The first is external to the official. It includes formal, institutional arrangements of observation and sanctions (Finer, 1941). Those arrangements have emphasized both rules of proper (or legal) behavior and principles of democratic political competition. Officials are bound and protected by rules. They are subject to punishment, including dismissal, if they fail to follow them. They are also held to account through competitive elections, agencies of countervailing power, independent courts of law, and audiences of clients and experts. More recently, reforms of the public sector have focused on making governmental offices and officials accountable directly to consumers and clients through competitive markets or marketlike mechanisms.

The attempt to introduce market sanctions into governmental accountability concerns is both honorable and promising. Markets are, however, different from other forms of sanctions, and their advantages are gained at the cost of some disadvantages from the standpoint of democratic principles. On the one hand, the use of price mechanisms in democracy presumes a distribution of resources consistent with the equality of citizens, and democratic experience clearly suggests the difficulty of achieving such a distribution with respect to any resources that form the basis of a market, most particularly money. The sanctions of the market establish accountability of officials only to those citizens with resources recognized by markets.

A deeper problem with market sanctions also stems from one of their great strengths. The market deals simultaneously with the demands of numerous autonomous actors pursuing their own interests. In principle, and to a substantial extent in practice, those demands are efficiently reflected in a price that provides most of the information required by each individual actor to make an individual decision. In fact, as markets become more efficient, the market as a place in which individuals come to meet physically, haggle over price, and get to know each other tends to disappear. The social relations summarized in the market become invisible to experience. The depersonalized property of markets is, of course, also a property of many other modern institutions, particularly those that substitute distant, impersonal bilateral contact for close, personal multilateral contact. The democratic presumption of discourse among citizens may be hard to sustain when the occasions of such discourse are replaced not only by television programs, opinion polls, and recorded messages but also by markets.

A second source of sanctions is internal to the official, particularly internalized personal senses of moral obligation, honor, and duty. An official who acts inappropriately is punished by guilt and a loss of self-respect (Friedrich, 1940). Through education and socialization of citizens and officials, the polity mobilizes conscience in the service of accountability. Such sanctions can be effective, but they presume a socialization procedure and a powerful culture of reference groups that cannot be assumed in modern democracies. The traditions of democratic accountability through internal sanctions have developed under assumptions of a strong community and conscience. They may need to be adapted to a world in which both community and conscience are less important. One aspect of the adaptation might be, of course, to reintroduce notions of community and conscience to modern life. In the short run, however, the decline of community and conscience suggests the necessity of increased use of explicit instruments of accountability, instruments that will almost certainly make public life less tolerable to potential officials, public institutions less capable of action, and democracy less effective.

Accounts and Democratic Governance

The construction of accounts is both an exchange of information and a negotiation among social groups and subcultures with different ideas and modes of thought. Those encounters often involve cooperative pursuits of mutual understanding, problem-solving, and diffusion of beliefs. Stories develop through the comparison and merger of disparate accounts and the pooling of information. The encounters are sometimes less cooperative. Accounts are contested. There is competition over interpretations between authorities and outside experts and partisans (Kelley, 1990, p. 57). Advocates of contrasting interpretations demand the right to construct, maintain, modify, or extend accounts, and thereby define themselves and their societies. There are contests among the main interest groups in a polity—the state, the church, the political party, the professional association, the mass media, the multinational corporation, and other organized entities. The democratic governance of accounts is the management of this process of cooperation and conflict to allow development of shared understandings, arguments, and reasons.

Democratic Ambivalences

Democratic political traditions and institutions are particularly sensitive to the benefits and dangers involved in the governmental shaping of accounts. Democracy depends simultaneously on a set of shared values and beliefs and on tolerance for variety in commitments and accounts. It is built on a conception of individual autonomy in judgment and on processes for exposing that autonomy to challenge by others. Democratic procedures for the governance of accounts are conditioned by these ambivalences.

AMBIVALENCE ABOUT UNITY (AND DIVERSITY)

Organized systems seek to gain both the short-run, local efficiency advantages of exploitation and the long-run, global adaptiveness advantages of exploration (March, 1991, 1994c). Although the terms of discourse vary from one literature to another, the problem of balancing exploitation and exploration is as familiar to theories of evolution as to philosophies of politics (Morengo, 1993). The political version of the problem is that of balancing the short-run requirements of the society for unity and coherence with the long-run necessity of diversity and change in accounts. Some of the grandest complications of democratic governance surround the processes for sustaining a balance between unity, solidarity, community, rules, integration, and efficiency (on the one hand) and diversity, differentiation, individual autonomy, individual liberty, disintegration, and experimentation (on the other hand). If it were possible to define and maintain an optimal balance between any of the pairs, life would be relatively easy. However, defining the optimum is elusive, and the natural adaptive dynamics of democracy tend to make any balance unstable. Each side of the balance requires the other, yet tends to eliminate it.

Democracy thrives on instruments for creating and maintaining unity. It profits from feelings of solidarity; stable, shared values and rules; and senses of commonality and similarity that are conducive to empathy and mutual trust. Integrated communities can engage in graceful, intelligent, and civil discourse over political directions and alternatives. They can grant authority to officials and make claims on citizens with confidence that responsibilities will be met. They can more effectively represent the unborn. On the other hand, a democratic system with a hegemonic monopoly of interpretation (whether sustained by government, a political party, a social class, a culture, or an intelligentsia) faces the possibility of ossification.

Consequently, democracy also thrives on instruments for creating and maintaining diversity. It profits from public criticism and debate, from conflict over values and rules, and from differences that lead to experimentation with alternative practices and exploration of new visions. Societies of conflict and differences challenge established ideas and prevent ossification. They avoid the blindness of collective ignorance. They stimulate change and the development of new capabilities. However, highly differentiated and fragmented societies face the possibility of communicative entropy and of losing coherence in their systems of law and justice (Dworkin, 1986, p. 407). Loss of a common language and concepts is a loss of political community, argumentative and rhetorical resources, and a shared understanding of the world (Ball, Farr, and Hanson, 1989, pp. 1–2). People who differ fundamentally in their causal and moral beliefs find it impossible to reason together in ways that produce causal and ethical understanding (MacIntyre, 1988; Taylor, 1992). Participants in debates across deep cultural cleavages share so little in the way of values, expressive norms, and principles of persuasion as to be unable to reach agreement through reasoning and deliberation (Frazer, 1992, p. 126). Debate drives them apart rather than together.

The modern democratic vision embraces the idea that unity and diversity can be made not only mutually consistent but also mutually supportive through a system of informed, empathic tolerance. Citizens are supposed to live together without insisting on agreement or certainty (Crick, 1983, pp. 33, 160). They are encouraged to maintain diverse attitudes, beliefs, and commitments and to express those elements of diversity within arenas involving other citizens similarly displaying their own distinctive characters. Public discussion and criticism, opposition, and regulated competition and conflict, are tolerated, even encouraged and institutionalized. This traditional democratic creed of tolerant unity, however, has proved difficult to sustain within large modern democracies. In the absence of external threat, social forces of subgroup differentiation threaten to overcome relatively weak pressures toward democratic unity both within nation-states and within larger international unions.

The problem is complicated by the way in which unity at one level of a system is a source of diversity at another. One of the most powerful ways of fostering differentiation and conflict among subgroups, for example, is to strengthen internal subgroup unity (Coser, 1956). Ideologies embedded in accounts of conflict, violence, repression, victories, and defeats preserve differences established at critical times in a nation's history (Lipset and Rokkan, 1967). Commitments to subgroup identities are sources of enduring diversity in a society. Perceptions of abandonment by others and idiosyncratic virtues tend to combine the subgroup confidence that might facilitate integration at a more inclusive level with the intergroup antagonisms that inhibit it. Variety is sustained not by a general system preference for diversity but by subgroup pride and power and by a stalemate between hostile opposing groups (Hirschman, 1991, p. 168). Subgroup unity and differentiation serve to preserve system diversity, but without commitment to it. Support for diversity (like much of the support for decentralization or equality) tends to be a tactical strategy of groups currently out of power or exhausted by conflict. It is very likely to be abandoned by the same groups when they come to power or have caught their breath.

As a result, democratic governance involves a continual unresolved ambivalence, continuous struggle and oscillation between the polarities of unity and diversity. As diversity and individual autonomy move inexorably toward the destruction of unity and community, or as rules and efficiency move inexorably toward the destruction of liberty and experimentation, wise governors interpose countervailing pressures. Governors are chosen democratically, however, and until the imbalance becomes severe, they are more likely to contribute to the momentum of imbalance than to correct it.

AMBIVALENCE ABOUT THE ROLE OF GOVERNANCE

The liberal democratic tradition has emphasized a free flow of ideas and ways of thought. It has also emphasized the constraints on the role of government in the construction and dissemination of accounts and the boundaries within which government has to act if it is going to maintain legitimacy. The liberal position has been to argue for the neutrality of the public sphere. The state should have no philosophical or religious projects of its own. It should recognize different subcultures but not use state power to give privileges to any one of them. The primary role of the state, from such a perspective, is to support the development of a self-regulating civil society.

The practice of democratic polities has been somewhat different. Governments habitually intervene in discussions of public policy. Taking part in account formation through deliberation, analysis, and persuasion, and in the development of institutions and communities of account construction, has been recognized as a legitimate role of modern democratic government. Governments are expected to express public ideas and visions, including beliefs about how citizens and officials should behave and relate to each other. They are expected to explain their actions and to describe their interpretations of social reality and available political opportunities. They are expected to influence the institutional context within which public accounts are developed, authorized, legitimized, and disseminated.

Many of those interventions are designed to influence the outcome of discussions, to make one set of policies more likely to be supported than another. Since such cases are likely to involve significant political actors with competing worldviews, senses of appropriateness, and resources of their own, changing interpretations enough to affect outcomes is not trivial. Consequently, governments ambitious for control have long engaged in techniques of censorship and control over the instruments of debate (Hannerz, 1993). As early as 1560 censorship of books was universal in Europe, and since then censorship has been a key instrument of official control over discussions of public policy (Rice, 1970, p. 10).

European nation-states helped build national institutions for account construction and dissemination as part of nation-building and the creation of a unified, national mass culture. A complex mix of account-producing institutions and a variety of competing actors and accounts at the supranational, national, and subnational levels were to some extent replaced by one dominant locus of account construction and dissemination and thus one authorized public truth. Such efforts at nation-building resulted in the construction of cultural boundaries, identities, and accounts of the nation as a shared culture (Eisenstadt and Rokkan, 1973; Flora, 1983; Turner, 1990). They promulgated such things as comprehensive standardizations of language, mass forms of compulsory education, shared ethical and causal beliefs, and expectations of everyday behavior—even norms of child-bearing and childrearing (Watkins, 1991). Over time, governments initiated or supported the development of account-producing and record-keeping institutions—national systems of education, central bureaus of statistics, libraries, national universities, museums, art galleries, armies, and national public service broadcasting corporations. History writing was a significant part of the nation-building project, and the modern democratic state and policy-relevant scholarly disciplines developed together (Wagner *et al.*, 1991).

The development of national accounts (as well as identities and capabilities) supported by an active government was of special significance in small and relatively homogeneous polities such as those found in Scandinavia. There, democracy included a strong role for government in formal education, often with the explicit idea of constructing the citizens needed for a new kind of society (Boli, 1989). Government had a leading role in adult education, in establishing public libraries, in the development of mass communications, and in supporting culture and the arts (Allardt *et al.*, 1981). Scandinavian democratic governance has involved constructing both accounts and the institutional frameworks (including a state church) for account construction. It has involved securing the survival of interpretative communities and maintaining a certain balance among them, modifying their relative status and significance, supporting and legitimizing their roles, and regulating their influence.

Contemporary students debate the extent to which governance properly involves helping to create these frameworks for accounts. The inclination to grant a more active role to governance in the management of account competition than the one suggested by traditional liberal theories stems partly from the fact that the state is

not the only threat to the free construction of accounts. Other organized actors also have a potential for establishing dominant positions
in the competition over accounts. Like the government, they may be
able to secure support by misinforming the public and corrupting
the accounts (Hannerz, 1992, p. 104). But those who see a more active role for governance in creating interpretations generally recognize the dangers of governmental tyranny that arise, and those who
are most adamant in denying such a role to governance generally
concede the risks of nongovernmental tyranny.

Democratic Possibilities

The ambivalences with respect to unity and with respect to the role
of government in fostering it create genuine difficulties for democratic governance. Democracy requires substantial unity, a considerable
commitment to a common fate and a common set of understandings.
At the same time it requires that such unity be consistent with diversity both across people and across time. The values and norms reflected in democratic unity are to be imposed neither by the
governors of the moment nor by those who happen to control the
instruments of information. They are to arise from more thoughtful
convergences of a free citizenry. The democratic solution to these
difficulties involves two myths. The first is the myth of obscure authorship. Democratic polities create and sustain evolving interpretive communities, systems of accounts that maintain continuity yet
are open to change. Meaning emerges without being imposed. Authorship is obscured, not by deception but by the ambiguity of
sources in emergent meaning. The second myth is the myth of immaculate truth. Democratic polities honor conflict and bargaining,
but they also see truth as something that exists outside those instruments. Knowledge is innocent, to be discovered rather than created
or negotiated. Expertise exists and can be made to serve a community of nonexpert equal citizens.

THE SOCIAL CONSTRUCTION OF ACCOUNTS

Modern democracies are changing inventories of meanings, identities, and accounts distributed over a population and woven into social and political relationships (Hannerz, 1992). They exhibit conflict among institutionalized rules and rule regimes, institutional pluralism, and hybrid organizations. Democratic political institutions seem to be based on layers of partly ambiguous, inconsistent, changing, and competing ideals and beliefs, rather than on coherent stable doctrines. Different actors adopt different identities and learn different rules at different times as the varieties of their histories are coded into the varieties of their institutions.

Those premises of democratic action evolve in the context of politics. Identities, preferences, capabilities, accounts, and experience change in the course of being acted upon. Capabilities are augmented and depleted through use. Experience is shaped by learning reactions to it. Accounts are changed in the process of creating and communicating them. Individual changes are not autonomous but occur in an ecology of changing premises. Citizens and officials discover their identities and preferences by observing, imitating, and avoiding the identities of others. Capabilities are transferred. The lessons of history are captured and diffused through rules and practices. Fads come and go. Individuals are formed by contemplation of reflections of themselves.

Moreover, at any point in the process of development, identities, preferences, capabilities, and experience are likely to be unclear. The problems of providing an adequate knowledge base for future-oriented planning models based on calculated consequences are well known. Similar problems complicate learning from experience, a process of central importance in most accounts of progress. The drawing of inferences from history may produce misunderstandings as well as understandings. The imperatives of identity are often simultaneously compelling and ambiguously specified. They need to be interpreted in specific situations (which are also ambiguous). Individuals know that they are citizens or officials and accept the necessity of fulfilling those identities without knowing exactly what it means to be a citizen or official in a particular situation.

Because of those uncertainties, democracy is more than a system for making and implementing collective decisions. It is also, and perhaps preeminently, a collection of interlocking interpretive communities. It is organized around talk, around establishing temporary understandings adequate to human communication, acceptance, and action. Some of the chief institutions of democracy are institutions for discourse, and the quality of democratic governance is measured by the quality of the discourse that it stimulates. Talk includes, of course, not only the vocalizations of meaning but also written and pictorial representations that allow meaning to be shared and contested. Talk evokes, interprets, and legitimizes identities, focusing attention on certain aspects of beliefs and away from others. Talk exhibits, elaborates, and shares competencies. Talk develops accounts by which history is understood and responsibility established. Conventions of talk restrict and organize considerations that can be attended at one time, thereby reducing the cacophony of possible meanings to a comprehensible chorus. They impose requirements of communication on the babble of the mind, thereby making meaning explicitly social.

Since the processes of interpretation and reinterpretation are ordinarily less episodic than the process of action and serve more purposes, the links between democratic talk and democratic action are not straightforward. Talk often affects action and is affected by it, but the two are also often buffered from each other in ways that encourage different arenas to reflect different concerns. Talk may deviate considerably from action, conforming to different imperatives at different rates. Accountability may be attached sometimes to one, sometimes to the other.

DEVELOPING INTERPRETIVE COMMUNITIES

In Western democracies political accounts are often constructed in encounters among contending accounts. The construction of "public truth" takes place in the context of those encounters, as well as in the context of discussions among professional communities, administrative agencies, and others, competing for attention and support. As ideas are exchanged and modified, the specific group or force responsible for a course of action becomes unclear. From this point of view, the objective of democratic account management is not to secure plebiscitary support for desired actions but to assure the existence of interpretive communities within which mutual understanding and an anonymously authored and generally comprehended policy can emerge (Habermas, 1992a, p. 449). Recent styles of journalistic accounts, with their emphasis on telling stories that interpret political outcomes as victories for some and losses for others, undermine such interpretive communities.

The idea of an interpretive community is illustrated by the community of law and legal interpretation. Legal reasoning is an exercise in constructive interpretation. In the context of a specific case, legal officials argue about the facts, the law, and their joint implications for action. The argument takes place within a structure of rules and traditions. For instance, in 1159 Emperor Frederick Barbarossa bestowed the right of interpreting civil law to authorized *doctores legis*, thereby creating a new institution of interpretation. The decision was taken in the context of a debate over whether jurists would usurp the functions of legislators and a discussion of who could legitimately interpret a law (Kelley, 1990, pp. 58, 65). Modern courts and rules of interpretation provide room for argument about which claims are sound and why. Judges add to the tradition they interpret. But any single case is part of a long story that the judge must interpret and continue (Berman, 1983; Dworkin, 1986, p. 239).

An interpretive community involves informed citizens and governors capable of undertaking competent evaluations of individual matters or able to evaluate the prerequisites for delegating decision-making authority to others (Dahl, 1987, p. 203). Traditions of liberal democracy, including traditions of Habermasian communicative rationality, imply unconstrained communication and free exchange of arguments, where the participants are convinced by the truth of the better argument, the rightness of a norm, and the authenticity of a conviction (Habermas, 1989). Democratic polities try to safeguard such discourse first by creating an institutional space between the state and civil society supported by a legal framework of freedom of association, speech, and press (Rodger, 1985), and second by building a common framework of understandings of how citizens think about the world and how they act within it.

In modern democracies the construction of meaning and the legitimation of accounts are exercises in contested imagination (March and Olsen, 1983). Because accounts influence the flow of political events, political actors struggle to invent, correct, control and interpret them (Wildavsky and Tenenbaum, 1980; Alonso and Starr, 1987). The development, dissemination, authorization, and legitimation of accounts engage leaders, commentators, and audiences as they try to understand and assess what is happening, to explain why things go well or wrong, to evaluate the performance of political actors, and to solicit support for their understandings. Shared meanings and understandings are created and discovered in the context of inconsistencies in preferences and identities and struggles for dominance. Perceptions are twisted to serve desires.

Because the scale and technologies of modern democracies differ significantly from the scale and technologies of democracies that functioned as recently as the nineteenth century, the meaning of an interpretive community is different in detail from what it was. Nevertheless, the spirit is largely unchanged since the earliest writings on democracy. The spirit includes the idea of communication among identifiable human beings who can know and respond to each other over an extended period of time. It includes the idea of shared responsibility for developing and exchanging authentic information and for maintaining the community. It includes the idea of openness, a conception that differences should be expressed and recognized, that questions and answers should evolve collectively within a culture of empathetic consideration. These concerns are as relevant to (and as frequently expressed in) many modern electronic bulletin board communities as they are to (and in) neighborhood political groups. The role of governance is to foster such communities.

Modern interpretive communities, however, are more richly textured and structured than such examples suggest. They are not autonomous clusters of people but interrelated groups linked together in networks organized to reflect differences in location, specialty, expertise, and interest. Directly or indirectly, each individual is tied to numerous other overlapping communities, each of which is, in effect, part of a discussion. Knowledge, values, and frames are created not only through interactions within a particular group but through cobwebs of connections in an ecology of communities. Ideas of communication, shared responsibility, and openness frame the development of accounts in parts of that ecology, but they shade into ideas of limited communication, contracts, and restraint in other parts. The resulting "community" is often in danger of losing a collective sense of integration, but it is also often remarkably interconnected.

DISCOVERING AND CONTROLLING KNOWLEDGE

There is a tension in democratic thought between the idea of knowledge as something sought and discovered collectively and the idea that knowledge involves the application of specialized competence. Democratic pursuits of appropriate policies through intelligent discourse proceed from confidence in the former and suspicion of the latter. The contrast is somewhat obscured by the fact that a commitment to knowledge is a convention of civilized discourse. Questions of value and interest are habitually couched in the linguistic form of questions of knowledge. The convention serves a democratic polity in two important ways: First, it civilizes debate and allows sentiments of shared destinies to shape expressions of conflict. By substituting the language of inquiry for the language of conflict, democratic polities reduce the potential for violence and unresolvable confrontation. Second, it provides (in principle) a counterbalance to the unequal distribution of monetary and physical resources. Knowledge purports to serve Truth, thus is imagined not to serve Mammon or Power except by happenstance (Wildavsky, 1979). Although modern conceptions of knowledge make it somewhat less innocent, its role as a democratic counterweight to economic power is well established.

Nevertheless, the relation between democracy and expert knowledge is troubled. Democracy assumes effective access to citizens to coherent information about the functioning of the government, a set of institutions ensuring opportunities for the free exchange of information and opinions, and a culture of confidence in the sustainability of meaningful discourse. Such assumptions are brought into question by specialized knowledge. Historical arguments that governance must be based on the interpretations and accounts of philosopher kings and enlightened representatives are renewed in contemporary claims that it is impossible for lay people to understand the complexity of public policy issues and that justifications can be developed and understood only by experts and in institutions protected against ignorance, like courts of law, military general staffs, scientific institutes, universities, and central banks.

On the surface at least, an unequal distribution of knowledge seems as problematic for democracy as an unequal distribution of other resources. Effective participation in many contemporary issues of public policy requires knowledge. Democratic aspirations are, however, not based on a belief that all individual citizens can understand equally well all policy justifications in detail (Marcus and Hanson, 1993). Expertise is recognized as a useful resource for reasoning citizens. Democratic discourse mixes the accounts believed and accepted by ordinary citizens on the basis of informed discussion, critical inquiry, and experiential learning with various forms of expert knowledge. In some decision areas, citizens express at least as much trust in experts as in elected officials, and claims of undue political influence over domains of expertise are commonplace (Olsen and Aardal, 1989). In other areas, however, professional expertise receives less deference. Discussions are deprofessionalized to protect them from technocratic manipulation (Nelkin, 1979; Taylor, 1984).

The governance of expertise is made easier by the way democratic discourse is organized into functionally specialized spheres (Walzer, 1983, 1984). Experience is, for instance, created, interpreted, and acted upon differently within the contexts of politics, science, law, ethics, markets, warfare, families, art, and organized religion. Those institutionalized spheres provide different arenas for argumentation, learning, the clarification of knowledge, and the creation of meaning. The weaving together of expert and lay beliefs occurs within each sphere. The different spheres develop different logics and criteria of relevance, claiming thereby some degree of autonomy from other spheres. A hegemony of expertise across spheres is thereby made more difficult. Separation and autonomy lead to collisions and conflicts among discourses (Teubner, 1992). Democratic politics is filled with attempts to clarify and redefine the division of labor, responsibility, and competence among different spheres. It is also filled with imperialistic attempts to subordinate the discourse of one sphere to the logic, norms, and discourse of another institutional sphere. These conflicts pit combinations of experts and nonexperts against each other in ways that weaken the homogeneity of experts and make them more accessible to lay accounts of reality.

Democratic Accounts

Political accounts are both the product of a political order and a force in its creation, maintenance, and change. Accounts are conservative in the sense that they reflect the basic organizing ideas, symbols, and interpretations of a polity. They usually accommodate discrepant facts without undermining the social fabric of fundamental causal and moral beliefs (Gambling, 1977). At the same time, however, the process of constructing and negotiating political accounts contributes to the modification of shared meanings.

The quality of accounts available in a polity is not guaranteed. Increased ignorance, barbarism, and decline are real alternatives to improved knowledge, wisdom, and growth. Political discourse can easily become a vehicle for the distortion of reason and justice in the service of political, economic, and professional power. Information is a strategic weapon, as well as a means for discovering truth and improving the common good. The use of secrecy and selective information in the service of personal or group interest is well known. Influencing the criteria and targets that define successes and failures, and controlling the attribution of blame and praise are key political objectives (March and Olsen, 1976). The ability to gain acceptance for a special language, a type of discourse, specific interpretative communities and institutions, or particular interpretations is a source and indication of political power.

Democratic governance involves managing those contests over meaning and building institutions that allow citizens to create, sustain, and change interpretations of reality in an ambiguous and uncertain world (Smirich and Morgan, 1982). It involves making the process of account-building one that contributes to collective intelligence, institutional learning, and political equality. It involves improving the capabilities of a society for moral and cognitive reasoning, thoughtful argumentation, and constructive compromise and organizing the processes of politics around discussion and respect in the service of a community of reasoning equal individuals, rather than around power and distrust in the service of selfishness and privilege. Democratic institutions and processes make it possible for democratic citizens and officials to construct a moral account of the good society, recognize appropriate tasks, ends, and forms of governance, and develop confidence in their mutual good spirit and capabilities for reason. They develop and protect an autonomous public sphere and civil society, not controlled by political, ideological, or economic power (Habermas, 1989). They define and maintain informal and formal accounting systems that make it possible to learn from experience and to call citizens, officials, and other powerful institutions and individuals to account in terms of democratic standards.

Chapter Six

DEVELOPING
POLITICAL ADAPTIVENESS

Political institutions change. Although institutional histories describe processes of change that are often halting, the institutions of long-lived democracies are in some respects notably different now from what they were one hundred years ago. Political transformations have sometimes involved substantial modifications in the boundaries of a polity, in definitions of identities, in the ways accounts are maintained and capabilities are distributed. At other times, changes appear to have been more piecemeal and gradual. In neither case do the changes produce a precise matching of institutional features to environmental requirements. Institutions seem to meander through modifications that occasionally are, or accumulate into, significant ones but often seem to have no consistent direction. Historical processes are inefficient in the sense that they move haltingly in the direction of one nonunique equilibrium after another in a co-evolutionary way.

During recent decades, as consciousness of the significance of adaptiveness has grown, democracies have been urged to allocate more attention and resources to learning (OECD, 1991; World Bank, 1991). Political institutions have been described as requiring greater learning capacity, improved ability to produce experiments, better skills at monitoring results, greater capabilities for evaluating and interpreting experience, and more effective procedures for storing and retrieving the lessons of history. Many of the components of institutional adaptiveness have become bases for growth industries in consulting (Derlien, 1990).

In this chapter we ask whether political adaptiveness can be harnessed in some way that is consistent with democratic hopes, whether the mistakes of change (and stability) can be reduced, and whether political institutions can lessen the significance of crisis, turbulence, and violence in political development. In short, we ask whether it is possible to build political institutions that civilize transformational political change and achieve intelligence through learning.

ADAPTIVENESS IN POLITICAL SYSTEMS

Democratic governance of institutional change seeks to further institutional survival while serving democratic ideals. Survival requires a reasonable match between an institution and its changing political, social, cultural, and economic environments. Serving democratic ideals requires a commitment to popular consent, informed discourse, and individual rights.

Stories of Institutional History

Political institutions are transformed through the mundane processes of everyday life, as well as through the rare metamorphoses at breaking points in history—institutional breakdowns and revolutions (March and Olsen, 1989). They evolve structures and routines for responding to their unfolding histories (March, 1981a). These institutional structures both routinize some kinds of changes and routinize resistance to others (Broderick, 1970; Bromiley and Marcus, 1987; Krasner, 1988; Blichner, 1995). Three rather different stories of institutional history and change are common. They are not mutually exclusive, but they are different. The first emphasizes the fitfulness of institutional adaptation to environments. It is a story of punctuated equilibria. The second story emphasizes the rich internal dynamics of institutional adaptation to environments. It is a story of processes that accelerate, decelerate, or redirect externally initiated change. The third emphasizes the co-evolution of institutions and environments. It is a story of the ways in which the environments to which political systems adapt are simultaneously adapting to them.

Historically, many of the more important changes in political institutions have been discontinuous, contested, and problematic (Skowronek, 1982; Orren and Skowronek, 1994). They are often described as relatively dramatic events linked to critical junctures which stimulate departures from established routines and practices (Collier and Collier, 1991). Change is pictured as a result of governmental crises that are too immense to be ignored (Weaver and Rockman, 1993, p. 464). Those breaking points in history have often been associated with devastating wars, including civil wars, and violent political struggles, with rare cataclysms and metamorphoses where considerable resources have been mobilized and one definition of appropriateness has replaced another (Krasner, 1988; March and Olsen, 1989). Many modern political regimes trace their beginnings to illegitimate, violent conquest and usurpation (Hinsley, 1986, p. 141), and major systemic reforms or revolutions have often been preceded by breakdowns of order accompanied by atrocities to the human spirit (Linz, 1978). The old institutional order collapses, and a new order is created.

During such transformative moments in history, institutionalized accounts and institutionalized ways of constructing accounts break down. The basic conceptions, categories, and presumptions on which standard accounts are based are no longer perceived as helpful in ordering and understanding ordinary experience. Political life is perceived as less comprehensible and more coercive than before. The standings of traditional stories and of the groups favored by them are brought into question. People become more uncertain in their conduct. They ask why certain things are prescribed or proscribed. Conventions that have been taken for granted become problems. Questions are raised about differences in codes of conduct among countries and contexts (Elias, 1982, p. 325). Key concepts, basic values, and habitual routines fail to make sense of the world. Old categories change content as citizens reconsider, clarify, or redefine what they want or believe, and renegotiate the terms of living together in a community (Herzog, 1989). In time, new groups come to dominate the construction of accounts within new institutionalized structures and procedures. A new public understanding of politics, society, and history, including what counts as reasonable and just, is developed (Collins, 1989; Herzog, 1989; Viroli, 1992).

Once created, an institution usually becomes relatively stable, its initial character being sustained by internal dynamics that resist change even though environmental conditions continue to evolve. Changes in the environment are likely to be ignored, fought, or buffered if they can be. Core practices and beliefs are likely to be defended rather than made consistent with new environmental pressures. Accounts and rules are constructed and furnished with meaning that can be diffused among current generations and passed on to new ones. In this way political institutions create elements of temporary and imperfect order and historical continuity that limit the possibilities for rapid change (Deutsch, 1966, pp. 131–32; Shklar, 1990, pp. 90, 120). This pattern of stabilization and resistance to change is not perverse, nor is it limited to political institutions (Tyre and Orlikowski, 1994). Successful institutions are usually associated with routinization and repetition, persistence and predictability, rather than with change, creativity, and free discretion. The record of institutional innovation is primarily a record of failure. Surviving institutions seem to be those that have successfully stabilized their norms, rules, and meanings, and procedures; forms adopted at critical junctures have surprising durability in institutions that survive (Stinchcombe, 1965; Hannan and Freeman, 1989).

Consequently, institutions and identities adapt to changes in their environments, but they typically do not adapt instantaneously, smoothly, or necessarily in the way that is intended by reformers (March, 1981a; Basu, Jones and Schlicht, 1987; North, 1990). Radical transformations are associated with major performance crises resulting from substantial changes in the environment and creeping obsolescence of stable systems (March and Olsen, 1989, p. 64). Typically, the crisis serves to expose the obsolescence. The mechanisms and advantages of stability maintain an institution until it is overpowered by a moment of environmental drama and collapses (March, 1994c). External changes in the conditions of survival combine with internally stabilized obsolescence to make change both difficult and dramatic (Johnson, 1982, p. 188). An institution crumbles, a new institution is put in its place, and the same story starts all over again. The result is a history characterized by extended periods of stability and little change, punctuated by occasional episodes of turmoil associated with rapid and substantial change (Krasner, 1988; March and Olsen, 1989).

There are numerous critics of this common story. The critics point particularly to institutional histories that seem to suggest more continuous institutional transformation and change that is less obviously attributable to external shocks. They argue that institutions sometimes drift great distances through combinations of modest steps, and that substantial change is sometimes triggered more by internal than by external forces. The critics also observe that the standard punctuated equilibrium story tends to obscure the extent to which rapid change that is ordinarily attributed to external forces is usually a joint consequence of those forces and process dynamics that accelerate (rather than resist) change.

INTERNAL DYNAMICS

Punctuated equilibrium histories commonly locate the source of institutional change in the environment and the source of institutional stability in process dynamics internal to institutions, but institutions are not simply instruments of stability occasionally driven to change by external pressures. Political institutions also change through mundane internal processes. In many respects they consist in a set of stable procedures that respond routinely to the worlds they face (March, 1981a). One example is the acceleration of motion that is common in organized action. A decision stimulates actions throughout the organization that sustain the momentum of change. Rules and routines are established, capabilities are refined, and controls are introduced. Justifications are codified and become bases for subsequent actions. New identities, preferences, and values consistent with the changes are created or evoked. Skills and roles are created and become the source of increasing movement. Experience with change yields competencies consistent with changing. Changes in one part of an institution increase the likelihood of imitative changes in other parts. Each additional change stimulates new actions that elaborate and extend the original one.

Within such processes, moreover, there are also ample possibilities for modifying directions or momentum. The processes of securing stability, for example, introduce two important sources of change: First, as we have seen, the same institutional stability that provides advantage (and may even be essential to survival in the short run) can easily become a source of vulnerability. Institutional competence and reliability become a barrier to change, thus a likely precursor of long-run obsolescence (Levinthal and March, 1993). Second, communicable meaning is subject to interpretation, reasoning, education, imitation, and adaptation. Institutions change as individuals learn the culture (or fail to), forget (parts of) it, revolt against it, modify it, or reinterpret it (McNeil and Thompson, 1971; Lægreid and Olsen, 1978; 1984). The resulting drifts in meaning lead to changes that explore alternative political paths and create the divergences of politics.

Many studies of organizational processes have reported ways in which organizational motion is slowed, reversed, or redirected. Studies of the displacement of goals (Selznick, 1949; Sills, 1957) and of evolving jobs and missions (Miner, 1990) have examined the ways changes stimulate subsequent changes that alter the direction of the original movement. Studies of organizational reform and policy implementation similarly record examples of process dynamics that slow or reverse institutional change (Bardach, 1977; Olsen and Peters, 1995a). Policy coalitions held together by optimistic ambiguity about the consequences of the policy fall apart when actual outcomes are realized. Commitments to absorb short-run costs in order to secure long-run benefits become less attractive as the costs are actually incurred. Collective identities evoked by adoption of reforms give way to more local identities characteristic of day-to-day life.

Finally, conflict among rules and identities as well as among institutional worldviews often makes institutional stability difficult to sustain regardless of its potential advantages (Broderick, 1970, p. xvi; Orren and Skowronek, 1994). Competitive internal politics dictate change as aspirants for power seek to differentiate themselves from current rulers. Comprehensive intentional changes occur when advocates marshal strong organizational and political capabilities to focus attention, mobilize resources, and cope with resistance (Peters, 1988, p. 10; March and Olsen, 1989). Since changes (and changing) usually lead to increased vulnerability, such changes may well be disastrous, but the short-run dynamics of political competition is often relatively inattentive to the long-run requirements of political survival.

CO-EVOLUTION OF ENVIRONMENTS AND INSTITUTIONS

Democratic institutions do not start from some external Archimedian point and proceed from there, for the starting point is itself created by social and political processes. Human actors are willful, but their wills are not exogenous to the system. They are at once "institutor and instituted" (Hilb, 1994, p. 108). Definitions of progress and improvement are transformed in the process of striving to achieve them (Alexander and Sztompka, 1990; Giddens, 1991). Thus, changes in institutions are not unique adaptations to exogenous environmental pressures and internal dynamics but sequences of steps summarizing interactions between external forces and internal processes. Change involves mutual learning and co-evolution. Environments adapt to institutions at the same time as institutions adapt to their environments. As the environment changes, the conditions for institutional survival change, but as the institutions change, so also does the environment. The adaptations are simultaneous and interactive, and there may be several (even many) stable equilibria. The final outcome may depend critically on the relative rates of adaptation and on the nature of fortuitous steps at critical moments.

Consider, for example, the process by which governmental agencies change accounting procedures. Proper procedures for any particular agency depend on the procedures used by others. A particular accounting procedure gains legitimacy by being adopted by many agencies, by becoming conventional practice. Thus, the environment of one agency consists of other agencies, each of which has an environment that consists, in part, of the first agency. The legitimacy of accounting procedures evolves over time by a co-evolutionary process of diffusion. The collective problem of survival is to come to agree on a code of practice, for each agency's survival depends on having procedures similar to those of other agencies. But there are many possible "solutions" (Bergevärn and Olson, 1989; Mezias, 1990).

Similarly, competition among interests for political support yields a co-evolutionary process in which the environment for each competitor consists in the actions of the others. The situation is well known to students of the topography of economic and political competition in the Hotelling (1990) tradition. Where rational political competitors locate themselves in a policy space depends on where others locate themselves (Riker, 1962). Even more generally, any situation where cooperation or competition might make a difference (a rather large class of situations) makes a simple history of adaptation to an exogenous environment impossible. We return to this issue below in discussing ecological complications in learning.

One familiar form of a co-evolutionary relationship among political institutions is the "armaments" race. Each institution seeks to have superiority in tanks, airplanes, lawyers, advertising, productivity, research, or budget. Each adjustment by one institution leads to a response by the others (their environment). Aspiration-level adjustments to past experience have similar effects, producing what might be called an "insatiable" environment. In such worlds, the governance problem may not be to speed up institutional adjustment to the environment but to slow it down so as to slow down a positive feedback cycle of escalation.

Democratic Factors in Adaptiveness

Adaptiveness is influenced by two important features of a democratic institutional context. First, the environment of democracy is a normative environment with values and expectations about political structures and processes. Satisfying democratic norms is not only a source of personal commitment but also a requirement of survival. Second, the institutions of democracy introduce particular political features to adaptiveness, features that affect adaptation in a democratic context. There is a politics of adaptiveness.

ENVIRONMENTS OF DEMOCRATIC NORMS

Democratic norms are part of the environmental requirements that must be met by democratic political institutions. Survival depends, in part, on matching democratic ideology and fulfilling democratic normative expectations. Institutions that are inconsistent with democratic norms are maladaptive in a democratic culture, and much of the history of democratic transformations has been a story of modifying individual and group privileges that have become normatively unacceptable. For example, a basic democratic norm is that adaptiveness is to be built upon informed democratic consent and therefore on a process of gaining popular support for institutional changes. Regimes that do not enhance such principles as popular consent and participation in government; individual liberties and rights; representative, responsive, and accountable government; impartial, honest, and competent bureaucrats and judges; and free opinion formation fail to survive in cultures where such democratic values are deeply held.

The compelling nature of democratic norms is obscured somewhat by their imprecision and by uncertainty about which institutional structures and processes are most likely to foster various democratic ideals and objectives in different environments. The norms are imprecise, self-reflecting (Nussbaum, 1990, p. 237), and evolving (Lefort, 1988, p. 16; Bobbio, 1987, p. 17). Satisfying imprecise, changing norms involves negotiating their meaning and their implications for institutions and behavior. The process of social construction by which norms and values are negotiated is one in which current officeholders have some advantages, but they are constrained by standards of political competition and free flows of information and by the fact that democratic ideals, despite their flexibility, are not completely amorphous.

The potential conflict between democratic norms and technical efficiency is a problem. Democratic institutions have to meet requirements for operational effectiveness while contending with democratic traditions and norms that are more attentive to protecting individuals from the dangers of an oppressive state than to enabling state institutions to function efficiently from a strictly technical or economic point of view. Requirements that disparate values be reconciled can conflict with requirements of consistent, clear objectives. Requirements that solutions be understandable by and acceptable to the people can conflict with requirements of technical sophistication. Requirements for prolonged public discourse and debate can conflict with requirements for speed. Requirements of equal treatment can conflict with requirements of discriminating management.

The challenge is to design institutions that survive and flourish in the face of changing environmental pressures while maintaining commitment to the primacy of democratic values. A standard solution when external pressures are severe, well known in democratic political systems in time of war, is to meet a crisis by a temporary suspension of democratic rules and institutions. The idea is that times of great environmental demands require a different form of government, and democracy will be restored (with apologies for excesses) when the crisis is resolved. The practice can become an unfortunate habit, but the capability of citizens to recognize the rare occasions on which some requirements of democracy can be forgone in order to attend to others is a capability of some importance, as is the capability to recognize the rarity of such occasions.

Democratic ambivalence over bureaucracy is a more day-to-day case in point. Weber (1978, p. 983) saw the development, indestructibility, and irreversibility of bureaucratic organization as an inevitable consequence of capitalism and mass democracy, and few of the activities of a modern democracy are imaginable without administrative organization. The efficiencies of bureaucratic organization are conspicuous. At the same time, the principles of bureaucracy deviate from the principles of democracy and are self-reinforcing. The development of bureaucratic expertise, position, and isolation becomes an oligarchic threat to democracy (Michels, 1968). The processes of bureaucratization are counterbalanced, however, by others stemming from democratic values. When bureaucratic oligarchy develops, bureaucracy becomes a political issue. When immediate experience with political institutions cannot be reconciled with democratic values, the bureaucratic system loses legitimacy, ordinary citizens mobilize their common resources, and political institutions are transformed. The restoration of democracy is not certain, but tales of the "inevitable" creation of oligarchy need to be moderated by tales of "inevitable" democratic revolt against such trends.

ADAPTING THROUGH DEMOCRATIC INSTITUTIONS

Adaptation is a political and social process structured by the nature of democratic institutions and processes (Weiss, 1979, p. 23). Two features of democratic institutions and processes are especially relevant to the development of adaptiveness. First, democratic ideologies value stability, and democracies use rules to achieve it. The rules of a constitutional democracy impose constraints on changing the political order. They protect democratic polities from too-rapid acquiescence in political, technological, or economic changes that threaten human dignity and political community (Polanyi, 1944; Deutsch, 1966, pp. 131–32). They limit the capability of individuals or institutions to respond to or initiate changes. Bureaucracies implement policies and learn how to do so from their experience, but they are limited in the degree to which they can make structural changes in response to their own idiosyncratic experience. Judges may contribute to legal transformations through their interpretations, but they cannot change the court system directly in simple response to their own idiosyncratic experiences. Rules are carriers and instruments of learning at one level, but they are deliberate inhibitors of learning at another.

Stability and reliability in institutional arrangements are valued particularly as being vital to equity. Rules and the rule of law insulate the actions of officials and the treatment of citizens from corruptions due to unequal distributions of resources and unequal access to networks of personal loyalty. Patience with rules is a way of reducing differences in competence at self-interested manipulation of the rules. Although any specific rule may have implications for different interests and thus may be favored or opposed by self-interested citizens because of its particular contents, rules that change rapidly generally favor those citizens who can adapt quickly. Rigid rules that change slowly permit more plodding citizens to figure out the game and play it reasonably effectively. Binding officials by stable rules reduces the advantages of the quick and the manipulative in their competition with the slow and the straightforward. This is, of course, one of the reasons that democratic political systems are often less than totally enthusiastic about modern financial markets.

Second, democratic institutions are built on a presumption of conflict. There may be conflicts over fundamental issues in democratic life, over what kinds of social policies to adopt, and over interpretations of policies and their outcomes. From the present perspective, the significant thing about democratic conflict is not so much its existence as its legitimacy and permanence (Crick, 1983, p. 31). Conflict is not completely resolved; it is likely to be deflected to another place or ignored. Implicit and explicit voting procedures within multiple settings, combined with the difficulties of securing broad agreement, lead to outcomes that are negotiated compromises among opponents. They involve political trades and the substitution of symbols for substantive action. Changes are contested after they are adopted as well as before. Democratic processes for engaging and exercising conflict sometimes produce change, but the politics of conflict seems more likely to lead to stalemates or incomplete actions that preserve the status quo. Changes tend to be relatively infrequent, relatively small, and relatively inconsistent.

The conflict and stability of democratic decision processes have mixed consequences for adaptiveness. Democratic processes tend to lead to small, incremental experiments and to difficulties in implementing planned experiments, two features that are not obviously useful from the standpoint of effective adaptation (Brunsson, 1985; Lounamaa and March, 1987). For the same reasons, however, democratic systems have a tendency to experiment infrequently and to be slow in abandoning experiments, two features that have been suggested as positive aids to effective adaptation (Lounamaa and March, 1987). At the same time, on a more systemic level, the rules and structures of politics provide a stable fulcrum for more dynamic innovations and adaptations in civil society and the economic system (Slagstad, 1981).

THE CASE OF ADMINISTRATIVE REFORM

One of the most common forms of democratic institutional adaptation is comprehensive administrative reform. Since administrative reform is a standard, repetitive feature of government, it is also a natural phenomenon to use to illustrate some complexities of political adaptiveness. Governments engage in administrative reform more or less continuously and routinely, instituting changes in administrative structures and procedures in response to external and internal pressures as well as experience. Despite such standard, ongoing programs of renewal, political leaders reliably portray existing administrative structures as major problems for democratic governance and encourage similar attitudes on the part of constituents.

Consequently, most democracies undertake comprehensive reforms of administration from time to time. They create special commissions or parliamentary initiatives to overhaul the administrative machinery of government. Those efforts regularly have their beginnings hailed, their aspirations praised, and their recommendations ignored (March and Olsen, 1983).

A study of comprehensive administrative reform in eight countries—Australia, Britain, France, Germany, Japan, Norway, Switzerland, and the United States—observed that administrative reforms, as a rule, seemed to result in neither improved administrative performance nor improved economic performance, nor did they lead to increased adaptability (Olsen and Peters, 1995a). Reformers learned from their experiences, but often they learned more about the difficulties of learning than about what worked. There was significant variation in capacities for monitoring, analyzing, assessing, and acting upon experience in a systematic way, but the correlation between capacities for analysis and capacities to adapt behavior and structures in the light of experience was modest. Strengthening the capabilities of agencies seemed to improve the analytical sophistication of the system and its capacity to interpret results. But strengthening the analytical hands of competing agencies simultaneously made the implementation of suggested reforms more difficult (Peters, 1995). Reformers learned about political feasibility and political rewards. Some governments started out with reform enthusiasm and ended up disappointed. They learned that programs of reform often had greater effects on aspirations than on performance. On the other hand, reform efforts were a source of pleasant surprises for others. The lesson learned was that is was possible to do more, and to gain more political credit, than was expected at the outset (Hood, 1995).

The similarities of reforms in different countries and at different times were conspicuous. Although programs of administrative reform were not all identical, different political systems had a strong tendency to identify the same problems as those identified by others with whom they had contact and to propose the same solutions. One interpretation of this phenomenon is that all administrative systems experience the same dynamics of bureaucracy. For example, perhaps they continually undermine their own effectiveness and require periodic correction. Since the processes by which bureaucratic systems become ineffective are universal, it is reasonable to expect that all systems will fall off course in about the same way and require about the same treatment. Alternatively, perhaps fluctuations in system reliability can be seen less as fluctuations in inefficiency than as fluctuations in experimentation. In such an interpretation, reform efforts are best described as attempts to reduce experimentation and to reassert orthodoxy.

In either case, the same deviations from standard practice will recur repeatedly and will give rise to repetitive uses of the same reforms to correct them. From this Sisyphean perspective, political institutions can be seen as learning from experience how to control administrative drift through reform and doing so as required. Like most control procedures, cycles of administrative decay (or experimentation) and administrative reform produce fluctuations in short-run performance as well as long-run trends. It is possible that the process could maintain a long-run stable equilibrium that balances the mistakes of internal administrative change with the corrections of changes through reform, but such a fine balance was not observed.

A somewhat different interpretation of repetitive reform is one that observes a loose coupling between reform programs (the talk of reform) and their implementation (the action of reform). Reforms seem more likely to stimulate demands for new reforms than to eliminate the problems to which they are manifestly addressed. As a result of initiating reform programs, reformers secure rewards that have little to do with their effects on administrative practice (Brunsson and Olsen, 1993). At the same time, experience with problems encourages new problems. Administrative systems discover both how to cope with problems and how to profit from them. As a result, reforms stimulate reforms, and problems stimulate problems. From this point of view, learning in administrative systems tends to confirm whatever action is taken. Political actors gain reinforcement from the feasibility of action rather than from its (ultimate) outcomes. They draw support for a course of action from the fact that they have been able to pursue it in the past.

The joint stimulation of problems and reforms is augmented by the way both problems and solutions (reforms) diffuse among political systems. Problems that are discovered in one system seem thereby to become more easily discovered in another. Reforms that are adopted in one system seem thereby to become more likely candidates for adoption by another system. Broad international organizations like the World Bank and OECD, as well as more focused organizations such as professional associations and interagency or intergovernmental committees and a variety of consultants, facilitate epidemics in problems and solutions. Whereas the administrative decay interpretation leads to a prediction that the same problems and reforms will occur time after time in a given political system, the epidemic interpretation leads to a prediction of similarity among reforms and problems in different political systems at a particular time, but not to as strong a prediction of similarity across time.

PROFITING FROM EXPERIENCE

The administrative reform case suggests that the process by which democratic institutions profit from their experience may be filled with complications that make an easy assumption of political adaptiveness suspect. The ambiguities of experience; conflicts of interest; contexts of competition, cooperation, and imitation; and difficulties of implementing action all make the process of gaining intelligence from the lessons of political history both intricate and unreliable.

Nevertheless, political institutions try to achieve adaptive intelligence. They anticipate their futures and act to shape them. They contemplate their pasts and learn from them. They observe the actions of others and reproduce them. They engage in discourse, debate, and discussion and derive insights from conflict and contradiction. They experiment with competing alternatives and preserve those that show advantages. We examine particularly the possibilities for using experience as a basis for adaptive intelligence.

The Pursuit of Intelligent Change

Political institutions must cope with three grand problems of intelligent change (Levinthal and March, 1993): (1) *Ignorance*: uncertainties about the future and the past and the causal structure of the experience. It is hard to determine what has happened or will happen in the world, or why. (2) *Conflict*: inconsistencies in identities and interests. The rules and preferences that guide some people conflict with the rules and preferences that guide others. (3) *Ambiguity*: lack of clarity, instability, and endogeneity in identities and interests. Rules and preferences are poorly defined, changing, and modified in the process of being implemented.

Collective efforts to achieve democratic intelligence in the face of the problems of ignorance, conflict, and ambiguity are marked by persistent disappointments. The disappointments are partly implicit in the elusive definition of intelligence (March, 1994b). There is a tension between the intelligence of analysis, with its emphasis on clear objectives and precise knowledge, and the intelligence of democracy, with its emphasis on conflict and open-endedness. Moreover, actions that are intelligent (by either criterion) in the short run are often not intelligent in the long run. Actions that are intelligent from the point of view of some people and groups are not intelligent from the point of view of other people and groups. It is not easy to specify a criterion of democratic intelligence that is robust against these tradeoffs across the time and space of a polity.

But the disappointments experienced with efforts to solve the problems of ignorance, conflict, and ambiguity are not entirely a consequence of elusiveness in the meaning of intelligence. Intelligence—however conceived—is imperfectly achieved. The history of efforts to act intelligently in democracies is a history of mistakes. In retrospect, some of those mistakes seem enormous. Great hopes and ambitious programs frequently not only failed to yield their promises but also seemed to generate more problems than they solved. If history teaches one thing to practitioners of democratic intelligence, it teaches that the harvest of hubris is chagrin.

Despite (or perhaps because of) this history of imperfection, intelligent change is persistently extolled and pursued. In recent years the pursuit of intelligent political change has been organized primarily by a vision of anticipatory human action. Within such a vision, action is based on anticipation of its consequences and anticipation of the values that will be associated with those consequences when they are achieved. Although most modern theories of action pay homage to this vision, it is persistently portrayed as flawed (March, 1978, 1988a, 1994a). Too many atrocities of stupidity and immorality have been based on anticipatory rationality, and too many efforts to improve human action through importing technologies of decision engineering have been disappointing. The pursuit of democratic intelligence has increasingly turned to other visions.

Among the instruments of intelligence that have been "discovered" as a result of the disappointments with rationality none is more prominent than learning from experience. From an enthusiasm for long-term planning, clear objectives, forward-looking estimations, information, and calculation, prophets of intelligence have shifted to an enthusiasm for learning from experience and the transfer and use of knowledge (Senge, 1990). The vision is one of contemplating the past rather than anticipating the future, of adapting to changes rather than trying to guess what they will be, of developing capabilities to respond to various possible worlds after one of them is realized rather than gambling on the ability to forecast which of them will occur.

Aspirations for improvement through experiential learning appear to fit democratic traditions of progress through incremental adjustments in human and institutional capabilities and democratic faith in the possibilities for progress through knowledge (Olsen and Peters, 1995a, 1995b). Recent political proposals have called for more systematic monitoring of the consequences of policies and actions and improved links between results and subsequent behavior. The explicit object has been to create institutional mechanisms capable of organizing experience in the service of improved learning. Increased interest in how political organizations and decision-makers consult the past has led to increased efforts to understand basic features of collective learning (Fiol and Lyles, 1985; Levitt and March, 1988; Huber, 1991; Dodgson, 1993), as well as to create institutions that learn more effectively (Deutsch, 1966; Argyris, 1977, 1982; Argyris and Schön, 1978; Rose, 1993).

Experiential Learning Processes

Experiential learning modifies (or reinforces) behavior as a result of inferences drawn from the consequences of previous behavior. Learning in its simplest form takes place within a cycle of adaptation in which individual beliefs lead to collective actions, which lead to outcomes, which lead to revised beliefs (March and Olsen, 1975).

Learners observe the apparent consequences of previous actions. They distinguish success from failure and develop interpretations of the links between their actions and the outcomes they experience. They repeat behaviors associated with successes and avoid behaviors associated with failures (Levitt and March, 1988). Accumulated experience is retained in the form of habits, traditions, customs, legends, belief systems, language, scientific theories, techniques, and organizational routines. Thus, experiential learning involves three classic steps of adaptation: Variation through experimentation and risk-taking, selection through forming inferences from experience and translating those inferences into action, and retention through routinizing action implications into rules that can be passed on to others who have not had the same experience.

VARIATION AND RISK-TAKING

Effective variation and experimentation in governance involve (1) a willingness and capability to take risks and (2) a willingness and capability to persist in a course of action despite early adverse signals. Without the first, political systems cannot try new directions. Without the second, they cannot discover whether new directions are desirable. In noisy worlds, learning requires big steps taken infrequently (Lounamaa and March, 1987). A nagging problem of producing effective variation in political systems is the fact that these two can conflict. Some of the conditions that produce experimentation in politics tend to produce, at the same time, impatience with the results of that experimentation.

Empirical studies suggest that risk-taking is less an individual or cultural trait than a product of the context of success and failure (Lopes, 1987; Shapira, 1995). As long as performance is interpreted as being in the neighborhood of their aspirations, learners produce greater variation in experience in the face of moderate failure than in the face of moderate success (Kahneman and Tversky, 1979). But in those circumstances, they tend to refine existing paradigms, technologies, and competencies rather than experiment with dramatically new alternatives (March, 1991, p. 85).

More extreme risk-taking and variation are associated with either major performance crises or considerable success (Levinthal and

March, 1981; March and Shapira, 1992). In the former case, experimentation is stimulated by the ambition to achieve a target and the difficulty of doing so using established routines. In the latter case, success emboldens both organizations and individuals. Success leads to organizational slack, and slack leads to relaxation of controls and tolerance of local deviations. At the same time, success leads to reduced individual fear of failure, a sense of self-confidence, and an overestimation of the likelihood of success in a new endeavor (Hamilton, 1978; Singh, 1986; March and Shapira, 1987; Taylor and Brown, 1988).

Success and failure (and their magnitudes) are socially constructed. They are defined by two values. The first value is a measure of political performance. Stories of political events create interpretations of what has happened: How many lives were saved? How are children doing in school? How many inventions were made? What is the unemployment rate? What is the gross national product?. The second value is a measure of political aspirations, expectations, or targets for performance: What is hoped for? By interpreting and comparing those two values, political actors define themselves as successful or not, and that definition affects their willingness to experiment and thereby affects the level of variation in a polity.

The construction of success and failure is affected by a structural bias in decision-making. In general, if alternatives are evaluated in terms of expectations of their probable consequences, and even if the error in those expectations is unbiased, any procedure that chooses the best apparent alternative will (on average) produce post-decision disappointment. That is, the actual realized return will usually be less than the expected return (Harrison and March, 1984). The disappointment effect among supporters of a policy is even greater if their errors in expectations are biased by political competition in which supporters inflate their estimates. The result is that even good experiments will fail to match the hopes for them, and the patience required for effective experimentation is made more difficult.

The structural bias toward disappointment is reduced by systematic bias in interpreting experience (Aronson, 1968; Salancik, 1977; Taylor and Brown, 1988). Supporters tend to reinterpret outcomes as more favorable than they were, thus to redefine apparent failures as successes. Similarly, if political competition leads opponents of a policy to deflate their expectations, experience with the consequences of a policy one has opposed should generally be better than expected. Opponents of a policy, however, tend to reinterpret outcomes as less favorable than they were, thus to redefine successes as failures. In this way, political competition interferes with convergence to a common evaluation of experience, but it may well increase the effectiveness of variation by augmenting persistence with apparently unsuccessful programs. The latter effect—the slowness of political leaders to recognize failures in their own policies or successes in the policies of opponents—is normally recorded as a defect of learning in politics. It undoubtedly is a defect in the short run; whether it is a defect in the longer run is a more difficult question.

SELECTION AND INFERENCES FROM EXPERIENCE

The worlds within which the selection of political learning takes place are confusing. Decisions are made in situations that are unique or rare, rather than recurring. Criteria of success and failure are ambiguous, changing, or conflicting. Environments are unstable, and their dynamics are not well understood. Many things, not controlled by political actors, change simultaneously. Evidence and causal relationships are unclear. The significance of events and actions, their relevance for the future, and their implications are not well understood. Interpretations offered are often intended to legitimize events and behaviors rather than to create improved understanding.

Confusion is seldom a legitimate reason for not acting in political life (Taylor, 1984). Faced with the confusions of ambiguity, uncertainty, conflict, and impotence, political actors try to impose order and meaning upon the world around them. They develop coherent stories of experience, theories of why the world is the way it is. They use organized procedures for articulating, sharing, and retaining collective accounts and assessments, including instruments to record and retrieve the past. They exploit organized ways of producing collective accounts, as well as a stock of competing accounts. They codify experience through everything from formal accounting systems to tradition (Giddens, 1991, p. 37).

In particular, political actors try to develop accounts of history from which they can form inferences about the world. The accounts of experience affect inference forming and selection in two important ways: First, experiential learning takes place within preestablished patterns of moral and causal beliefs and conventional constructions of myths and stories. Learning processes and outcomes are influenced by those frames. They are affected by the general frameworks for accounts accepted in democratic politics, and they are affected by the specific, historically developed accounts of a single country or a region. Those stable elements of interpretive life provide continuity to experience and its interpretation (Skowronek, 1982; Ashford, 1986; March and Olsen, 1989).

Second, political actors construct more concrete accounts of particular events in order to learn from them. The difficulties involved in making inferences from the naturally occurring events of politics are legendary. Political life consists of small samples of observations taken from situations of considerable causal complexity. The experiments of history are poorly controlled, often hopelessly confounded. Political learning often involves learning from critical incidents, which means learning from samples of one. As a consequence, interpretations and responses "tend to be adopted more as a result of their temporal proximity, cognitive availability, or political convenience than by virtue of their obvious validity" (March, Sproull, and Tamuz, 1991, p. 7).

RETENTION IN RULES AND ACCOUNTS

The lessons of experience are often lost, but not always. Knowledge is retained in an institution and endures beyond the tenure of the original learner by being captured in rules and accounts (Levitt and March, 1988). As an example of the way political accounts are retained in the form of stories of political traditions and interpretations of events, consider the way in which conceptions of the relation between political democracy and the economic system have evolved in somewhat different ways in different democratic systems, with attendant political mythology and stories of history. One account sees democracy as having evolved through a gradual extension of power to the previously weak, the gradual reduction of privilege. Political power has been extended to the bourgeoisie, to workers, to women, and to noncitizens. Wealth and access to education and personal security have been redistributed. In this case, the story of democracy is a story of increasing political equality and extends easily into a story of reducing economic disparities.

A second account sees democracy as having evolved through a gradual extension of freedom to the previously enslaved, the gradual reduction of limitations on human independence. Freedoms of speech, religion, press, assembly have been secured and extended to wider and wider groups. Restrictions on personal behavior and economic activities have been minimized. In this case, the story of democracy is a story of increasing political liberties and extends easily into a story of reducing constraints on economic liberties.

Each of these accounts is a major theme in almost any telling of democratic history. They condition current political actions and the justifications for those actions, thus frame democratic political life. However, different democratic systems have developed somewhat different emphases in interpreting the democratic experience as a result of somewhat different political experiences. Stories of democracy in the United States, built around stylized constructions of the American Revolution, the American Civil War, and westward expansion, have come to place somewhat greater emphasis on the relation between democracy and liberty than have Northern European stories, with their somewhat greater emphasis on the relation between democracy and equality. The relative tolerance of American political democracy for disparities in economic wealth and the relative reluctance of American democracy to interfere with economic freedoms are reinforced by (and reinforce) those stories of democracy.

Students of rules and accounts have been particularly interested in the ways in which they change and develop over time as deposits of history and the ways they are transferred and retained (Schulz, 1992; Zhou, 1993). One question is whether the lessons of history change the rules and accounts of a particular domain with decreasing marginal effect or with increasing marginal effect. In the first case, each additional modification reduces the likelihood of a subsequent modification. This is a story of depletion of possible new knowledge in which each additional refinement makes it harder to find new refinements. In the second case, each additional modification increases the likelihood of a subsequent modification. This is a story of explosion of possible new knowledge in which each additional change makes it easier to find new changes. (Notice that explosion of new "knowledge" is not always a good thing. For example, in the case of technological refinements, the explosion case includes the case in which each modification introduces more problems than it solves.)

The development and teaching of formal knowledge are prime examples of the way in which lessons of history are changed, codified, and transferred. The lessons of thousands of observations are summarized in the accounts of physics and economics and transferred to novices who do not know and cannot reproduce the experiential and evidential base for the accounts. Similarly, experiences with new technologies or political strategies are transferred to new technicians and new politicians in the form of rules and accounts that reflect but do not reproduce the experiences on which they are based. The retention of accounts in the rules of politics is exemplified by the rules of parliamentary procedure. A full understanding of the rules would require an understanding of the history of their development, the occasions in which any particular rule was imposed, and the circumstances of its revision. Novice parliamentarians learn the rules, however, simply as arbitrary regulations on debate, accepting them in much the same way as they might accept the laws of physics or rules of personal politeness.

The retention of the lessons of history in rules, procedures, and organizational forms is one of the sources of stability and intelligence in politics. It is a possible source of stability because political institutions and their rules are usually taken as given, perhaps frustrating but not easily changed, and in a conflict situation involving many different interests, the status quo is favored. Retention of rules is a possible source of intelligence because rules reflect a wider range of experience than do the memories of current actors. If that experience is relevant, and in some cases it may not be, rules may make good sense in a particular case that is not specifically obvious to current actors. Retention of rules counterpoises the conceit of experience to the arrogance of thought.

Complications in Experiential Learning

There is considerable evidence indicating that the rules and practices of institutions can be improved through a learning process involving experimentation, monitoring of results, and modifying future rules on the basis of interpretations of those results. There is also considerable evidence that institutions can accumulate and diffuse knowledge and that such a process often leads to improvement. And there is considerable evidence that such uses of experiential learning and knowledge transfers may have substantial advantages over anticipatory calculation in many circumstances. Learning is a key instrument of collective intelligence, and contemporary enthusiasms for learning are well founded (Burgelman, 1988; Levitt and March, 1988; Senge, 1990).

Processes for learning from confusing experience are not perfect, however, and effective use of learning requires balancing an awareness of its potential with consciousness of its difficulties (Taylor, 1984; Douglas, 1986; Levitt and March, 1988). In particular, there are numerous ways in which manifestly efficient processes of learning reduce long-term adaptiveness (Levinthal and March, 1993; March, 1994c). The difficulties stem partly from features of human behavior, partly from structural features of political processes, and partly from features embedded in the logic of adaptation. Experiential learning is complicated by the particular ways human actors experiment, form inferences, and code the lessons of history in rules. It is complicated by the way political systems authorize action and legitimize interpretations of results. It is complicated by features of the sampling plan that it produces, systematically undersampling certain kinds of experiences. It is complicated by problems in maintaining a balance between exploration and exploitation. And it is complicated by the ecological structure of adaptation, the way in which the environments of political institutions consist of other adapting institutions. In many ways, experience is a poor teacher, and human beings are poor historians.

LIMITATIONS OF LEARNING CAPABILITIES

Each of the steps in a learning process involves capabilities. Since we have discussed issues of institutional capabilities in Chapter 4, we shall not consider them in detail here, but it may be appropriate to note their criticality to adaptiveness. As a result of limitations in capabilities, there is a significant discrepancy between what is wished, expected, and claimed on behalf of experiential learning in contemporary democracies and actual political experience with learning. Policy-makers are not reliably able to experiment and look for lessons in their experience (Rose, 1993). When they do try to learn, they are subject to cognitive limitations (March, 1994b). When they are successful in learning, they do not have the capabilities to implement, retain, and transfer the knowledge they have gained.

First, a political institution needs the *capability to experiment*, or at least the capability to observe the natural experiments of political life. Some standard features of political democracy reduce capabilities for experimentation, particularly rules enforcing jurisdiction, standardization, and accountability. Jurisdictional rules inhibit experimentation that would violate such rules, for example, experiments across the division of powers in a federal system. Principles of standardization in treatment inhibit experimentation by subunits of a polity. The "free commune" initiatives of the Scandinavian countries have persistently been faulted for imposing such severe restrictions on local experimentation as to make the experiments trivial. Principles of accountability tied to rules of appropriate behavior inhibit experimentation that might explore alternative possible rules.

Moreover, experiments often require resources of time, energy, political commitment, and money that are demanded elsewhere. In competition for scarce resources, experiments suffer from their riskiness and their relatively low expected value. New initiatives may have substantial political and social return, but they also may be a waste, or worse. On average, they are likely to do worse than a well-established procedure. Experiments also suffer from a characteristic distribution of costs and benefits that places costs nearer in time than benefits. Even if an experiment pays off politically, the returns are likely to be reaped by a subsequent set of political actors.

Second, a political institution needs the *capability to form inferences* from experience. That capability is limited by the ways in which political accounts are constructed and the ways humans form inferences about experience. Learning may be impeded by numerous failures in accounting for and responding to experience. Search behavior and exposure to events may not generate adequate experience. The demands of the environment may be too slack to demand excellence (Deutsch, 1966, p. 108). Experience may be treated as a symbol of learning rather than as a source of knowledge (Feldman and March, 1981). The inadequate data of experience are confronted by learners who have the usual human limitations. Their interpretations introduce systematic biases (Brehmer, 1980; Levitt and March, 1988). They interpret outcomes and desires for them in a way that tends to conserve confidence in prior actions. This introduces a strong bias to see the results following a decision as confirming its appropriateness. Individuals tend to use simple causal theories to interpret events, assuming that causes are to be found in the neighborhood of effects rather than separated from them by time and space. This introduces a strong tendency to overlook second-order effects and to prefer tautological theories. Interpretations of events are constructed socially in such a way that shared understandings (reliability) become more important than correct understandings (validity). This introduces a strong bias in favor of pooling judgments rather than pooling data.

Two of the better-known biases of human interpretation are an anthropocentric bias—the overattribution of effects to human intentions—and an egocentric bias—the overattribution of personal success to personal intention and ability. As a general rule, individuals seem more inclined to attribute their successes to themselves and their failures to the fates of fortune (bad luck) or the intentions or abilities of others than the other way around. Places where successful people congregate (for example, selective schools, international athletic competitions, and first-class cabins of passenger aircraft or ships) will be crowded with people who, on average, exaggerate their own importance and underestimate the role of uncontrollable variation in life's outcomes. Political leadership is such a place. Leaders are selected by a process that confirms their capabilities and past successes. They can be expected to hold theories of their worlds that systematically underestimate the uncontrolled variability (risk) in most situations.

Those limitations of individuals are often accentuated by limitations of institutions. Democratic institutions have difficulty assessing the results of history. Democratic milieus of conflict and political competition make understanding the results of political experiments difficult. The lessons to be drawn from history are contested. The process of interpreting the events of experience is filled with efforts to assign and evade responsibility and to establish politically favored stories (Sagan, 1993). Information as a source of knowledge is contaminated by its use as an instrument of control (Lawler and Rhode, 1976; O'Reilly, 1983). Even such relatively simple technical issues as the assessment of the causes of an aircraft accident become entangled in issues of legal liability and political responsibility that serve to make discourse confrontational and information suspect (Tamuz, 1988). Political action requires political advocacy, and political advocacy undermines judicious consideration of experience. Collective learning processes may lead to shared and stable interpretations of its experience, without necessarily leading to valid ones (March, Sproull, and Tamuz, 1991, p. 6).

Third, a political institution needs the *capability to act on the basis of knowledge*. Students of public policy-making (Etheredge, 1985), political institutions (March and Olsen, 1986b, 1989; Weaver and Rockman, 1993; Olsen and Peters, 1995a) and formal organizations (Levitt and March, 1988) report that actions do not change easily in response to experience. Sometimes the problem is a problem of will, the desire to change, but often the problem is one of capability. Principles of the rule of law and the pursuit of reliability in governmental action militate against immediate adaptation of action to experience. The democratic emphasis on clear and stable rules removes discretion from political authorities and thereby restricts their capability to act on the basis of their own knowledge. It is quite possible to know what to do without being able to do it because of limited authority. Political institutions often require wars or threats of war to institute major change (Tilly, 1975).

It is also possible to lack necessary resources or organizational capacity. Developing countries often lament their inability to capture the benefits of their knowledge due to lack of resources and external constraints imposed by such agencies as the World Bank or the International Monetary Fund. At the same time, as we have noted, international agencies report that they cannot implement their knowledge because of Third World political, social, and cultural constraints. Bureaucratic agencies often complain about their inabilities to implement known solutions to problems because of resource limitations or political and organizational conflicts.

In general, the capability to enact knowledge in a democracy depends on the extent to which that knowledge is shared and the length of time it has been shared. Knowledge known to only a few and for only a short time is disadvantaged (possibly because experience shows that such knowledge is also likely to be wrong). As a result, any political actor with specialized or new experience is likely to lack the capabilities to translate that experience into action.

Fourth, a political institution needs the *capability to retain knowledge*. Democracies have difficulty retaining the lessons of history. Institutional memories recall experience imprecisely. They use rules and stories to record the lessons of history, but rules and stories are sometimes lost, and often their messages are garbled by the way they are stored and retrieved. Knowledge is lost as well as ignored. Problems of reorganization and decentralization make it difficult to retain the lessons of experience, but the largest source of problems lies in changes in regimes. Democratic institutions depend on active conflict between contending parties and regular turnover in control over the apparatus of governance. Such an arrangement is essential to democracy, but it poses problems for the transfer of capabilities within a political system. At every occasion on which one party or coalition succeeds another in control over government, knowledge is lost. Stories of turnover in regimes are filled with anecdotes of required regaining of knowledge, ranging from the most mundane abilities needed for communicating to the grandest abilities of making policy and managing political power.

The threats to retention come primarily from two rather different sources. The first is the necessary consequence of the simple turnover in personnel. Rules change slowly in response to experience and knowledge, but they sometimes change quickly and easily with turnover and forgetting. Democratic systems vary substantially in the magnitude of the personnel turnover created by a change in regime, but they all presume significant turnover at the top of the government hierarchy. Even with the most conscientious efforts to transfer knowledge from the old officials to the new, the shock to the system is substantial. The simultaneous exit of many top officials removes the specific knowledge that those officials carry in their heads as well as the interlocking practices and procedures that tied them together as a distinct cadre.

The second source of difficulty is the competitive nature of politics. When turnover involves a substitution of one constellation of political interests for another, neither party to the transfer is wholeheartedly committed to an effective transfer of knowledge. The incoming government is ambivalent about accepting assistance from its predecessors. It recognizes the substantial degree to which knowledge determines policies, thus is reluctant to adopt the beliefs developed previously unless it is sure that they are unbiased in their effects on policies. The outgoing government is ambivalent about assisting the new government. It recognizes that such assistance may help a smooth transition and may help solve the problems of the country, but it is also conscious that it simultaneously provides the new regime with knowledge useful in political competition.

BIASED SAMPLES

For experiential learning to be effective, historical records must provide reasonable samples of possible histories. As we have seen, natural experience and the inferential habits of human actors conspire against having records that are good samples. The problem with learning is, however, deeper than that. Experiential learning is (precisely) a process that ensures a biased sample of possible histories. It confounds two processes: The first is the process of sampling the universe, estimating what the world is like. The second process is acting in the universe, taking advantage of knowledge about what the world is like. The second process interferes with the first. The essence of learning is changing rules and structures on the basis of experience. The consequence of those changes is to alter subsequent experience to make it less useful for learning, though it may be more successful (Wildavsky, 1988; Levinthal and March, 1993).

Undersampling rare events. Life is filled with possibilities of rare events—unlikely accidents, unlikely illnesses, unlikely triumphs, unlikely discoveries. The events are possible, but they are unlikely. Small samples of experience with a process having some very unlikely outcome will overwhelmingly be samples that do not contain any realization of the rare event. Since learning ordinarily is a process that modifies behavior continuously (thus on the basis of small samples), it typically will deal poorly with domains in which significant possible events have not been realized.

Consider, for example, the case of extremely rare catastrophic events (e.g., a nuclear disaster). When the likelihood of a nuclear disaster becomes very small, most people in the system will never experience such a thing. Because they have done such a good job in making a nuclear facility safe, most people involved in nuclear safety are likely to come to believe they are capable of producing a safer environment than they actually are. In this case, learning may be self-correcting—though not in an entirely happy way. As learners come to believe that the system is safer than it really is, they underestimate the risks and take greater risks than they realize they are taking, thus producing a less safe environment. When the environment becomes unsafe enough, the chances of an accident rise to a point where accidents become frequent enough for most people to obtain a reasonable experiential estimate of the risks.

Consider, alternatively, the case of extremely rare, major positive events (e.g., a competitive outcome in which a highly favored competitor loses to an unknown competitor). Most lowly rated people or institutions involved in competition never experience the event of defeating a highly favored competitor. As a result, they are likely to come to believe they are less likely to win than they actually are. This lack of confidence probably makes them likely to compete in a way that makes them even less likely to win than they would be without the belief, thus confirming the erroneous estimate. In this case, the estimates based on biased sampling are self-confirming.

Undersampling failures. As political systems and actors endure, they learn different things from success and failure and from the contrast between the two. Success leads to self-confidence, which leads to self-confirmation of success—learning from expectations of consequences before they occur and reinterpreting results to make them favorable. Failure leads to lack of confidence, which leads to self-confirmation of failure—learning from anticipation of failure before it occurs and reinterpreting results to make them unfavorable. The contrast between success and failure allows learners to discriminate between good strategies and poor ones.

The symmetry between the effects of success and failure and the power of the contrast between success and failure, however, is eroded by learning. Learning systematically undersamples failures. It adapts to experience by producing more and more successes. Learners settle into domains in which they have confidence and experience few failures. As a result, learning from failure and from the contrast between success and failure is compromised. The effects are accentuated by any tendency to reinterpret experience to make it more supportive of past actions, thus to define most outcomes as successes.

To some extent, the problem of undersampling failures is controlled by adaptive aspirations. Success and failure are subjective terms defined by an aspiration level. As long as aspirations adjust to experience fairly rapidly, failure will continue to be fairly common. There is a tradeoff, however. Adaptive aspirations refine the calibration of success and failure, but they do so in a way that simultaneously makes the distinction more sensitive to random fluctuations. In a similar way, political competition assures that almost any political action will be interpreted as successful by its initiators and as a failure by its opponents, thus reducing the problem of undersampling of failures but at the cost of making the assessment of policy outcomes relatively insensitive to their realizations.

EFFICIENCY AND ADAPTIVENESS

A central issue of individual and institutional change is the relation between efficiency and adaptiveness (Schumpeter, 1934; Holland, 1975; Kuran, 1988; March, 1991). Efficiency refers to the short-term improvement, refinement, routinization, and elaboration of existing ideas, paradigms, technologies, strategies, and knowledge. It thrives on focused attention, precision, repetition, analysis, sanity, discipline, and control. Adaptiveness refers to the long-term substitution of new ideas, paradigms, technologies, strategies, and knowledge for old ones. It thrives on serendipity, experimentation, novelty, free association, madness, loose discipline, and relaxed control.

Efficiency and adaptiveness are linked in an enduring symbiosis. Each requires the other in order to contribute effectively to survival and prosperity. Institutions that fail to engage in the exploration required for adaptiveness suffer from an inability to discover and adopt new forms and practices. Institutions that fail to engage in the exploitation of current knowledge, on the other hand, suffer from continually using forms and practices at which they are relatively incompetent. A balance between efficiency and adaptiveness is required, but each interferes with the other. Not only do they compete for scarce resources, but the processes of one interfere with the other. Consequently, politics persistently fails to maintain an effective balance between the two.

The problem of achieving a favorable balance between the exploitation of old certainties and the exploration of new possibilities has been discussed in the context of rational choice, bounded rationality, economic development, technological change, learning, and selection. The terms "efficiency" and "adaptiveness" are not the only pair used to describe the marriage. Different commentators on developmental processes examine the relation between exploitation and exploration, between static equilibrium and dynamic equilibrium, between refinement and innovation, between selection and variation, between stability and change, between rationality and foolishness, between intelligence and creativity. Although the different terms have sometimes reflected somewhat different connotations, they reflect a common concern with the two sides of change.

The exploration/exploitation balance in politics. Polities need a political and social order based on shared understandings and knowledge. They need reliability, consistency, and coherence. At the same time, they need to encourage experimentation and exploration, variance and deviance. Creating political adaptiveness involves building institutions and identities that are able to maintain a delicate balance between exploitation and exploration (March, 1991). Choices between the two are reflected in many features of institutional forms and practices, for example, in procedures for accumulating and using political support, in voting rules and practices, in the ways in which budgets are set and changed, and in patronage systems. Forms and practices that increase exploitation (e.g., centralization, party discipline, tightly coupled bureaucratization, shared cultures and languages) militate against exploration. Forms and practices that increase exploration (e.g., decentralization, coalition governments, loose coupling, diverse cultures and languages) militate against exploitation (Morengo, 1993).

Defining the optimal balance between exploitation and exploration is particularly difficult in the face of a changing environment. In addition to the computational difficulties, determining an optimum involves specifying trade-offs across time and space that are rarely trivial. The optimum is hard to specify, but it is not hard to see that the natural dynamics of adaptation are likely to drive an adaptive system to relative extremes of exploitation or exploration, thus probably away from a desirable mix. Those are particularly notable in the tendency for adaptive processes to be more responsive to feedback in the temporal and spatial neighborhood of the actor than to more distant feedback.

Balancing the short run and the long run. Learning responds to results by modifying behavior in terms of short-run feedback (Levinthal and March, 1993). This feedback leads to three kinds of shaping of behavior. First, learning leads to *focused search*. By doing things that are known to be effective, learning reduces exposure to alternatives. Thus, it reduces the chance of discovering any improvement in alternatives not currently being pursued. Second, learning leads to *focused practice*. The emphasis on successful alternatives increases practice on those alternatives and reduces practice with other alternatives that might become superior when experience with them has generated enough competence. Third, learning leads to *focused sampling*. By reducing the sampling of apparently inferior alternatives, learning increases the chance that their values are experienced incorrectly.

Each of these forms of the shaping of behavior through learning endangers long-term adaptiveness in the name of short-term efficiency. Consider, for example, a dynamic that might be called the *failure* (or *incompetency*) trap. The failure trap is produced by a cycle in which failure leads to search, which leads to failure, which leads to more search, and so on (Cyert and March, 1992; March and Simon, 1993). The key to the cycle is the way in which the process conspires against finding a good alternative. Each new alternative that is considered fails, leading to a search for another. The failure trap is likely to be particularly common if three simple features of the learning environment are present: (1) If most new ideas are bad ones, search will usually lead to disappointment. (2) If even good ideas require practice and experience to realize their value, developing capabilities on a specific alternative requires patience with its failures. Organizations trapped in the failure cycle will abandon alternatives before enough experience is accumulated to make them successful. (3) If aspirations adjust downward more slowly than upward, aspiration adjustments more quickly turn successes into failures than they turn failures into successes.

Failure traps are frequent in contemporary political systems. Learning from feedback on the performance of an alternative interferes with the persistence in pursuing that alternative that is required to achieve intelligence. The process of adopting policies, the complexities of political environments, and the dynamics of political mobilization tend to make most actions and reforms unrewarding. Programs are adopted on the basis of unrealistic expectations. Problems are not anticipated (or at least not publicly admitted); prospects are exaggerated. The political necessities of implementation conflict with the political necessities of policy adoption. Unless a new alternative is so dominant that even an incompetent can do well with it, political institutions are doomed to endless cycles of new reforms and disappointments.

Although the failure trap is common, students of adaptiveness have been more concerned in recent years with a dynamic that might be called the *success* (or *competency*) trap (Herriott, Levinthal, and March, 1985; Arthur, 1989). The success trap is the consequence of mutual local positive feedback between experience and competence. Having competence with an activity leads to success, which leads to more experience with the activity, which leads to greater competence. A learner becomes better and better at one technology while doing it more and more and being continually successful. This positive local feedback quickly pushes the learner into a competency lock-in, where efficiency in using one alternative (technology, strategy, etc.) makes trying other alternatives unlikely. This in turn makes it unlikely that the learner will accumulate the experience necessary with other alternatives to realize their potential. Examples are innumerable: Competence and experience at a particular technology, paradigm, or political program feed each other until other (potentially better) technologies, paradigms, or programs are—in the short run—less advantageous. Success in using power to impose an environment and competence in doing so feed each other until capabilities to adapt to an exogenously changed environment atrophy.

The success trap is fed by the fact that returns from exploration are systematically less certain, more remote in time, and politically more distant from the locus of action and adaptation than are returns from exploitation. Those features tie exploitation to its consequences more quickly and more precisely than is the case with exploration. The result is that adaptation serves exploitation better than exploration, and the system becomes better and better at doing what it already knows how to do. It fails to discover or develop competence in new forms and practices.

For example, political parties (and political institutions) develop constituencies to support their actions. Maintaining an existing constituency typically results in quicker and more certain rewards than does experimenting with possible alternative constituencies. Parties and their constituents develop specialized competencies at dealing with each other so that neither is likely to find the exploration of alternative arrangements preferable in the short run. As existing coalition members become more and more specialized to each other, they become less and less able to consider alternatives. When circumstances force a realignment, the mutual specialization makes the process of finding new constituencies fitful and sometimes unsuccessful. For example, when West European parties based heavily on organized labor faced a declining industrial labor force and the necessity of appealing to different voters, the process of shifting was painful in the short run and required experience to become successful.

It should be noted that what we have called a success trap is closely related to what is sometimes called "development of distinctive competence" or "exploitation of a niche." As long as the set of action alternatives is stable, there is much to be said for a strategy of pursuing greater and greater competence in one technology and strategy, eschewing the (usually unrewarding) explorations of alternatives. Indeed, political institutions that fail to be responsive to their immediate audiences in this way are likely to suffer for their sluggishness. Competency traps become a problem particularly when the set of alternatives is changing over time, so that competencies with existing alternatives (or niches) interfere with the discovery of new ones. Insofar as political institutions are effective in adapting to their immediate pressure for short-run efficiency, they often weaken their preparedness and fitness in the face of change.

In short, adaptiveness may often be made more effective by slowing short-run learning processes than by speeding them up. The long-run adaptiveness of political institutions will frequently be improved by decreasing the rate of experimentation in the face of failure (in order to avoid the failure trap and gain the advantages of experience) and increasing the rate of experimentation in the face of success (in order to avoid the success trap and gain the advantages of exploration).

Balancing local concerns and distant concerns. The imbalances of exploration and exploitation with respect to time occur because learning is more localized in time than its effects are. There are similar imbalances of exploration and exploitation that stem from the fact that learning is also more localized in space than its effect are. The problem is an old one in studies of adaptation. The mix of exploitation and exploration that is best for an individual is not necessarily best for a collectivity, and the mix that is best for a collectivity is not necessarily best for a system of collectivities (March, 1994a).

Two quite different stories are commonly told about the relation between institutional learning and the adaptation of populations of institutions. The first story pictures local learning as providing a local (but not systemwide) advantage. It focuses on the local learning threat to exploration. The basic idea is that many fruits of exploration are public goods. They spread easily to others. The costs, on the other hand, tend to be localized. Since learning is a local process, it experiences the local costs more than the distant benefits. As a result, it tends to extinguish experimentation in favor of imitation of the successful experiments of others. Such a result on the part of all units in the system, however, leads to systemwide underinvestment in exploration, with the result that no one is able to imitate because no one is experimenting.

The second story pictures local learning as providing a sys-temwide (but not local) advantage. The basic idea is that there is a division of labor between local and population-level adaptation in serving the latter. Local-level units specialize in exploitation, devel-oping their specialized competencies through learning, refinement, and efficient attention to local pressures. This learning makes them very efficient in their existing environments, very vulnerable to change. When environments change, old local units die and are re-placed with new ones that subsequently develop competencies spe-cialized to the new environments, become vulnerable to change, and die. And so on. Provided there is a ready pool of new local units with new capabilities, this system of rigid, disposable local units is an effective way of providing systemwide adaptation. Local rigidity provides short-run efficiency and easy replacement, thus has some clear systemwide attractiveness (Hannan and Freeman, 1989; Baum and Singh, 1994).

For instance, Michels argued that while existing organizations eventually turn into self-interested oligarchies, new social move-ments arise (in an unexplained way) and bring forward new values and identities (Michels, 1968). The process produces a developmen-tal pattern in which mature democratic organizations turn into oli-garchies that are subject to social criticism—*Zivilisationskritik* —from young organizations that force the older organizations out by substituting action in the name of the interests and good of the general public, only to become oligarchies themselves in their turn (Brand, 1990; Dalton, Kuechler, and Bürklin, 1990, p. 8). From the standpoint of the history of any one organization, this is a story of self-destruction, hardly to be admired as a pursuit of survival. From the standpoint of the population of organizations, however, the process can yield a quite effective mixture of young experimenting organizations and old nonexperimenting organizations (March, 1994c).

ECOLOGIES OF EXPERIENCE

The adjustment of political institutions to their environments is fur-ther complicated by the fact that they adapt in and to an environ-ment consisting of other adapting institutions and individuals. The resulting ecological interactions produce results that depend on the ways in which the learning units fit together rather than on the individual motives or adaptation (Schelling, 1978). For example, nation-states simultaneously adapt to their international environments and their internal environments of political competition. Different political institutions within a single state react to the same environment in ways that make the consequences for each dependent on the actions of the others.

Problems of interaction complexities are well known to students of partial and general equilibria in systems of interacting rational actors, for example students of rational political strategies. The consequences of actions by one actor, and therefore their optimality, depend on the actions of others. Any strategic action requires attention to the fact that other strategic actors are simultaneously affecting actions in other sites, that each strategic actor is a political system itself with internal conflict and strategic action, and that the actions of each are affected by expectations of others. For example, in 1994 several European countries (Austria, Finland, Sweden, Norway) considered the possibility of joining the European Union. Political leaders in each of those countries, as well as in countries within the European Union, shaped their behavior—including particularly the timing of national referenda—with consciousness of the effects of internal party disputes, competition with other political parties within the country, developments in other countries (including other countries not in the European Union but with significant impact on related alliances), and developments within the European Union.

The same kind of interactions affect learning processes. The mechanisms are not strategic anticipations of the strategic actions of others but simultaneous learning in contexts in which outcomes are jointly determined. These situations of interdependent learning introduce a number of ecological complications into institutional adaptation. They are complications for observers of political systems, but they are even more substantial complications for adaptive political actors.

Competition and cooperation. Interactive complications are particularly obvious in competition among political actors. When electoral, legislative, bureaucratic, or international position is determined competitively, environments are adapted to and created simultaneously. For example, one of the main claims for democratic political systems is that competition for political favor among politicians creates an environment that forces politicians to be responsive to the wishes of citizens. Individual incentives in pursuit of political power produce a competition in responsiveness.

As neoclassical economics reminds us, however, the conditions in which the competitive construction of environments makes life better are not universal. In particular, there are externalities (Hardin, 1968, 1982). Some of the more obvious examples in politics are competitive "races" in which each participant's actions induce an acceleration of other participants' actions. The prototype is an armaments race among nations, but accelerating positive feedback loops are not limited to military competition. They are commonplace in political competition. They lead to "races" in campaign expenditures and promises, staffs, technology, urban development and resulting blight, and corruption. In such situations, locally adaptive learning by individual participants often creates an environment that makes little collective sense.

Situations involving cooperation among political actors are similarly cases in which mutual learning both creates an environment and adapts to it. For example, members of the European Union adapt to existing EC/EU standards at the same time as they try to influence the development of those standards (Jacobson, 1993). Studies of cooperation and the occasions under which it is, or is not, sustainable are primarily studies of the interaction of multiple, rational actors (Axelrod and Hamilton, 1981; Axelrod, 1984; Taylor, 1987; Glance and Huberman, 1993), but many of the same general interactive effects apply to learning processes. If cooperative action encourages cooperative action in others and noncooperative action encourages noncooperation, a culture of cooperation may be rather sensitive to such things as the strength of the two imitative effects, the size of the group, the distribution of awareness of cooperative and noncooperative acts, and the institutional structure guiding initial interactions (Dawes, 1980; Bendor and Mookherjee, 1987; Oliver and Marwell, 1988).

Learning substitutions. A learning system adapts simultaneously through several different mechanisms at several different points. The different learning mechanisms and locales are learning substitutes for each other (Levinthal and March, 1993). Adaptation in one part of a system inhibits adaptation in another, and the parts of a system that are active develop greater adaptive competence than do the parts of the system that are not used. The result is a short-run substitution of one part of the system for the other in learning and a long-run differentiation in learning competence (which in turn sustains the substitution).

The proposition that rapid adaptation by one part of a system reduces the need for, and likelihood of, adaptation by another is well known in theories of bargaining, learning, and search. Hard bargainers attempt to exhibit their inability to adapt (Schelling, 1960). When two learning collaborators learn from each other, the fast-learning collaborator changes more than the slower partner (Lave and March, 1975). In satisficing models of decision-making, changes in search, slack, and targets function effectively as substitutes for each other (Cyert and March, 1992). Preferences also adapt in response to experience (March, 1988b), and preference change is an adaptive substitute for search or change in an activity. Citizens can respond to dissatisfaction with a political party by either shifting to another party (i.e., "exit") or by complaining to the party leadership (i.e., "voice"). The two are substitutes in the story of how a political system corrects declining quality (Hirschman, 1970). Exit can substitute for voice, and vice versa. Since the two alternatives have different long-run consequences for the development of quality in political policies, a responsible governor might look for ways of slowing adaptation through exit in order to increase the likelihood of adaptation through voice. Hirschman suggests that loyalty is, in effect, a way of slowing the exit mechanism, thus inducing a greater use of voice.

Learning substitutions also occur within a particular institution. Learning is nested. A learner learns both which strategy, technology, or rule to use and how to operate within various alternatives (Herriott, Levinthal, and March, 1985). If learning is nested in this way, refining an existing strategy, technology, or rule substitutes for recognizing a better one, and vice versa. For example, political effectiveness often involves inventing and improving techniques for affecting interpretations, what is often called "packaging" or "spin control" in the language of political marketing. In effect, the learning of skills at packaging is a substitute for the learning of skills at designing and producing a program. More importantly from the present point of view, learning from experience with the former interferes with accumulating learning experience with the latter, and skills at inventing new programs are lost. Similarly, fast adaptation at one place in a political system leads to slow adaptation at other levels. For example, flexible administration of a policy that is attentive to local feedback enhances a political institution's position in its present environment. In the longer run, however, such first-order learning inhibits second-order exploration of new policies.

More generally, at every level in a political system, power allows a political actor to impose a new environment rather than adapt to an existing one (Deutsch, 1966, p. 111). This substitution of power for adaptiveness leads to refinement in the skills of power and decay in capabilities to respond to change. When the ability to exercise arbitrary control over an environment is lost to changing economic, political, or demographic forces, the withering of adaptive skills puts the system at risk. The phenomenon is an essential element in the decline of great empires and exists to a lesser degree in all domains.

GOVERNING ADAPTIVENESS

The complications and imperfections of learning processes are not so much reasons for abandoning efforts to improve them as they are a warning that no adaptive process can promise magic in the pursuit of intelligence. Learning can be improved and used, but learning organizations will often learn the wrong lessons, will often be more effective locally than globally, and will often sacrifice long-run adaptiveness to short-run efficiency. The role of governance is to surround learning with institutional structures and processes that reduce its errors and exploit its strengths.

Facilitating Experimentation

Without a precise definition of the optimum balance between exploration and exploitation it is hard to know whether the adaptive problem in any particular political setting is a problem of too much or too little experimentation. Some learners seem particularly prone to the failure cycle, jumping from one solution to another without ever accumulating competence at any. They may be "rigid" in the sense that they fail to implement any innovation, but their main characteristic is a tendency to abandon one idea and adopt another before fully comprehending the first. They experiment too often.

By far the more commonly noted problem in recent years, however, has been the problem of sustaining and stimulating adequate experimentation. Democracy is not rich in alternative structures and processes. Choices appear to be limited. Rapid learners and successful institutions seem systematically to reduce the resources allocated to new alternatives. They sacrifice adaptiveness to efficiency. From one democratic polity to another, basic institutional structures are variations on a few themes rather than many conspicuously different forms. An institutionalized, free public sphere based on popular participation, public reasoning, criticism, and justification is supposed to guarantee truth-oriented opinion formation and the development of authentic identities. Public deliberation and majority voting institutionalized in representative assemblies are supposed to secure political equality in political decision-making. Bureaucratically organized agencies are supposed to assure efficient, qualified, and impartial implementation of policies. Constitutions and courts of law are supposed to guarantee individual rights and liberties. Compared to the multitude of utopias, values, interests, beliefs, and tasks with which democratic polities have been blessed, there have been rather few institutional forms and few competing theories of the organization of democracy. As a result, as democracies develop new ideals, values, and tasks, there is no guarantee that there will be institutions that can implement them.

The implications are twofold. First, it is possible that democratic norms and environments favor only a few robust forms of institutions across a wide variety of tasks, at least within the historical context of existing democracies. In a world where problems are plentiful and institutional solutions are not, it may be necessary to replace a focus on purposes and values to be pursued with a focus on what institutions are feasible. Rather than derive institutional specifications from human purposes, we may want to ask what institutions are viable in the current democratic-historical context. If only a few different institutional structures are feasible, then the organized pursuit of democratic ideals is limited to those options. The organizational and institutional imagination of democracy should be directed to adapting traditional institutions to new uses rather than to inventing new ones.

Second, the invention of new democratic forms might well be separated from a sense of current democratic objectives. Democratic engineering has usually been linked to specific democratic problems. For example, a good deal of effort has been devoted to designing institutions, as well as a new political language, to meet the needs of European integration. In practice, this has usually, as it has in the European case, meant adapting traditional democratic forms to a new situation. Given the abundance of problems and the paucity of solutions, however, it might be more sensible to be more daring or utopian in design. Purposes and ends are less likely to find forms relevant to their problems than new institutional forms are to discover or create purposes and ends for which they are relevant.

As a result, the main concern expressed by modern commentators on the exploration–exploitation balance is finding ways to encourage exploration. The concern has been reflected in increased emphasis on explicit public sector experiments in order to create more varied experience (Olsen, 1995). National governments have attempted to stimulate both exploratory activity and systematic evaluation of the results. An example is the Nordic attempt to encourage local community experimentation with various procedures of local governance (Baldersheim and Ståhlberg, 1994). Two tactics for stimulating exploration have attracted attention: The first is to provide incentives for exploration; the second is to slow the learning that tends to extinguish risk-taking.

ALIGNING MOTIVATIONS

In various ways, the problems of exploration are problems of motivation. Individuals who calculate the consequences of their action require that the returns from experimentation be commensurate with the costs and opportunities elsewhere. Individuals who match situations and identities to determine appropriate action require that experimentation be consistent with a conception of self. Individuals who vary their risk-taking as a function of their target aspirations require that the difference between aspirations and achievement make experimentation attractive.

The role of incentives. Strengthening the incentive base for exploration involves providing large rewards for successful explorations or protection from the consequences of exploratory mistakes. Traditional economic strategies involve providing large rewards for successful explorations, assigning property rights to the initiators of explorations by means of such instruments as patents and copyrights. Protection from the consequences of exploratory mistakes is provided through bankruptcy procedures and devices (such as stock companies) that allow experiments using other people's money.

For the most part, the structure of economic incentives inhibits political exploration in a democracy. On the one hand, the economic rewards for successful explorations are rarely very large. Providing large economic rewards for political successes is characteristic of many nondemocratic systems but is defined as corruption in a democracy. Political leaders who produce successful experiments in a democracy—for example those who revitalize a local or regional community to bring together good physical and social environments, good citizens, good schools, good homes, and good jobs—normally cannot expect to capture personally any significant share of the increased economic value that is produced.

Noneconomic rewards for successful explorations are more likely in democratic political systems. Personal flattery and political power come to those who are successful with new electoral, legislative, or administrative tactics. Moreover, the rewards seem sometimes to be linked as much to the novelty of programs as to their ultimate value. New initiatives are rewarded more than efforts to implement old ones, and many professionals within the political system are likely to see their own identities as demanding differentiation from, rather than consistency with, the plans of others. Planners seek to make new plans; lawyers seek to make new law. Moreover, the winner-take-all character of some democratic political competition gives advantage to political risk-taking (March, 1991).

It is hard, however, for a successful political innovator to claim exclusive rights to an innovation. There is no law or tradition of patents or property rights for political inventions. Except in cases where the fit between a tactic and its creator is so unique that it cannot easily be mimicked, political innovations are rather easily appropriated by others. As a result, the political gains for their creators tend to be modest and short-lived. Moreover, exploratory mistakes, far from receiving protection, are ordinarily subject to sanctions in politics. Political systems seem to punish errors that result from overt deviation from standard procedures more severely than errors that result from failing to deviate from standard procedures. For the most part, they respond to observed mistakes; they do not respond to the unobserved potential opportunities that lie in strategies that failed or the opportunities lost by failing to pursue them.

The role of accountability. Democratic political systems generally seek to make public services and entitlements predictable and equitable. Democracy (by virtue of both its philosophy and its procedures) will generally surrender some advantage in average return in order to reduce variance in returns. Thus it often discourages spontaneous local experimentation that might lead to variability and has to depend on special programs of experimentation (Baldersheim and Ståhlberg, 1994). As was observed earlier, those discouragements are accentuated by political traditions of accountability. The practice of political accountability generally responds faster and more forcefully with penalties for failures than it does with rewards for successes.

Accountability, moreover, frequently is not tied to outcomes. Despite efforts in the last twenty years to create standard measures of performance in the public sector, such measures are not a dominant feature of public sector administration. Whether a particular program, strategy, or practice has favorable outcomes is frequently unclear, even after the fact. As a result, it is not easy to link accountability to performance outcomes. That lack of clarity in outcomes leads political systems to seek to control structures and processes rather than outcomes. Not wanting to risk unreliability in the impact of a program on individuals, and not being able to measure the effectiveness of a program, political systems seek to standardize and stabilize practices. The standardization and stabilization of processes normally reduces experimentation.

The role of aspirations. Exploration depends on the relation between performance and aspirations. Generally, exploration increases with the absolute difference between performance and aspiration (unless survival is threatened), and for equal absolute differences greater exploration is associated with failure than with success (March and Shapira, 1992). Since the effects of performance are moderated by the subjective target for performance, the rate and character of exploration are affected by those targets as well as by "objective" changes in performance. In particular, exploration is affected by the way aspirations adapt to experience (Lant, 1992).

Self-referential aspirations tend to be optimistic moving averages of past performance, thus tend in a stable environment to keep a political actor in the position of having a target slightly above performance, and in a slowly improving environment to keep an actor in a position of having a target slightly below performance. The former leads to modest experimentation of the refinement type; the latter leads to little experimentation. With self-referential aspirations, substantial experimentation is associated with slowing aspiration adjustment. With stable or slowly changing aspirations, it is possible for performance to deviate substantially from the target (positively or negatively) and thus to induce substantial exploration. Individual aspirations that adapt slowly to the performance of others are also likely to be far from individual performance and thus to lead to exploration, but so also will aspirations that adjust quickly to a reference group whose possibilities are substantially different from those of the actor. By this analysis at least, "unrealistic" reference groups (for example, reference groups that do much better or much poorer than the individual) will lead to more exploration than will "realistic" ones.

There is no assurance, of course, that the rate and nature of exploration produced in this way bear any close connection to the rate and nature of exploration that is optimal (whatever that may mean in this context). Although some models of exploration indicate that there are fairly general survival advantages to variable rates of exploration linked to adaptive aspirations (March, 1988b; March and Shapira, 1992), those advantages depend in detail on the rate and character of aspiration adaptation, the correlation between risk and return, the level of competition, and the nature of the "birth process" by which new entries replace actors who fail to survive.

SLOWING LEARNING

For reasons detailed above, learning tends to eliminate exploration. As a result, individual attributes and institutionalized practices that reduce the rate of learning contribute to exploratory activity. Among those mechanisms are various practices that reduce the efficiency of coding, interpreting, and using history.

The role of ignorance. Exploratory activity may be sustained by ignorance. Ignorance is furthered by devices that make it harder to communicate about current problems or to exchange feedback on the consequences of action. It is furthered by things that make it harder to implement past solutions to problems or to recall past lessons gained from history. These include playfulness in relating action to knowledge, in using memory, and in implementing procedures (March, 1971).

Ignorance useful to exploration may also be found in overestimations of the likelihood of success (Taylor and Brown, 1988). Optimistic illusions have the (system) advantage of overcoming risk aversion, thus making those who overestimate their prospects into unwitting altruists who maintain exploration that is useful for the institution or political system at, on average, a cost to themselves and their own institutions. Such overestimations may have a basis in deeply ingrained, and not easily changed personality styles or cultural regularities. For example, overestimations of the likelihood of future success have been found to be more characteristic of males than of females in contemporary Western cultures (Maccoby and Jacklin, 1974).

Within any particular cultural setting, a standard way of generating systematic biases in expectations of future success is by selecting on past success. Since successful people overestimate the contribution of their ability to their success and to underestimate the contribution of good fortune, they underestimate the probable costs of experimentation and overestimate their ability to distinguish between experiments that are likely to be successful and those that are not. This pattern of beliefs is fomented by a meritocratic promotion scheme in a hierarchy. Individuals who are promoted in such a scheme are people who have done well in the past. By virtue of their past successes, they have illusions of control (Langer, 1975). Those illusions are confirmed and magnified by reinterpretations that emphasize the favorable consequences of past actions. As a result, successful people are likely to engage in more exploratory behavior than they would if they understood the odds correctly (March and Shapira, 1987; Kahneman and Lovallo, 1993).

The role of ideology. Ideology is a set of beliefs about what should be done and how it can be done. The democratic tradition is one of nurturing ideological discontent, criticism, opposition, civil disobedience, and revolt in order to challenge laws, institutions, and authority (Dahl, 1966). Democratic institutions seek to support some differentiation, preserving, rather than submerging or eliminating, contending individual, group, and institutional identities, beliefs, and ways of life (Selznick, 1992, pp. xi, 313, 369). Ideological beliefs are tied to cognitive and social structures that sustain them in the face of short-run experience. In particular, democratic rights, laws, and customs provide a framework within which mutually supportive citizens and public officials can maintain ideologies. When ideologies change in response to political fortunes and policies, they do so slowly and in ways only loosely connected to the short-run local feedback. Changes seem to be driven more by fashions in enthusiasms than by feedback from experience.

Strong ideologies derived from such things as religious orthodoxy (Festinger *et al.*, 1956) or professional belief systems (Davis, Menon, and Morgan, 1982) and maintained by political principles of tolerance, interfere with the responsiveness that is vital to selection in learning. At the same time, however, they support variation. Ideology interferes with the short-run learning processes that normally eliminate exploration. Political leaders and administrative officers persist in the face of evidence suggesting they are misled. They reinterpret the evidence and solidify the beliefs. For example, during the 1980s such political leaders as Ronald Reagan in the United States and Margaret Thatcher in England argued that radical, systemic reform of government was needed. Their proposals were based primarily on ideas about appropriate social organization derived from economic theory and the proclamations of private sector ideologues. Their enthusiasms were not particularly sensitive to short-run experience.

True believer reformers and their consultants usually argue that appropriate policies are obvious. The problem is adoption and implementation complicated by the opposition of wrongheaded groups. Thus a 1991 World Bank report announces: "The problem is not that one does not know what to recommend; on the contrary, the goals and instruments are clear. But governments continue to have difficulties implementing PSM [public sector management] reform. The quandary is that sociopolitical and bureaucratic obstacles in each country impede or block the implementation of good practices" (World Bank, 1991, p. 38). That is, failures are to be attributed not to the policies (which are protected by World Bank ideology) but to the perversities of politics and bureaucracies.

Ideological dreams support explorations when experience does not. True believers construct accounts that are robust against events that are inconsistent with core normative and causal beliefs. They are unlikely to modify beliefs, behavior, or institutions in the light of new experience. Believers tend to see what they expect to see and what they hope to see (March and Olsen, 1975). They tend to interpret apparent failures not as a sign that they are on the wrong track but as a sign that they should push harder along the track they are on. All of these attributes lead true believers both to try deviant things (deviant, that is, from the views of the establishment) and to persist in the face of evidence that their experiments do not work. The difficulty in securing both experimentation and also patience with the results of experimentation is one possible reason for defending "true believers" in politics, and democratic politics has traditionally profited from the exploratory activities of utopian politicians who resist learning from their own experience or the experience of others.

The role of turnover. Important sources of exploratory activity in a political system are found in the deviant behavior and ideas of new citizens or officials (Lægreid and Olsen, 1978). Turnover is likely to bring people into a system who, on average, differ more from system norms than did the people they replace. The subsequent dynamic of turnover involves mutual learning between new arrivals and established practice. Political institutions seek to instruct new citizens and officials in the norms and practices of a political order. They diffuse collective knowledge and faiths to new arrivals through various forms of instruction, indoctrination, and exemplification (Whyte, 1957; Van Maanen, 1973). At the same time, institutions absorb the knowledge held by new arrivals, gaining new ideas from them. Such mutual learning is generally beneficial to the institutions and individuals involved, but it involves conflicts between short-run and long-run concerns and between gains to individual knowledge and gains to collective knowledge (March, 1991).

Political institutions benefit from having individuals adopt forms and practices that have become standard. Those gains from homogeneity in values and convergence of identities and practices, accentuated by modern methods of communication, move political institutions toward standardization and shared meaning. At the same time, the institutions also benefit (in the longer run) from a certain amount of exploratory deviance on the part of some individuals. If everyone is socialized too fast, the system as a whole fails to learn from its exploratory deviants, thus is buffered from possible favorable changes. Those advantages from exploratory deviance, however, are realized primarily by the system as a whole rather than by the deviant individual or group. Ordinarily there are clear advantages to any specific individual or subgroup in learning and conforming to standard institutional practice, particularly if the individual's objective is to succeed within the establishment. As a result, the best position for a self-interested individual is to be one who learns approved practices quickly in a political system in which there are others persisting in experimenting with possible new directions. This is, of course, the story of co-optation and reflects the complications (and opportunities) for governance produced by the divergence of individual and group interests. In the face of these processes, diversity is sustained by turnover and by structural arrangements (e.g., decentralization, autonomous cultures, competition) that slow the socialization of deviant new arrivals (March, 1991).

Facilitating Knowledge

As we have noted at several places, experience is ambiguous. It is made particularly ambiguous by the small samples of experience available and the presence of multiple, interacting causes. Small samples introduce large sampling errors. Multiple causes tend to bury the effects of any particular action in the "noise" of other factors. Those two features of experience combine with the time required before political outcomes are clear to frustrate the understanding of political history. It often takes ten years or more to evaluate the results of a particular policy intervention (Sabatier, 1991, p. 257). In the short run it is hard to assess the results, while in the long run it is hard to separate the various factors that influence the results achieved and trace their cause to a particular reform (Olsen, 1995, p. 5). Governance involves improving the capabilities of political institutions to gain knowledge from such ambiguous experience. Governments do this in a number of ways that have already been enumerated, but particularly by improving patience, improving accounts, improving memory, and improving learning from others.

IMPROVING PATIENCE

Increasing the sample size of experience with a particular practice, strategy, institution, or action involves increasing the patience that political actors have with actions once agreed upon. Patience increases the number of experiences with a particular course of action, thus provides a more reliable estimate of its effects. Patience is also important because of the way it allows skills to develop. Many practices and policies that are potentially very good are initially bad because of lack of competence in executing them. They require time and experience to realize their full potential.

Because it does not stem from anxiety about results, success-based experimentation is likely to generate greater patience than will failure-based experimentation. As a result, it is likely to produce more reliable estimates of the value of the experiment. Failure-based experimentation will tend to be impatient, thus to make more mistakes. Mistakes of believing a policy to be better than it really is will tend to be corrected by the tendency to continue the policy and accumulate additional experience. Mistakes of believing the policy to be poorer than it really is will not be corrected. Early failures are likely to produce demands for new strategies. The patience advantage of success-based experimentation over failure-based experimentation is likely to be particularly significant in discovering the value of practices or policies that require practice to realize their full value.

Patience and impatience can also be influenced by interpretive bias. The tendency of decision-makers to exhibit positive bias in interpreting the results of their actions makes them slow in reversing a direction, thus both inhibits an initial change from a previous course and encourages patience with a change once made. The tendency of political processes to encourage expectations of quick results as well as oppositional skepticism with respect to results probably does the reverse: It stimulates change but makes the system impatient with the results of change. Ideological commitments on the part of political actors make them impatient with the programs of others but patient with their own. Those interpretive biases are embedded in political traditions and practices that affect them. As we have observed in Chapter 5, a traditional source of patience in democratic politics has been the use of periodic, rather than continuous, political monitoring. When successful political coalitions are relatively stable and have capabilities and time to experiment, the biases of interpretation encourage patience. When political parties are inchoate and politics is a daily plebiscite, political patience is much harder to sustain.

IMPROVING ACCOUNTS

Political systems learn from their experience on the basis of the accounts they formulate to interpret their histories (Spring, 1992). Learning processes, however, can be as powerful in contributing to mistakes as they can be in making intelligence possible. False accounts can be constructed; false lessons can be learned. In order to facilitate intelligent learning, accounts of history need to be both valid and reliable. A valid account is one that correctly captures what happened and why it happened. A reliable account is one that is shared among individuals in the polity. A learning community needs valid accounts in order to ensure that the inferences made, rules changed, and actions taken as a result of learning improve the position of the community. A learning community needs reliable accounts in order to ensure that there is consistency in the changes that learning produces. Neither requirement is absolute. It is possible to improve actions on the basis of less than completely valid accounts, and unreliability in learning can be tolerated (even encouraged) within limits.

Contemporary enthusiasms for subjective interpretations of experience have led to considerable reluctance to make a sharp distinction between validity and reliability, seeing validity as simply reliability in another place. The point is well taken if it is interpreted as recording the considerable elements of social construction in any conception of "reality," but the observation that reality is socially constructed does not exclude the possibility that different realities are constructed in different parts of the social system and that some of those constructions are (socially) conceded to have greater validity than others.

Improving validity in accounts. The tension between those who seek to improve the validity of individual accounts through the development, professionalization, and use of expertise and those who seek to do so through strengthening competition among contending accounts is as long-lasting as political democracy. From the point of view of the former, learning intelligently from small samples of experience in complicated worlds involves three major possibilities in the elaboration of accounts (Lounamaa and March, 1987; March, Sproull, and Tamuz, 1991). The first possibility is to try to improve the experimental design of experience. The interpretation of experience is made difficult by the fact that the consequences of action are often lost in the noise of other factors, and by the way in which learners seek to adapt to their experience before they understand it, thus further confusing it. The obvious—though not always practiced—implication is that experience is more easily interpreted if learning is slowed so that actions are changed infrequently and if changes are large when they are made.

The second possibility for building accounts for learning is to try to augment the detail of any observations that experience provides.

On the one hand, when large samples of events are not available, it is possible to substitute large numbers of observers of single events. The idea is to focus on reducing measurement error in the observation of history rather than sampling error. Although it is impossible to avoid the large sampling errors produced by small sample sizes, it may be possible to reduce measurement error through multiple observers. At the same time, it is possible to elaborate the rich detail of experience in order to gain contextual understanding of the processes underlying historical events in the particular case.

The third possibility is to try to construct hypothetical histories. The specific events realized in history are viewed as draws from distributions of possible histories. They may, in fact, be relatively unlikely draws. By using the rich detail of a specific case it is possible to produce a theory of the process from which to simulate possible histories. In this way it is possible to learn not only from a single observed history but from the distribution of hypothetical histories. Making these counterfactual events compelling is fundamental to effective learning (March, Sproull, and Tamuz, 1991).

As a general rule, none of these possibilities is easy to implement, but political systems provide some advantages over less overtly conflictual systems. The idea of politics is to use conflict, not to reduce it. Politics provides an arena for competition among biased advocates. Although it is recognized that such a competitive structure accentuates individual biases, it is imagined that truth emerges from competition among advocates—witting or unwitting liars. With respect to improving the experimental design of experience, political systems seem better designed for frequent small changes than for infrequent large ones, but party competition and relatively long periods between elections provide a basis for somewhat less frequent, larger changes. With respect to augmenting the number of observers, although any one political actor tends to want to restrict the number of independent commentators interpreting history, political competition and traditions of competition among observers (e.g., journalists) lead to multiple, relatively independent observers. With respect to constructing hypothetical histories, politics seems particularly vulnerable to treating historical events as necessary results rather than as draws from a distribution, but competition and heterogeneity generate alternative, counterfactual stories to a greater extent than is found in other systems less committed to conflict.

Improving reliability in accounts. Many of the institutions and practices of politics are oriented toward creating reliable accounts. Collective discourse and journalism are often, from the standpoint of decision-making, essentially gossip (March and Sevón, 1984). They resolve no critical decision issues but provide occasions on which individuals share interpretations of their experience. They tell and elaborate stories. Through the retelling and listening, accounts come to be shaped and reshaped (Boje, 1991). For the process of storytelling to converge to a reliably confirmed account, exposure of a listener to a story must transform the listener's account in the direction of the storyteller's. Standard theories of cognitive and emotional consistency suggest that such a result depends on a predisposition toward agreement (Heider, 1958; Abelson, 1968). Stories told by friends tend to converge as a result of mutual exposure, but stories told by enemies tend to diverge, thereby confirming their opposition to each other. The development of accounts in politics involves interactions not only among mutual supporters but also among opponents, thus tends to lead not to complete reliability throughout the population but instead to reliably conflicting accounts.

Traditions of civility in debate can be seen as efforts to subordinate the emotionality of opposition to the emotionality of commonality, thus to make it easier for accounts to converge. As opponents talk in a civil way, they distinguish their differences in preferences from their differences in accounts and impose expectations of convergence on the latter. And although the path to that convergence is filled with complications of strategic action and potentials for misunderstanding, the rules of polite argument make the creation of a reliably shared account more likely.

Reliability in accounts contributes to democratic learning. The political community learns by sharing accounts and their implications. Reliability, however, is also a problem for learning. Political communities often come to share accounts that are systematically wrong as descriptions of reality, thus lead to systematic errors from learning. Moreover, reliability contributes to difficulties in correcting those errors. By reducing variety in interpretations, it reduces variety in experience and thereby slows learning.

IMPROVING MEMORY

Political systems have three major problems with memory. First, they forget some things. Lessons of history that are not coded into rules, traditions, and standard operating procedures are lost through turnover and the passage of time. Each political generation has difficulty retrieving the lessons of the previous one. Second, political systems remember some things too well. When experience is coded into rules and practices, the underlying history is suppressed. Rules take on their own justification, building alliances and beliefs that sustain them far beyond their original basis in experience. Third, political systems remember some things poorly. Memories are victimized by desires, tactics, and retrospective reinterpretations of experience. The present has difficulty learning usefully from a past that is reconstructed to confirm the prejudices of the present.

Although governments are notorious for accumulating records, democratic institutions appear to be loath to invest in usable memory (OECD, 1989, p. 9; Olsen, 1995, p. 36), and even more loath to invest in agencies or systems for maintaining and retrieving knowledge. Aside from some domains of vital statistics and economic indicators, most democracies have poor official memories. In large part, this is because there is relatively little demand for memory on the part of political officials and citizens. The one principal (and very important) exception is the law, including administrative law. The legal rules of democracy, along with the records of the history of their applications and interpretations, are usually maintained rather well.

It is perhaps instructive that, aside from the military, branches of governance and intellectual traditions linked to logics of consequence and to an understanding of the causal structure of history seem to have been less inclined to accumulate records of historical experiments than have branches of government and intellectual traditions linked to logics of appropriateness. Economic history has been a tiny branch of economics. Interpretive history has been the heart of jurisprudence. When action is seen as stemming from anticipations of the future, records of the past are disadvantaged. When action is seen as stemming from the lessons of history, records of the past become important. This suggests that improving memory may involve not only investing in records and the paraphernalia of adequate maintenance and retrieval but also a transformation of the worldviews of governance and human action.

IMPROVING LEARNING FROM OTHERS

A distinctive feature of the past few thousand years has been a fairly steady increase in the importance of formal systems for learning from others (Rose, 1993). Rather little of the knowledge base of a modern political institution is derived from direct experience. Most is gained from others. As a result, the relevance of the individual polity as a sustained accumulator of idiosyncratic experiential knowledge has declined. Processes of knowledge acquisition that emphasize direct experience within a particular political institution have become less important to success than those processes that emphasize more analytical and broader knowledge and exposure. Research, education, and exposure to the experiences and inferences of others have become more important; personal experience has become less relevant. Contemporary political and economic success involves gaining access to knowledge and having the capability to use it. Neither of those is assured. Access is inhibited by conscious efforts to limit knowledge exchange and by limitations in connections through which the exchange can take place. The returns to the relatively unfocused knowledge exchange that characterizes informal networks tend to be slow in coming and uncertain. The capability to use knowledge often depends on having other knowledge.

Three problems in particular are worthy of attention in the context of political institutions. The first is the difficulty of making transfers of knowledge from one political coalition to an opposing coalition. As we have noted previously, turnover hurts the transfer of knowledge, particularly when it involves transfer from one regime to an opposing one. Democratic traditions emphasize the role of a permanent civil service and the training of opposition parties in the competencies of governance. The permanent civil service and the massive structure of offices and rules that undergird it protect democratic governance from turnover paralysis. Most things go on. The knowledge of the state is rather substantially independent of the knowledge of the rulers, so is unaffected by the transfer of power. Similarly, the creation of "shadow" opposition governments in two-party cabinet systems and the involvement of opposition leaders in detailed knowledge about the workings of the government in others mitigate the ignorance of future rulers. Both of those practices strengthen continuity and the conservation of the lessons of history, but they pay for that gain by dulling the bite of political competition.

The second problem is the difficulty of learning across institutional boundaries. Political institutions in one country convert their experiences into rules, procedures, and knowledge. The sharing of experience and knowledge among countries or among institutions within a country can be facilitated by investing in networks of contacts (see Chapter 4) that connect the citizens and officials of one jurisdiction with those of another. Political institutions facilitate participation in such networks by providing resources to support them and by encouraging citizens and officials in one institution to view themselves as having identities that are consistent with those of citizens and officials elsewhere. Learning consistent with the polity's long-run needs for knowledge exchange is particularly facilitated when the short-run interests and identities of current officials support professional or collegial contact. The usual problem is that the returns to the polity of such contacts sometimes seem too remote and the returns to the officials too immediate.

The third problem is the problem of building long-term reciprocal relationships in a political context. The voluntary transfer of knowledge is an act of faith. The faith may reside in a definition of an identity—as it often does in relations among friends. It may reside in expectations of reciprocity—as it often does in relations among business partners. It may reside in desperation—as it often does in psychotherapy. Building an ethos of faith under conditions in which the returns to transferring knowledge are both unclear and delayed requires substantial patience, and the central logic of democratic politics is not patience. It is turnover through competition. As a result, networks need to be buffered from political turnover through the involvement of the opposition in them and through their professionalization.

Chapter Seven

PROSPECTS FOR GOVERNANCE

Democratic governance is a quaint topic, more consistent with the elaborate conversations of an eighteenth-century salon than the sound bites of contemporary television. It evokes images of archaic philosophers lost in the erudition of their distinctions and romantic patriots lost in the enthusiasms of their rhetoric. Nevertheless—or perhaps for those reasons—we think it is a proper topic. We have tried to suggest a few elements of an institutional perspective for comprehending, discussing, and improving democratic political life, for discovering ways in which human beings can live together with civility and grace. The effort is predicated on the idea that the perspectives of political discourse come to constitute political reality and the judgment that contemporary political perspectives create political realities that are both less consistent with democratic hopes and less durable than those of institution-based alternatives.

GOVERNANCE AND POLITICAL INSTITUTIONS

An institutional perspective on governance reflects and encompasses a history of debate over the appropriate role of governance in democracy. It is in many ways a synthesis of different programs for democratic governance, a synthesis that provides a distinct set of research questions.

Four Programs for Democratic Governance

We can contrast four conceptions of the agenda of democratic governance: The first is *minimalist* and emphasizes the role of governance in creating an effective set of rules for managing voluntary political exchanges among citizens. The second is *redistributive* and emphasizes the role of governance in influencing' substantive outcomes through redistribution of resource capabilities. The third is *developmental* and emphasizes the role of governance in building a political culture of beliefs and shared purposes. The fourth is *structuralist* and emphasizes the construction of political processes and rules. The different programs are based on different ideas about the nature of political community, the individual, and governance. Their advocates tend to be antagonistic, but they are not mutually exclusive. What we have called an institutional approach is attentive to aspects of each.

THE MINIMALIST AGENDA

In the minimalist agenda human beings are taken much as they are, with preferences and resources determined exogenously. The political community is seen as an aggregate of autonomous self-interested individuals. Actions are based on individual consent and voluntary contracts. Individual entrepreneurship rather than public action provides innovations and adaptiveness. Governance manages the organization of bargaining and exchange, including the formation of coalitions, in order to minimize the costs of finding and implementing mutually satisfactory exchanges among citizens. It is judged by its success in minimizing inefficiencies in these private exchanges.

Governmental goals, authority, and capabilities have to be justified; individual preferences, resources, and capabilities do not. Stable and impartial constitutive rules minimize the discretion and power of political authorities and allow individuals to plan their own conduct, use their own resources, and promote their own purposes. The rules specify procedural constraints on exchange, assuring rights to private property and fair competition among individuals, given their initial resources. In the minimalist conception, governance is indifferent among substantive outcomes and plays no legitimate role in the construction or transformation of identities, accounts, capabilities, or adaptiveness.

THE REDISTRIBUTIVE AGENDA

The redistributive agenda is committed to social and economic democracy and stresses the obligation of government to secure a more equal distribution of social and economic resources and capabilities in society. As in the case of the minimalist agenda, politics is seen as involving conflicts of interest among self-interested actors who gain power from the possession of resources. In contrast to the minimalist agenda, however, the redistributive agenda seeks to affect substantive outcomes. Political institutions are justified by their contribution to human development and public welfare and are expected to redress inequalities through the redistribution of economic and social resources.

The focus is on changing resource constraints, on redistributing resources and rights and thereby affecting the capabilities of groups in society. Such a focus stems from the conviction that popular consent must be free of the coercion that large differences in resources create. Some versions of the redistributive agenda emphasize explicit redistribution of key resources, particularly income and wealth. Others extend that emphasis to focus on regulation of exchange processes designed to limit the inequalities of resource-based advantages that remain.

Compared with the minimalist agenda, the redistributive agenda is less concerned with the dangers of public authority and more concerned with how private power concentrations may endanger democracy. The key slogans of the minimalist agenda—"authenticity," "autonomy," "freedom," "neutrality," "free exchange," and "consent"—are seen as diverting attention from the dangers of private power based on the possession of critical scarce resources. The task of democratic government is portrayed as being not only to regulate and limit the authority and power of government but also to regulate and limit inequalities in private resources and capabilities.

THE DEVELOPMENTAL AGENDA

Like the redistributive agenda, the developmental agenda presumes an active role of governance in producing a just society. Its primary focus, however, is less on resource constraints than on creating and sustaining a shared culture of democratic values and habits. The po-

litical community has a substantive foundation rather than a procedural one. The developmental perspective is educational and communitarian more than regulatory.

The idea that political participation and political reform should be
viewed as part of developing the people morally and cognitively is
an old one. Many classical humanists believed it possible and desirable for the polity to create civilized and free citizens of taste and
judgment. A view of politics as an arena for collective education and
development blurs some standard distinctions between "communitarian" and "liberal" views of the relation between the individual
and the political community. For example, a confirmed liberal such
as John Stuart Mill could argue:

> The first element of good government being the virtue and intelligence
> of the human beings composing the community, the most important
> point of excellence which any form of government can possess is to
> promote the virtue and intelligence of the people themselves. The first
> question in respect to any political institutions is how far they tend to
> foster in the members of the community the various qualities, moral or
> intellectual (as well as their well-being) (Mill, 1962, pp. 30–35).

The developmental agenda seeks to affect the operation of the
polity by affecting the values, beliefs, and identities of citizens. The
role of governance is to mold identities and accounts to create virtuous citizens and officials. The objective may include not only education into the obligations and rights of the key identities of the polity
but also the establishment of widespread agreement on many substantive purposes and ends for the polity, a sense of a common good
and common destiny. A key objective is to produce a political community within which citizens can discuss political issues in an atmos-
phere of mutual trust, tolerance, and sympathy (Mill, 1962, p. 32).

THE STRUCTURALIST AGENDA

The structuralist agenda sees an active role for governance, but an
indirect one. It emphasizes the role of governance in the construction of political structures (institutions). It is based on a democratic
vision, but that vision is substantively open-ended. It is a conception
of a set of open institutions through which citizens can define the na-

ture of the political life they seek and discover the extent to which they can achieve it. In that sense, it shares common ground with the minimalist agenda. Just as the minimalist agenda sustains institutions for efficient voluntary exchange without commitment to any particular Pareto-preferred outcome, the structuralist agenda sustains institutions for developing and implementing conceptions of democratic civic virtue without commitment to any particular version of that virtue.

Unlike the minimalist agenda, however, the structuralist agenda goes beyond managing coalition formation and exchange among preexistent interests and within prior constraints. The interests and constraints are managed as well. Unlike the redistributionist agenda, the structuralist agenda is inclined to see opportunities for affecting identities, accounts, and adaptiveness, as well as capabilities. Unlike the communitarian agenda, the structuralist agenda is concerned less with creating appropriate democratic values and identities directly by molding citizens into a specific political culture than with creating political structures that both respond to political demands and shape them.

An Institutional Synthesis

What we have called an institutional approach to governance combines elements of all four agendas. It recognizes the role of political institutions in managing exchange, in redistribution, in building a political culture, and in developing structures for the sustenance of civic virtue. It blends principles from traditions emphasizing substantive programs with those from traditions emphasizing procedures. The spirit is both activist with respect to a willingness to influence the constraints and structuralist with respect to emphasizing the building of institutions for influencing constraints in ways that leave the precise nature of the influence one of the things yet to be determined.

Political institutions have been described sometimes as instruments of command and coercion, helping one group to enhance its resources and capabilities and thereby to secure dominance over other groups; sometimes as tools for collective problem-solving, helping societies reach shared purposes and goals; sometimes as arrangements for regulating and facilitating exchange, helping individual citizens to fulfill their private desires; and sometimes as vehicles for constructing meaning and defining appropriate behavior, helping a society to construct individual and collective identities and accounts. They are all of these, and the task of an institutional approach to governance is to refine somewhat our understanding of how these various aspects can be made to fit together to further democratic hopes in a postmodern context.

An institutionalist agenda for governance portrays a world where a democratic order of rights, rules, and institutions is constructed and maintained through active education and socialization of citizens and officials; where individual and collective capabilities for action depend on the endogenous allocation of resources and competencies; where human action is based substantially on a conception of identity and a logic of appropriateness; where meaning, including an understanding of history and self, is based on accounts constructed through a political and social process; and where history matches institutions, behaviors, and contexts in ways that take time and have multiple, path-dependent equilibria.

From an institutionalist perspective, democratic governance involves improving the processes by which a society formulates ends, seeks to achieve them efficiently, elaborates and overturns its conceits, and weaves an understanding of the good life by experiencing its pursuit. It involves encouraging an examination of what constitutes a worthwhile life, how the lives individuals live compare with democratic ideals, what resources and actions are required to bring those lives closer to democratic aspirations, and how we are to understand and respond to our failures to achieve those ideals.

Democratic governance involves creating identities and preferences that define what is appropriate, right, desirable, and acceptable, the rules by which citizens and officials are constituted. It involves creating and limiting capabilities for action. Capabilities imply discretion—the flexibility to consider a broad array of options. Capabilities imply choice—the ability to influence what action is taken. And capabilities imply the ability to believe that choices make a difference. Governance involves creating accounts of the relation between human action and the flow of history, credible stories that distribute individual and group praise and blame for collective outcomes. It involves adaptiveness, sustaining change and stability, disorder and order, diversity and unity, conflict and consensus, disintegration and integration, ambiguity and coherence.

The institutional agenda organizes a program of questions for research on how a democratic political system can be achieved. The questions include:

1. A set of questions about the molding of identities and standards of appropriateness: How are standards of appropriateness created, changed, evoked, and interpreted? How are they organized into political identities of the citizen, the political agent, the professional, etc.? What are normative imperatives about identities? What is the proper tie between the self and the citizen? How are unity and diversity of identities balanced within a democratic society? What is the role of collective discourse in the construction of standards of appropriateness? What are the possibilities for improving the institutional processes by which identities and standards evolve and are activated?

2. A set of questions about political capacity: Who is able to do what in a political system? How does a society develop political capabilities and regulate their use? How are resources and rights distributed and utilized? How are capabilities for effective action created, rationed, and controlled? How is knowledge allocated and used? How are distributions of political capabilities and resources justified? How are considerations of equality, equity, and efficiency balanced? How can political obligations be matched with political capabilities? What are the possibilities for improving the institutional processes by which political capacities are distributed and organized for use?

3. A set of questions about the ways in which accounts are constructed and interpretive meaning established: How do political actors create stories of institutional history? How are those stories affected by the democratic context of norms and institutions? What are the processes of collective reasoning, experience, and socialization by which a political community learns, assigns responsibility, and attributes blame and honor? How does a society secure an enlightened public understanding? What are the proper roles of religion, tradition, science, family, and rationality in molding a

comprehension of political life? What is the proper relation between expertise and public discourse? What are the possibilities for improving the institutional processes by which understandings are shaped and shared?

4. A set of questions about political adaptiveness: How do political actors and institutions learn from their own experience and the experience of others? What is the proper balance between extending existing beliefs and identities and experimenting with possible new ones? Between efficiency and adaptiveness? What are the procedures of inference and how are they affected by the political process? What is the relation between capability and adaptation? Between accounts and adaptation? How do ecologies of adaptation result in outcomes due to the interactions of simultaneous nested learners? What are the possibilities for improving the institutional processes by which political institutions learn from their own experience and the experiences of others?

This book has tried to provide a few preliminary observations on parts of this agenda. The observations suggest some of the complexities of democratic governance in a modern context. Democratic governance reflects social norms, interests, and climate, but it also shapes the society it reflects and must accept the responsibilities that accrue from reflecting a society it has shaped.

GOVERNANCE, VIRTUE, AND FAITH

The democratic creed is predicated on the possibility of improving the organization of society and thereby the ability of citizens to achieve their purposes and better their lot. It assumes not only that it is possible to produce political change—which within a branching, meandering history may be relatively easy—but also that it is possible to produce change that is reliably an improvement. We have explored some of the complications in achieving democratic virtue—the ways in which the practices of democracy are permeated with indeterminacies and ambivalences and the difficulties democratic institutions have in sustaining a necessary commitment to a democratic ethos, a rich collection of procedures and rules, and a useful level of variety. We need also to acknowledge that although we know enough about processes of change to be able to affect history signifi-cantly, we do not know enough to be confident that the effects we produce will ultimately prove to be intelligent ones.

Ambiguities of Democratic Virtue

History provides little support for human claims of moral foresight. Although historical outcomes such as the abolition of slavery, the de-velopment of equal political and human rights, the expansion of liter-acy, and the humanization of justice are widely seen as improvements in the human estate and triumphs of democratic political regimes, many other past proclamations of progress now seem unwarranted. The objectives pursued in an earlier age are not necessarily confirmed as desirable in a later one, and the accomplishments of the former can become the tragedies of the latter. The record suggests that it will be persistently difficult to predict which currently admired reforms will be appreciated in the future and for what reasons.

The difficulties stem partly from the uncertainties of history. Hirschman (1991, pp. 11, 43, 81) identifies three standard theses about the role of politics in history: (1) The *futility* thesis: the idea that politics is impotent. Attempts at social transformation will be fruitless, resulting in cosmetic changes at best. (2) The *perversity* the-sis: the idea that political efforts at reform exacerbate the conditions they purport to improve. (3) The *jeopardy* thesis: the idea that a po-litical action, though possibly desirable in itself, invariably involves endangering previous, precious accomplishments. Many theories of history lead to a limited sense of political possibilities. Ideas that see history as driven by deep economic and social structures and laws recognize profound limitations on political action and personal re-sponsibility (Higgins and Apple, 1983), as do theories that attribute individual action to social or economic experience or conditions rather than to will.

The problems, however, are not limited to existential angst. De-spite a long tradition of discussion of the moral and ethical standards of civilized democratic conduct, the criteria for judging political ac-tions are often ambiguous, conflicting, and changing rather than clear, consistent, and stable. Political change involves a complicated mosaic of development over time by interacting nested units within an environment that is also developing. It is not obvious that improvement is achieved by preserving any particular institution or political form. There is no obvious metric for comparing long-run and short-run consequences or for comparing consequences across polities with seemingly incommensurable histories, cultures, and values. What is appropriate or optimal from the standpoint of the individual is not necessarily appropriate or optimal from the point of view of the institution within which he or she operates, which in turn is not necessarily appropriate or optimal from the point of view of the larger society. What is appropriate or optimal in the short run is not necessarily appropriate or optimal in the longer run. The consequences of alternative conduct are so uncertain, and individual behaviors interact within an ecology in such ways as to make definitions of appropriateness and calculations of optimality from any point of view problematic.

Willful political engineers seem to be left with two possible approaches to improvement, neither fully satisfactory. The first is to see the political system as an instrument for the pursuit of some vision of transcendent personal or collective goals in terms of which outcomes can be evaluated. Ideas of transcendent goals ranging from grand visions of an exemplary society and its implementation to mundane notions of strategic planning are important parts of contemporary politics, as they were of earlier politics. There has been a modest drift away from defining goals in terms of God's will and toward equating them with individual desires, but it is hard to see either as capturing the ethos of democracy.

The second approach is to emphasize strengthening the development of democratic processes without any commitment to particular substantive outcomes. This approach suffers from some obscurity about what it means to "strengthen" the processes, but such a tactic is implicit in much of this book, as well as others. We have argued that political development involves simultaneously improving the processes by which political institutions seek out or generate new options (exploration), implement options that prove effective (exploitation), and transform the criteria by which the outcomes of experience are judged (evaluation). The formulation may have merit, but it still leaves the criteria of virtue ill-defined and has little to say about how effort should be distributed among the three tasks.

Deliberate political intervention sometimes seems able to change the course of history, but there is no assurance that the changes will be desirable. Even though the institutions and accounts that are created today affect the standards that will be adopted and endorsed by future generations, our abilities to produce effects are not matched by similar abilities to guarantee that we (or our children) will assess those effects as desirable in the future. Relative to *post hoc* assessments of improvement and progress, human interventions in history sometimes seem to be almost as haphazard as mutations.

Democratic Governance as Faith

The ambiguities of democratic virtue clash with the optimism of democratic belief. Democratic thought thrives on a benign view of human nature and a vision of human control over the circumstances of life. It is an alluring imagination in which human intentions overcome adversities and control history, and political institutions are created by human will in the service of human purpose. Old institutions are changed to improve human conditions. New ones are constructed. We share some of those sentiments, but not all of them. Although we embrace the purposeful intervention into meandering political histories to change the course of political development, we do not embrace democratic governance out of confidence in its consequences. Neither ideas of strengthening the processes of political development nor ideas tied to specific human objectives and visions of destiny can claim profound consequential justification.

Critics of attempts to affect history through political action regularly postulate such problems as justification for maintaining a status quo (Merkl, 1967, p. 127). We do not. The justification for democratic governance and democratic change lies ultimately not in a logic of consequence but in a logic of appropriateness. To be a democratic citizen is to try to act within the democratic spirit as democratic traditions and discourse have come to define that spirit. To be a human being is to try to act within the human spirit as human traditions and discourse have come to define that spirit. It is a vision of a self-considered life. While there are many limitations to human capabilities, to be a democratic citizen is to accept responsibility for crafting the practices, rules, forms, capabilities, structures, procedures, accounts, and identities that construct democratic political life. In short, the essence of the democratic and human spirit is to try to do good, even while knowing that the efforts may be fruitless or misguided. It is an assertion of faith, not a claim of significance.

REFERENCES

Abelson, R. P., ed. 1968. *Theories of Cognitive Consistency: A Sourcebook.* Chicago: Rand McNally.

Adelberg, S., and C. D. Batson. 1978. Accountability and helping: When needs exceed resources. *Journal of Personality and Social Psychology*, 36: 343–50.

Alexander, J. C., and P. Sztompka, eds. 1990. *Rethinking Progress.* Boston: Unwin, Hyman.

Allardt, E., *et al.* 1981. *Nordic Democracy: Ideas, Issues, Institutions in Politics, Economy, Education, Social and Cultural Affairs in Denmark, Finland, Iceland, Norway and Sweden.* Copenhagen: Det Danske Selskab/Munksgaard.

Alonso, W., and P. Starr, eds. 1987. *The Politics of Numbers.* New York: Russell Sage.

Amenta, E., and B. Carruthers. 1988. The formative years of U.S. social spending policies. *American Sociological Review*, 53: 661–78.

Anderson, C. W. 1990. *Pragmatic Liberalism.* Chicago: University of Chicago Press.

Anderson, P. A., and G. W. Fischer. 1986. A Monte Carlo model of garbage can decision process. In J. G. March and R. Weissinger-Baylon, eds., *Ambiguity and Command: Organizational Perspectives on Military Decision Making*, pp. 140–64. Marshfield, MA: Pitman.

Apter, D. A. 1991. Institutionalism reconsidered. *International Social Science Journal*, August, pp. 463–81.

253

Argyris, C. 1977. Organizational learning and management information systems. *Accounting, Organizations and Society*, 2 (2): 113–23.

———. 1982. *Reasoning, Learning, and Action*. San Francisco: Jossey-Bass.

Argyris, C., and D. Schön. 1978. *Organizational Learning*. Reading, MA: Addison-Wesley.

Aristotle. 1980. *Politics*. Harmondsworth: Penguin.

Aronson, E. 1968. Disconfirmed expectancies and bad decisions—discussion: Expectancy vs. other motives. In R. P. Abelson, *et al.*, eds., *Theories of Cognitive Consistency*, pp. 491–93. Chicago: Rand McNally.

Arthur, W. B. 1984. Competing technologies and economic prediction. *IIASA Options*, 2: 10–13.

———. 1989. Competing technologies, increasing returns, and lock-in by historical events. *Economic Journal*, 99: 116–31.

Ashford, D. E. 1986. *The Emergence of the Welfare State*. Oxford: Basil Blackwell.

———. 1990. Social Democratic visions: Interpreting the postwar welfare states. Unpublished manuscript, University of Pittsburgh.

Ashforth, B. E., and F. Mael. 1989. Social identity theory and the organization. *Academy of Management Review*, 14: 20–39.

Axelrod, R. M. 1984. *The Evolution of Cooperation*. New York: Basic Books

Axelrod, R. M., and W. D. Hamilton. 1981. The evolution of cooperation. *Science*, 211: 1390–96.

Axelrod, R. M., and R. O. Keohane. 1986. Achieving cooperation under anarchy: Strategies and institutions. In K. A. Oye, ed., *Cooperation Under Anarchy*. Princeton, NJ: Princeton University Press.

Bachrach, P., and M. Baratz. 1962. The two faces of power. *American Political Science Review*, 56: 947–52.

Baier, V. E.; J. G. March; and H. Sætren. 1986. Implementation and ambiguity. *Scandinavian Journal of Management Studies*, 2: 197–212.

Bailey, R. W. 1991. *Images of English: A Cultural History of the Language*. Ann Arbor: University of Michigan Press.

Baldersheim, H., and K. Ståhlberg, eds. 1994. *Towards the Self-Regulating Municipality*. Aldershot: Dartmouth.

Ball, T.; J. Farr; and R. L. Hanson, eds. 1989. *Political Innovation and Conceptual Change*. Cambridge: Cambridge University Press.

Barber, B. 1984. *Strong Democracy*. Berkeley: University of California Press.

Bardach, E. 1977. *The Implementation Game*. Cambridge, MA: MIT Press.

Barker, E. 1984. Demokrati som aktivitet. In B. Hagtvet and W. M. Lafferty, eds., *Demokrati og Demokratisering*, pp. 360–66. Oslo: Aschehoug.

Barnard, C. I. 1938. *Functions of the Executive*. Cambridge, MA: Harvard University Press.

Barth, F. 1969. *Ethnic Groups and Boundaries*. London: Allen & Unwin.

———. 1993. Enduring and emerging issues in the analysis of ethnicity. Unpublished manuscript, Oslo.

Basu, K.; E. Jones; and E. Schlicht. 1987. The growth and decay of custom: The role of the new institutional economics in economic history. *Explorations in Economic History*, 24: 1–21.

Baum, J., and J. Singh, eds. 1994. *The Evolutionary Dynamics of Organizations*. New York: Oxford University Press.

Baumgartner, F. R., and B. D. Jones. 1993. *Agendas and Instability in American Politics*. Chicago: University of Chicago Press.

Bay, C. 1965. *The Structure of Freedom*. New York: Atheneum.

Becker, G. S., and G. J. Stigler. 1977. De gustibus non est disputandum. *American Economic Review*, 67: 76–90.

Bellah, R. N., *et al.* 1991. *The Good Society*. New York: Knopf.

Benavot, A.; Y-K. Cha; D. Kames; J. W. Meyer; and S. Ying. 1991. Knowledge for the masses: World models and national curricula, 1920–1986. *American Sociological Review*, 56: 85–100.

Bendix, R. 1968. Introduction. In R. Bendix, ed., *State and Society*, pp. 1–13. Boston: Little, Brown.

Bendix, R., and S. Rokkan. 1964. The extension of national citizenship to the lower classes. In R. Bendix. *Nation-building and Citizenship*, pp. 74–100. New York: Wiley.

Bendor, J., and D. Mookherjee. 1987. Institutional structure and the logic of ongoing collective action. *American Political Science Review*, 81: 129–54.

Bennett, L. M., and S. E. Bennett. 1990. *Living with Leviathan*. Lawrence: University Press of Kansas.

Berezin, M. 1991. The organization of political ideology: Culture, state, and theater in Fascist Italy. *American Sociological Review*, 56: 639–51.

Berg, E. 1965. *Democracy and the Majority Principle*. Stockholm: Ivar Heggströms Tryckeri.

Bergevärn, L. E., and O. Olson. 1989. Reforms and myths: A history of municipal accounting in Sweden. *Accounting, Auditing, and Accountability*, 2 (3): 22–39.

Berman, H. J. 1983. *Law and Revolution: The Formation of the Western Legal Tradition*. Cambridge, MA: Harvard University Press.

Berscheid, E. 1994. Interpersonal relationships. *Annual Review of Psychology* 45: 79–129.

Biddle, B. J. 1986. Recent developments in role theory. *Annual Review of Sociology* 12: 67–92.

Blichner, L. B. 1995. Radical change and experiential learning. Thesis, Norwegian Research Centre in Organization and Management, Bergen.

Bloom, W. 1990. *Personal Identity, National Identity and International Relations*. Cambridge: Cambridge University Press.

Bobbio, N. 1987. *The Future of Democracy*. Minneapolis: University of Minnesota Press.

———. 1990. *Liberalism and Democracy*. London: Verso.

Boje, D. M. 1991. The storytelling organization: A study of story performance in an office-supply firm. *Administrative Science Quarterly*, 36: 106–26.

Boli, J. 1989. *New Citizens for a New Society: The Institutional Origins of Mass Schooling in Sweden*. Oxford: Pergamon.

Boström, B. O. 1988. *Samtal om Demokrati*. Lund: Doxa.

Brady, D. W. 1988. *Critical Elections and Congressional Policy Making*. Stanford, CA: Stanford University Press.

Brand, K. W. 1990. Cyclical aspects of new social movements: Waves of cultural criticism and mobilization cycles of new middle-class radicalism. In R. J. Dalton and M. Kuechler, eds., *Challenging the Political Order*, pp. 23–42. Oxford: Oxford University Press.

Brehmer, B. 1980. In one word: Not from experience. *Acta Psychologica*, 45: 223–41.

Brief, A. P., and S. J. Motowidlo. 1986. Prosocial organizational behaviors. *Academy of Management Review*, 10: 710–25.

Broderick, A. 1970. *The French Institutionalists*. Cambridge, MA: Harvard University Press.

Brodkin, E. Z. 1990. Implementation as policy politics. In J. Palumbo and D. Calista, eds., *Implementation and the Policy Process*, pp. 107–19. New York: Greenwood Press.

Bromiley, P., and A. Marcus. 1987. Deadlines, routines, and change. *Policy Sciences* (The Netherlands), 20 (2): 85–103.

Brunsson, N. 1985. *The Irrational Organization*. Chichester: Wiley.

———. 1989. *The Organisation of Hypocrisy*. Chichester: Wiley.

Brunsson, N., and J. P. Olsen. 1993. *The Reforming Organization*. London: Routledge.

Burgelman, R. A. 1988. Strategy-making as a social learning process: The case of internal corporate venturing. *Interfaces*, 18: 74–85.

Burke, E. 1965. Speech to the electors of Bristol (November 3, 1774). *The Works of the Right Honorable Edmund Burke*. Rev. ed. 2: 89–98. Boston: Little, Brown.

Burkhart, R. E., and M. S. Lewis-Beck. 1994. Comparative democracy: The economic development thesis. *American Political Science Review*, 88: 903–10.

Burns, T. R., and H. Flam. 1987. *The Shaping of Social Organization: Social Rule System Theory with Applications.* Beverly Hills, CA: Sage.

Calhoun, C., ed. 1992. *Habermas and the Public Sphere.* Cambridge, MA: MIT Press.

Campbell, B. G. 1985. *Human Evolution: An Introduction to Man's Adaptations.* 3d. ed. Chicago: Aldine.

Carlsson, S. 1951. *Executive Behavior.* Stockholm: Strömberg.

Carroll, G. R., and J. R. Harrison. 1994. Historical efficiency of competition between organizational populations. *American Journal of Sociology*, 100: 720–49.

Cerny, P. G. 1990. *The Changing Architecture of Politics.* London: Sage.

Chapman, J. W., and W. A. Galston, eds. 1992. *Virtue.* Nomos XXXIV. New York: New York University Press.

Coase, R. H. 1994. *Essays on Economics and Economists.* Chicago: University of Chicago Press.

Cohen, C. 1971. The justification of democracy. *Monist*, 55: 1–28.

Cohen J. L., and A. Arato. 1992. *Civil Society and Political Theory.* Cambridge, MA: MIT Press.

Cohen, M. D., and J. G. March. 1986. *Leadership and Ambiguity.* 2d ed. Boston: Harvard Business School Press.

Cohen, M. D.; J. G. March; and J. P. Olsen. 1972. A garbage can model of organizational choice. *Administrative Science Quarterly*, 17: 1–25.

Cohen, W. M., and D. A. Levinthal. 1989. Innovation and learning: The two faces of R&D. *Economic Journal*, 99: 569–90.

Coleman, J. S. 1966a. Foundations for a theory of collective decisions. *American Journal of Sociology*, 71: 615–27.

———. 1966b. The possibility of a social welfare function. *American Economic Review*, 56 (5): 1105–22.

———. 1986. *Individual Interests and Collective Action.* Cambridge: Cambridge University Press.

———. 1990. *Foundations of Social Theory.* Cambridge, MA: Harvard University Press.

Collier, R. B., and D. Collier. 1991. *Shaping the Political Arena: Critical Junctures, the Labor Movement, and Regime Dynamics in Latin America.* Princeton, NJ: Princeton University Press.

Collins, S. L. 1989. *From Divine Cosmos to Sovereign State: An Intellectual History of Consciousness and the Idea of Order in Renaissance England.* Oxford: Oxford University Press.

Connolly, W. E. 1991. *Identity/Difference*. Ithaca, NY: Cornell University Press.

Coser, L. A. 1956. *The Social Functions of Conflict*. New York: Free Press.

Cox, G. W., and M. D. McCubbins. 1993. *Legislative Leviathan*. Berkeley: University of California Press.

Crick, B. 1983. *In Defence of Politics*. 2d ed. Harmondsworth: Penguin.

Crozier, M. 1964. *The Bureaucratic Phenomenon*. Chicago: University of Chicago Press.

Curley, S. P.; F. Yates; and R. A. Abrams. 1986. Psychological sources of ambiguity avoidance. *Organizational Behavior and Human Decision Processes*, 38: 230–56.

Cyert, R. M., and J. G. March. 1963. *A Behavioral Theory of the Firm*. Englewood Cliffs, NJ: Prentice-Hall.

———. 1992. *A Behavioral Theory of the Firm*. 2d ed.. Oxford: Basil Blackwell.

Dahl, R. A. 1956. *A Preface to Democratic Theory*. Chicago: University of Chicago Press.

———, ed. 1966. *Political Oppositions in Western Democracies*. New Haven, CT: Yale University Press.

———. 1980. The Moscow discourse: Fundamental rights in a democratic order. *Government and Opposition*, 15: 3–30.

———. 1982. *Dilemmas of Pluralist Democracy: Autonomy vs. Control*. New Haven, CT: Yale University Press.

———. 1985. *A Preface to Economic Democracy*. Oxford: Polity Press.

———. A., 1986. *Democracy, Liberty, and Equality*. Oslo: Norwegian University Press.

———. 1987. Sketches for a democratic utopia. *Scandinavian Political Studies*, 10 (3): 195–206.

———. 1989. *Democracy and Its Critics*. New Haven, CT: Yale University Press.

Dahl, R. A., and C. E. Lindblom. 1953. *Politics, Economics, and Welfare*. New York: Harper.

Dahl, R. A., and E. R. Tufte. 1973. *Size and Democracy*. Stanford, CA: Stanford University Press.

Dalton, R. J.; M. Kuechler; and W. Bürklin. 1990. The challenge of new movements. In R. J. Dalton and M. Kuechler, eds., *Challenging the Political Order*, pp. 3–20. Oxford: Oxford University Press.

David, P. A. 1985. Clio and the economics of QWERTY. *American Economic Review*, 75: 332–37.

Davis, L. 1964. The cost of realism: Contemporary restatements of democracy, *The Western Political Quarterly*, 17 (1): 37–46.

Davis, S. W.; K. Menon; and G. Morgan. 1982. The images that have shaped accounting theory. *Accounting, Organizations and Society*, 7 (4): 307–18.

Dawes, R. M. 1980. Social dilemma. *Annual Review of Psychology*, 31: 169–93.

Day, P., and R. Klein. 1987. *Accountabilities*. London: Tavistock.

DeBressen, C., and F. Amesse. 1991. Networks of innovators: A review and introduction to the issue. *Research Policy*, 20: 363–79.

de Jouvenal, B. 1949. *On Power*. New York: Viking Press.

Derlien, H. U. 1990. Genesis and structure of evaluation efforts in comparative perspective. In R. Rist, ed., *Program Evaluation and the Management of Government*. London: Transaction Publishers.

Deutsch, K. W. 1966. *The Nerves of Government*. New York: Free Press.

Dewey, J. 1927. *The Public and Its Problems*. Denver: Alan Swallow.

DiMaggio, P. J., and W. W. Powell. 1983. The iron cage revisited: Institutional isomorphism and collective rationality in organizational fields. *American Sociological Review*, 48: 147–60.

Di Palma, G. 1990. *To Craft Democracies*. Berkeley: University of California Press.

Dodgson, M. 1993. Organizational learning: A review of some literatures. *Organizational Studies*, 14 (3): 375–94.

Douglas, M. 1986. *How Institutions Think*. Syracuse, NY: Syracuse University Press.

———. 1990. Converging on autonomy: Anthropology and institutional economics. In O. E. Williamson, ed., *Organization Theory*, pp. 98–115. Oxford: Oxford University Press.

Dower, N. 1991. World poverty. In P. Singer, ed., *A Companion to Ethics*, pp. 273–83. Cambridge: Basil Blackwell.

Downs, A. 1957. *An Economic Theory of Democracy*. New York: Harper & Row

———. 1967. *Inside Bureaucracy*. Boston: Little, Brown.

Dryzek, J. S. 1990. *Discursive Democracy*. Cambridge: University of Cambridge Press.

Duncan, G., and S. Lukes. 1963. The new democracy, *Political Studies*, 11 (2): 156–77.

Dunn, J. 1990. *Interpreting Political Responsibility*. Princeton, NJ: Princeton University Press.

Dworkin, R. 1986. *Law's Empire*. Cambridge, MA: Belknap, Harvard University Press.

Dynes, R. R. 1970. *Organized Behavior in Disaster*. Lexington, MA: Heath Lexington Books.

Eggertsson, T. 1990. *Economic Behavior and Institutions*. Cambridge: Cambridge University Press.

Eisenstadt, S. N. 1987. *European Civilization in Comparative Perspective*. Oslo: Norwegian University Press.

Eisenstadt, S. N., and S. Rokkan, eds. 1973. *Building States and Nations*. Vols. 1 and 2. Beverly Hills, CA: Sage.

Elias, N. 1982 [1939]. *The Civilizing Process: State Formation and Civilization*. Oxford: Basil Blackwell.

Elster, J. 1983. Offentlighet og Deltakelse. In T. Bergh, ed., *Deltakerdemokratiet*. Oslo: Universitetsforlaget.

———. 1989a. *The Cement of Society*. Cambridge: Cambridge University Press.

———. 1989b. Demokratiets Verdigrunnlag og Verdikonflikter. In J. Elster, *Vitenskap og Politikk*, pp. 77–93. Oslo: Universitetsforlaget.

Elster, J., and R. Slagstad, eds. 1988. *Constitutionalism and Democracy*. Oslo: Norwegian University Press.

Eriksen, E. O. 1993. *Grenser for staten*. Oslo: Universitetsforlaget.

Eriksen, T. H. 1993. *Ethnicity and Nationalism*. London: Pluto Press.

Etheredge, L. 1985. *Can Governments Learn?* New York: Pergamon.

Evans, P.; D. Rueschemeyer; and T. Skocpol, eds. 1985. *Bringing the State Back In*. Cambridge: Cambridge University Press.

Farr, J. 1989. Understanding conceptual change politically. In T. Ball, J. Farr, and R. L. Hanson, eds., *Political Innovation and Political Change*, pp. 24–49. Cambridge: Cambridge University Press.

Fearon, J. D. 1994. Domestic political audiences and the escalation of international disputes. *American Political Science Review*, 88: 577–92.

Feldman, M. S. 1989. *Order Without Design: Information Production and Policy Making*. Stanford, CA: Stanford University Press.

Feldman, M. S., and J. G. March. 1981. Information in organizations as signal and symbol. *Administrative Science Quarterly* 26: 171–86.

Ferejohn, J. A. 1974. *Pork Barrel Politics: Rivers and Harbors Legislation, 1947–1968*. Stanford, CA: Stanford University Press.

———. 1986. Logrolling in an institutional context: A case study of food stamp legislation. In G. C. Wright, Jr., L. N. Reislebach, and L. C. Dodd, eds., *Congress and Policy Change*. New York: Agathon.

Festinger, L., *et al.* 1956. *When Prophecy Fails*. Minneapolis: University of Minnesota Press.

Finer, H. 1941. Administrative responsibility in democratic government. *Public Administration Review*, 1: 335–50.

Finley, M. I. 1973. *Democracy Ancient and Modern*. London: Chatto & Windus.

Fiol M., and M. Lyles. 1985. Organizational learning. *Academy of Management Review*, 10: 808–13.

Fischhoff, B. 1982. Debiasing. In D. Kahneman, P. Slovic, and A. Tversky, eds., *Judgment Under Uncertainty: Heuristics and Biases*, pp. 422–44. New York: Cambridge University Press.

Fiske, S. T., and S. E. Taylor. 1984. *Social Cognition*. Reading, MA: Addison-Wesley.

Flam, H., 1990a. Emotional "man" I: The emotional "man" and the problem of collective action. *International Sociology*, 5 (1): 39–56

———. 1990b. Emotional "man" II: Corporate actors as emotion-motivated emotion managers. *International Sociology*, 5 (2): 225–34.

Flora, P. 1983. *State, Economy, and Society in Western Europe, 1815–1975*. Frankfurt-am-Main: Campus.

Føllesdal, A. 1991. The significance of state borders for international distributive justice. Thesis, Harvard University, Department of Philosophy.

Fox, F., and B. M. Staw. 1979. The trapped administrator: The effects of job insecurity and policy resistance upon commitment to a course of action. *Administrative Science Quarterly*, 24: 449–71.

Frazer, N. 1992. Rethinking the public sphere: A contribution to a critique of actually existing democracy. In Craig Calhoun, ed., *Habermas and the Public Sphere*, pp. 109–42. Cambridge, MA: MIT Press.

Freud, S., and W. C. Bullitt. 1966. *Thomas Woodrow Wilson: A Psychological Study*. Boston: Houghton Mifflin.

Friedman, M. 1962. *Capitalism and Freedom*. Chicago: Chicago University Press.

Friedrich, C. J. 1939. Democracy and dissent. *Political Quarterly*, October–December, pp. 571–82.

———. 1940. Public policy and the nature of administrative responsibility. In C. J. Friedrich and E. S. Mason, eds., *Public Policy*. Cambridge, MA: Harvard University Press.

———. 1950. *Constitutional Government and Democracy*. Boston: Ginn & Company.

———. 1963. *Man and his Government*. New York: McGraw-Hill.

Fuller, L. L. 1971. *The Morality of Law*. New Haven, CT: Yale University Press.

Fürst, D. 1989. Reviving the discussion of the state: Changed demands on government and administration in Western industrial societies. In T. Ellwein *et al.*, eds., *Yearbook on Government and Public Administration, 1987/88*, pp. 205–24. Baden-Baden: Nomos.

Furubotn, E. G., and R. Richter, eds. 1984. The new institutional economics: A symposium. *Zeitschrift für die Gesamte Staatswissenschaft*, Special Issue, 140(1).

———. 1993. The new institutional economics: Recent progress, expanding frontiers. *Zeitschrift für die Gesamte Staatswissenschaft*, Special Issue, 149(1).

Gambling, T. 1977. Magic, accounting and morale. *Accounting, Organizations and Society*, 2 (2): 141–51.

Garrett, G., and B. R. Weingast. 1993. Ideas, interests and institutions: Constructing the European communities internal market. In J. Goldstein and R. O. Keohane, eds., *Ideas and Foreign Policy*, pp. 173–207. Ithaca, NY: Cornell University Press.

Gellner, E. 1993. *Nations and Nationalism*. Oxford: Blackwell.

Gergen, K. J. 1968. Personal consistency and the presentation of self. In C. Gordon and K. J. Gergen, eds., *The Self in Social Interaction*, 1: 299–308. New York: Wiley.

Gibbons, R. 1992. *Game Theory for Applied Economists*. Princeton, NJ: Princeton University Press.

Giddens, A. 1985. *The Nation State and Violence*. Oxford: Polity Press.

———. 1991. *The Consequences of Modernity*. Oxford: Polity Press.

Gilje, N. 1988. Det Gode Liv. Frihet eller Fellesskap. *Nytt Norsk Tidsskrift*, 5 (3): 92–107.

Gilligan T. W., and K. Krehbiel. 1993. The gains from exchange hypothesis of legislative organization. Unpublished manuscript, Graduate School of Business, Stanford University.

Glance, N. S., and B. A. Huberman. 1993. The outbreak of cooperation. *Journal of Mathematical Sociology*, 17: 281–302.

Goldstein, J., and Robert O. Keohane, eds. 1993. *Ideas and Foreign Policy*. Ithaca, NY: Cornell University Press.

Goldwin, R. A. 1986. Of men and angels: A search for morality in the constitution. In R. H. Horowitz, ed., *The Moral Foundations of the American Republic*, 3d ed., pp. 24–41. Charlottesville: University Press of Virginia.

Gould, C. C. 1988. *Rethinking Democracy*. Cambridge: Cambridge University Press.

Grafstein, R. 1992. *Institutional Realism*. New Haven, CT: Yale University Press.

Greber, E. R., and J. E. Jackson. 1993. Endogenous preferences and the study of institutions. *American Political Science Review*, 87: 639–56.

Greeley, A. M. 1967. *The Catholic Experience: An Interpretation of the History of American Catholicism*. Garden City, NY: Doubleday.

Greenfeld, L. 1992. *Nationalism: Five Roads to Modernity*. Cambridge, MA: Harvard University Press.

Greenwald, A. G. 1980. The totalitarian ego: Fabrication and revision of personal history. *American Psychologist*, 35: 603–18.

Gretschman, K. 1986. Solidarity and markets. In F. X. Kaufman, G. Majone, and V. Ostrom, eds., *Guidance, Control and Evaluation in the Public Sector*, pp. 387–405. Berlin: de Gruyter.

Gutman, A. 1985. Communitarian critics of liberalism. *Philosophy and Public Affairs* 14 (3): 308–22.

Habermas, J. 1981. *Theorie des Kommunikativen Handels*. Frankfurt: Suhrkamp.

———. 1988. Historical consciousness and post-traditional identity: Remarks on the Federal Republic's orientation to the West. *Acta Sociologica* 31 (1): 3–13.

———. 1989. Towards a communication-concept of rational collective will-formation: A thought experiment. *Ratio Juris*: 2 (2): 144–54.

———. 1992a. Further reflections on the public sphere. In Craig Calhoun, ed., *Habermas and the Public Sphere*, pp. 421–61. Cambridge, MA: MIT Press.

———. 1992b. *Faktizität und Geltung: Beiträge zur Diskurstheorie des rechts und des demokratischen Rechtsstaats*. Frankfurt-am-Main: Suhrkamp.

———. 1992c. Citizenship and national identity: Some reflections on the future of Europe. *Praxis International*, 12 (1): 1–19.

———. 1994. Three normative models of democracy. Unpublished manuscript.

Håkansson, H., ed. 1987. *Industrial Technological Development: A Network Approach*. London: Croom Helm.

———. 1992. Evolution processes in industrial networks. In B. Axelsson and G. Easton, eds., *Industrial Networks: A New View of Reality*, pp. 129–43. London: Routledge.

Hall, P. A. 1989. *The Political Power of Economic Ideas*. Princeton, NJ: Princeton University Press.

Hamilton, A.; J. Jay; and J. Madison, eds. 1964 [1787]. *The Federalist Papers*. New York: Pocket Books.

Hamilton, G. G. 1978. The structural sources of adventurism: The case of the California gold rush. *American Journal of Sociology*, 83: 1466–90.

Hannan, M. T., and J. Freeman. 1989. *Organizational Ecology*. Cambridge, MA: Harvard University Press.

Hannaway, J. 1989. *Managers Managing*. New York: Oxford University Press.

Hannerz, U. 1992. *Cultural Complexity*. New York: Columbia University Press.

————. 1993. State, culture and globalization. Unpublished manuscript, Uppsala.

Hanson, R. L. 1985. *The Democratic Imagination in America*. Princeton, NJ: Princeton University Press.

Hardin, G. 1968. The tragedy of the commons. *Science*, 162: 1243–48.

————. *Collective Action*. Baltimore, MD: Johns Hopkins University Press.

Harrison, J. R., and J. G. March. 1984. Decision making and Post-decision surprises. *Administrative Science Quarterly*, 29: 26–42.

Harsanyi, J. C. 1977. *Rational Behavior and Bargaining Equilibrium in Games and Social Situations*. Cambridge: Cambridge University Press.

Hart, O., and B. Holmström. 1987. The theory of contracts. In T. Bewley, ed., *Advances in Economic Theory*. Cambridge: Cambridge University Press.

Hayek, F. A. 1960. *The Constitution of Liberty*. London: Routledge & Kegan Paul.

Hechter, M.; K. D. Opp; and R. Wippler. 1990. *Social Institutions: Their Emergence, Maintenance and Effects*. New York: de Gruyter.

Heider, F. 1958. *The Psychology of Interpersonal Relations*. New York: Wiley.

Held, D. 1987. *Models of Democracy*. Oxford: Polity Press.

————. 1991. Democracy, the nation-state and the global system. In D. Held, ed., *Political Theory Today*, pp. 197–235. Oxford: Polity Press.

Henke, K. D., and D. Fürst. 1989. Between desire and reality: Ecological renewal of the institutionalized state. In T. Ellwein *et al.*, eds., *Yearbook on Government and Public Administration, 1987/88*, pp. 531–50. Baden-Baden: Nomos.

Herriott, S. R.; D. A. Levinthal; and J. G. March. 1985. Learning from experience in organizations. *American Economic Review*, 75: 298–302.

Herzog, D. 1986. Some questions of republicans. *Political Theory*, 14: 473–93.

————. 1989. *Happy Slaves: A Critique of Consent Theory*. Chicago: University of Chicago Press.

Higgins, W., and N. Apple. 1983. How limited is reformism? *Theory and Society*, 12: 603–30.

Hilb, C. 1994. Equality and the limit of liberty. In E. Laclau, ed., *The Making of Political Identities*, pp. 103–12. London: Verso.

Hinsley, F. H. 1986. *Sovereignty*. 2d ed. Cambridge: Cambridge University Press.

Hintze, O. 1968. The state in historical perspective. In R. Bendix, ed., *State and Society*, pp. 154–69. Boston: Little, Brown.

Hirschman, A. O. 1970. *Exit, Voice, and Loyalty*. Cambridge, MA: Harvard University Press.

————. 1991. *The Rhetoric of Reaction*. Cambridge, MA: Harvard University Press.

Hobsbawm, E. J. 1992. *Nations and Nationalism Since 1780*. 2d ed. Cambridge: Cambridge University Press.

Hobsbawm, E. J., and T. Ranger, eds. 1983. *The Invention of Tradition*. Cambridge: Cambridge University Press.

Hoffmann, S. 1993. Thoughts on the French nation today. *Dædalus* 122 (3): 63–79.

Hogg, M. A., and D. Abrams. 1988. *Social Identifications: A Social Psychology of Intergroup Relations and Group Processes*. London: Routledge.

Holland, J. H. 1975. *Adaptation in Natural and Artificial Systems*. Ann Arbor: University of Michigan Press.

Homans, G. C. 1961. *Social Behavior: Its Elementary Forms*. New York: Harcourt Brace & World.

Hood, C. 1995. Shock and long tenure: From second chance to near miss: Learning in UK public service reform? In J. P. Olsen and B. G. Peters, eds., *Lessons from Experience*. Pittsburgh, PA: University of Pittsburgh Press, in press.

Hook, G. D., and M. A. Weiner, eds. 1992. *The Internationalization of Japan*. London: Routledge.

Hotelling, H. 1990. *The Collected Economics Articles of Harold Hotelling*. New York: Springer Verlag.

Huber, G. P. 1991. Organizational learning: The contributing processes and the literatures. *Organization Science* 2 (1): 88–115.

Inglehart, R. 1990. *Culture Shift in Advanced Industrial Society*. Princeton, NJ: Princeton University Press.

Jackson, R. H. 1990. *Quasi-states: Sovereignty, International Relations and the Third World*. Cambridge: Cambridge University Press.

Jacobsson, B. 1993. Europeisering av Förvaltningen. *Statsvetenskaplig Tidsskrift*, 96 (2) 113–37.

Johansson, U. 1993. The concept of responsibility in housing management: A study of the construction of the responsible caretaker. Unpublished manuscript, University of Lund, Sweden.

Johnson, C. 1982. *Revolutionary Change*. 2d ed. Stanford, CA: Stanford University Press.

Jones, E. E. 1979. The rocky road from acts to dispositions. *American Psychologist*, 34: 107–17.

Kahneman, D., and D. Lovallo. 1993. Timid choices and bold forecasts: A cognitive perspective on risk taking. *Management Science*, 39: 17–31.

Kahneman, D., and A. Tversky. 1979. Prospect theory: An analysis of decision under risk. *Econometrica*, 47: 263–91.

Kaufman, H. 1960. *The Forest Ranger*. Baltimore, MD: Johns Hopkins University Press.

Kedourie, E. 1993. *Nationalism*. 4th ed. Oxford: Blackwell.

Keech, W. R. 1992. Rules, discretion, and accountability in macroeconomic policy making. *Governance*, 5 (3): 259–78.

Kelley, D. 1990. Civil science in the Renaissance: The problem of interpretation. In A. Pagden, ed., *The Languages of Political Theory in Early-Modern Europe*, pp. 57–78. Cambridge: Cambridge University Press.

Kenny, C., and M. McBurnett. 1994. An individual-level multi-equation model of expenditure effort in contested House elections. *American Political Science Review*, 88: 699–707.

Keohane, R. O. 1984. *After Hegemony*. Princeton, NJ: Princeton University Press.

Kiesler, A. C. 1971. *The Psychology of Commitment*. New York: Academic Press.

Kingdon, J. W. 1984. *Agendas, Alternatives, and Public Policies*. Boston: Little, Brown.

Kitcher, P. 1985. *Vaulting Ambition*. Cambridge, MA: MIT Press.

Klosko, G. 1993. Rawls' "political" philosophy and American democracy. *American Political Science Review*, 87: 348–59.

Knoke, D. 1990. *Political Networks: The Structural Perspective*. New York: Cambridge University Press.

Kogut, B.; W. Shan; and G. Walker. 1993. Knowledge in the network and the network as knowledge: The structuring of new industries. In G. Grabher, ed., *The Embedded Firm: On the Socioeconomics of Industrial Networks*, pp. 67–94. London: Routledge.

Kramer, R. M. 1991. Intergroup relations and organizational dilemmas: The role of categorization processes. *Research in Organizational Behavior*, 13: 191–228.

———. 1993. Cooperation and organizational identification. In J. K. Murnighan, ed., *Social Psychology in Organizations: Advances in Theory and Research*, pp. 244–68. Englewood Cliffs, NJ: Prentice Hall.

Krasner, S. D. 1988. Sovereignty: An institutional perspective. *Comparative Political Studies*, 21: 66–94.

———. 1991. Global communications and national power: Life on the Pareto frontier. *World Politics*, 43: 336–66.

Krehbiel, K. 1991. *Information and Legislative Organization*. Ann Arbor: University of Michigan Press.

Kreps, D. 1990. Corporate culture and economic theory. In J. Alt and K. Shepsle, eds., *Perspectives on Positive Political Economy*. New York: Cambridge University Press.

Kuhn, T. S. 1962. *The Structure of Scientific Revolutions*. Chicago: University of Chicago Press.

Kuran, T. 1988. The tenacious past: Theories of personal and collective conservatism. *Journal of Economic Behavior and Organizations*, 10: 143–71.

Lægreid, P., and J. P. Olsen. 1978. *Byråkrati og beslutninger*. Bergen: Universitetsforlaget.

———. 1984. Top civil servants in Norway: Key players on different teams. In E. N. Suleiman, ed., *Bureaucrats and Policy Making*. New York: Holmes & Meier.

Laitin, D. D. 1985. Hegemony and religious conflict: British imperial control and political cleavages in Yorubaland. In P. Evans, D. Rueschemeyer, and T. Skocpol, eds., *Bringing the State Back In*, pp. 285–316. Cambridge: Cambridge University Press.

Langer, E. J. 1975. The illusion of control. *Journal of Personality and Social Psychology*, 32: 311–28.

Lant, T. K. 1992. Aspiration adaptation: An empirical exploration. *Management Science*, 38: 623–44.

Lave, C. A., and J. G. March. 1975. *An Introduction to Models in the Social Sciences*. New York: Harper & Row.

Lawler, E. E., and J. G. Rhode. 1976. *Information and Control in Organizations*. Pacific Palisades, CA: Good Year Publishing.

Leca, J. 1992. Questions on citizenship. In C. Mouffe, ed., *Dimensions of Radical Democracy*, pp. 17–32. London: Verso.

Lefort, C. 1988. *Democracy and Political Theory*. Minneapolis: University of Minnesota Press.

Lehmbruch, G. 1984. Concertation and the structure of corporatist networks. In J. H. Goldthorpe, ed., *Order and Conflict in Contemporary Capitalism*. Oxford: Clarendon.

Lepsius, M. R. 1988. *Interessen, Ideen und Institutionen*. Opladen: Westdeutscher Verlag.

Levinthal, D. A. 1988. A survey of agency models of organizations. *Journal of Economic Behavior and Organization*, 9: 153–85.

Levinthal, D. A., and J. G. March. 1981. A model of adaptive organizational search. *Journal of Economic Behavior and Organization*, 2: 307–33.

———. 1993. The myopia of learning. *Strategic Management Journal*, 14: 95–112.

Levitt B., and J. G. March. 1988. Organizational learning. *Annual Review of Sociology*, 14: 319–40.

Levitt, B., and C. Nass. 1989. The lid on the garbage can: Institutional constraints on decision making in the technical core of college-text publishers. *Administrative Science Quarterly*, 34: 190–207.

Lindsay, A. D. 1914. The state in recent political theory. *Political Quarterly*, February, pp. 128–45.

Linz, J. J. 1978. *The Breakdown of Democratic Regimes: Crisis, Breakdown, and Reequilibration*. Baltimore: Johns Hopkins.

Lipset, S. M. 1990. *Continental Divide*. New York: Routledge.

Lipset, S. M., and S. Rokkan. 1967. Cleavage structures, party systems and voter alignments: An introduction. In S. M. Lipset and S. Rokkan, eds., *Party Systems and Voter Alignments*, pp. 1–64. New York: Free Press.

Locke, J. 1690. *Second Treatise on Civil Government*.

Lopes, L. L. 1987. Between hope and fear: The psychology of risk. *Advances in Experimental Social Psychology*, 20: 255–95.

Lott, B. E. 1961. Group cohesiveness: A learning phenomenon. *Journal of Social Psychology*, 55: 275–86.

Lounamaa, P. H., and J. G. March. 1987. Adaptive coordination of a learning team. *Management Science*, 33: 107–23.

Löwith K. 1982. *Max Weber and Karl Marx*. London: Allen & Unwin.

Lundquist, L. 1988. *Byråkratisk Etik*. Lund: Studentlitteratur.

MacArthur, D. 1964. *Reminiscences*. New York: McGraw-Hill.

Maccoby, E. E., and C. N. Jacklin. 1974. *The Psychology of Sex Differences*. Stanford, CA: Stanford University Press.

MacCormick, N., and O. Weinberger. 1986. *An Institutional Theory of Law*. Dordrecht: D. Reidel.

MacIntyre, A. 1984. *After Virtue*. 2d ed. Notre Dame, IN: University of Notre Dame Press.

———. 1988. *Whose Justice? Which Rationality?* Notre Dame, IN: University of Notre Dame Press.

Majone, G. 1988. Policy analysis and public deliberation. In R. B. Reich, ed., *The Power of Public Ideas*, pp. 157–78. Cambridge, MA: Ballinger.

Mandeville, B. 1755. *The Fable of the Bees*. Oxford: Clarendon Press, 1957.

Manin B. 1987. On legitimacy and deliberation. *Political Theory*, 15 (3): 338–68.

Mann, M., 1993. Nation-states in Europe and other continents: Diversifying, developing, not dying. *Dædalus*, 122 (3): 115–40.

Mansbridge, J. J., ed. 1990. *Beyond Self-Interest*. Chicago: University of Chicago Press.

Mansfield, E. 1985. How rapidly does new industrial technology leak out? *Journal of Industrial Economics*, 34: 217–23.

March J. G. 1970. Politics and the city. In K. Arrow, J. S. Coleman, A. Downs, and J. G. March, eds., *Urban Processes as Viewed by the Social Sciences*, pp. 23–37. Washington, DC: The Urban Institute Press.

———. 1971. The technology of foolishness. *Civiløkonomen* (Copenhagen), 18 (4): 4–12.

———. 1978. Bounded rationality, ambiguity, and the engineering of choice. *Bell Journal of Economics*, 9: 587–608.

———. 1980. Science, politics, and Mrs. Gruenberg. In *National Research Council in 1979*. Washington, DC: National Academy of Sciences.

———. 1981a. Footnotes to organizational change. *Administrative Science Quarterly*, 26: 563–77.

———. 1981b. Decisions in organizations and theories of choice. In A. Van de Ven and W. Joyce, eds., *Assessing Organizational Design and Performance*, pp. 205–44. New York: Wiley Interscience.

———. 1984. How we talk and how we act: Administrative theory and administrative life. In T. J. Sergiovanni and J. E. Corbally, eds., *Leadership and Organizational Cultures*. Urbana: University of Illinois Press.

———. 1987. Ambiguity and accounting: The elusive link between information and decision making. *Accounting, Organizations, and Society*, 12: 153–68.

———. 1988a. *Decision and Organizations*. Oxford: Basil Blackwell.

———. 1988b. Variable risk preferences and adaptive aspirations. *Journal of Economic Behavior and Organizations*, 9: 5–24.

———. 1991. Exploration and exploitation in organizational learning. *Organization Science*, 2: 71–87.

———. 1994a. The evolution of evolution. In J. Baum and J. Singh, eds., *The Evolutionary Dynamics of Organizations*, pp. 39–49. New York: Oxford University Press.

———. 1994b. *A Primer on Decision Making: How Decision Happen*. New York: Free Press.

———. 1994c. *Three Lectures on Efficiency and Adaptiveness in Organizations*. Helsinki: Swedish School of Economics.

March, J. G., and J. P. Olsen. 1975. The uncertainty of the past: Organizational learning under ambiguity. *European Journal of Political Research*, 3: 147–71.

———. 1976. *Ambiguity and Choice in Organizations*. Bergen, Norway: Universitetsforlaget.

———. 1983. Organizing political life: What administrative reorganization tells us about government. *American Political Science Review*, 77: 281–97.

———. 1984. The new institutionalism: Organizational factors in political life. *American Political Science Review*, 78: 734–49.

———. 1986a. Garbage can models of decision making in organizations. In J. G. March and R. Weissinger-Baylon, eds., *Ambiguity and Command: Organizational Perspectives on Military Decision Making*, pp. 11–35. Cambridge, MA: Ballinger.

———. 1986b. Popular sovereignty and the search for appropriate institutions. *Journal of Public Policy*, 6: 341–70.

———. 1989. *Rediscovering Institutions*. New York: Free Press.

March, J. G., and P. Romelaer. 1976. Position and presence in the drift of decisions. In J. G. March and J. P. Olsen, *Ambiguity and Choice in Organizations*, pp. 251–75. Bergen, Norway: Universitetsforlaget.

March, J. G., and G. Sevón. 1984. Gossip, information, and decision-making. In L. S. Sproull and J. P. Crecine, eds., *Advances in Information Processing in Organizations*: 1; 95–107. Greenwich, CT: JAI Press.

March, J. G., and Z. Shapira. 1987. Managerial perspectives on risk and risk taking. *Managerial Science*, 33: 1404–18.

———. 1992. Variable risk preferences and the focus of attention. *Psychological Review*, 99: 172–83.

March, J. G., and H. A. Simon. 1958. *Organizations*. New York: Wiley.

———. 1993. *Organizations*, 2d ed. Oxford: Blackwell Publishers.

March, J. G.; L. S. Sproull; and M. Tamuz. 1991. Learning from samples of one or fewer. *Organization Science*, 2: 1–13.

Marcus, G. E., and R. L. Hanson. 1993. *Reconsidering the Democratic Republic*. University Park: Pennsylvania State University Press.

Marcus, H., and R. B. Zajonc. 1985. The cognitive perspective in social psychology. In G. Lindzey and E. Aronson, eds., *The Handbook of Social Psychology*, 3d ed., vol. 1. Reading, MA: Addison-Wesley.

Marin, B., and R. Mayntz, eds. 1991. *Policy Networks*. Frankfurt-am-Main: Campus.

Marshall, T. H. 1950. *Citizenship and Social Class and Other Essays*. Cambridge: Cambridge University Press.

Martin, C. J. 1994. Basic instincts? Sources of firm preferences for national health reform. Unpublished manuscript, Boston University.

Mayntz, R. 1989. Political control and societal control problems: Notes on a theoretical paradigm. In T. Ellwein *et al.*, eds., *Yearbook on Government and Public Administration, 1987/88*, pp. 81–98. Baden-Baden: Nomos.

McCubbins, M. D.; R. G. Noll; and B. R. Weingast. 1987. Administrative procedures as instruments of political control. *Journal of Law, Economics and Organization*, 3 (2): 243–77.

McKeown, T. J. 1994. The epidemiology of corporate PAC formation, 1975–84. *Journal of Economic Behavior and Organization*, 24: 153–68.

McNeil, K., and J. D. Thompson. 1971. The regeneration of social organizations. *American Sociological Review*, 36: 624–37.

McPherson, M. S. 1982. Mill's moral theory and the problem of preference change. *Ethics*, 92 (January): 252–73.

Merkl, P. H. 1967. *Political Continuity and Change.* New York: Harper & Row.

Meyer, J. W. 1986. Social environments and organizational accounting. *Accounting, Organizations and Society,* 11 (4/5): 345–56.

Meyer, J. W., and B. Rowan. 1977. Institutionalized organizations: Formal structure as myth and ceremony. *American Journal of Sociology,* 83: 340–63.

Meyer, J. W., and W. R. Scott. 1983. *Organizational Environments: Ritual and Rationality.* Beverly Hills, CA: Sage.

Meyers, D. T. 1989. *Self, Society, and Personal Choice.* New York: Columbia University Press.

Mezias, S. J. 1990. An institutional model of organizational practice: Financial reporting at the Fortune 200. *Administrative Science Quarterly,* 35: 431–57.

Michels, R. 1968 [1915]. *Political Parties.* New York: Free Press.

Mill, J. S. 1956 [1859]. *On Liberty.* Indianapolis: Bobbs-Merrill.

———. 1962 [1861]. *Considerations on Representative Government.* South Bend, IN: Gateway Editions.

———. 1969. *Autobiography.* Boston: Houghton Mifflin.

Miller, D. 1990. *Market, State and Community.* Oxford: Clarendon Press.

Miller, N. 1983. Pluralism and social choice. *American Political Science Review,* 77: 734–47.

Milward, A. S. 1992. *The European Rescue of the Nation State.* London: Routledge.

Miner, A. S. 1990. Structural evolution through idiosyncratic jobs: The potential for unplanned learning. *Organization Science,* 1: 195–210.

Mintzberg, H. 1973. *The Nature of Managerial Work.* New York: Harper & Row.

Moe, T. 1984. The new economics of organization. *American Journal of Political Science,* 28 (4): 739–77.

———. 1990. Political institutions: The neglected side of the story. *Journal of Law, Economics and Organization,* 6: 213–66.

Moe, T., and M. Caldwell. 1993. The institutional foundations of democratic government: A comparison of presidential and parliamentary systems. Unpublished manuscript, Stanford University.

Moore, B., Jr. 1966. *Social Origins of Dictatorship and Democracy.* Boston: Beacon Press.

Morengo, L. 1993. Knowledge distribution and coordination in organizations: On some social aspects of the exploitation vs. exploration trade-off. *Revue Internationale de Systémique,* 7: 553–71.

Morley, F., ed. 1958. *Essays on Individuality*. Philadelphia: University of Pennsylvania Press.

Morrisey, W. 1986. The moral foundations of the American Republic: An introduction. In R. H. Horowitz, ed., *The Moral Foundations of the American Republic*, 3d ed., pp. 1–23. Charlottesville: University Press of Virginia.

Mouffe, C., ed. 1992. *Dimensions of Radical Democracy*. London: Verso.

Mowery, D. C., and N. Rosenberg. 1989. *Technology and the Pursuit of Economic Growth*. New York: Cambridge University Press.

Mulhall, S., and A. Swift. 1992. *Liberals and Communitarians*. Oxford: Blackwell.

Muller, E. N.; T. O. Jukan; and M. A. Seligson. 1982. Diffuse political support and anti-system behavior: A comparative analysis. *American Journal of Political Science*, 26: 240–64.

Muller, E. N., and M. A. Seligson. 1994. Civic culture and democracy: The question of causal relationships. *American Political Science Review*, 88: 635–52.

Myrdal, G. 1967. *Beyond the Welfare State*. New York: Bantam.

Næss, A. 1968. *Democracy, Ideology and Objectivity*. Oslo: Oslo University Press.

Nauta, L. 1992. Changing conceptions of citizenship. *Praxis International*, 12: 20–34.

Nelkin, D. 1979. Scientific knowledge, public policy, and democracy: A review essay. *Knowledge*, 1 (1): 106–22.

Nisbett, R. E., and L. Ross. 1980. *Human Inference: Strategies and Shortcomings of Social Judgment*. New York: Appleton-Century-Crofts.

Nisbett, R. E.; H. Zukier; and R. Lemley. 1981. The dilution effect: Nondiagnostic information. *Cognitive Psychology*, 13: 248–77.

Niskanen, W. A. 1971. *Bureaucracy and Representative Government*. Chicago: Rand McNally.

North, D. C. 1981. *Structure and Change in Economic History*. New York: Norton.

———. 1986. The new institutional economics. *Zeitschrift für die Gesamte Staatswissenschaft: Journal of Institutional and Theoretical Economics*, 142: 230–37.

———. 1990. *Institutions, Institutional Change and Economic Performance*. Cambridge: Cambridge University Press.

Nozick, R. 1974. *Anarchy, State and Utopia*. New York: Basic Books.

Nussbaum, M. 1990. Aristotelian social democracy. In R. B. Douglass, G. M. Mara, and H. S. Richardson, eds., *Liberalism and the Good*, pp. 203–52. New York: Routledge.

Oakes, P. J., and J. C. Turner. 1980. Social categorization and intergroup behavior: Does minimal intergroup discrimination make social identity more positive? *European Journal of Social Psychology*, 10: 295–301.

OECD. 1991. *Public Management Service, Public Management Committee: Programme Policy and Planning*. Paris: Organisation for Economic Co-operation and Development, PUMA 3/ADD1 (March 19).

Offe, C. 1989. The theory of the state in search of its subject matter: Observations on current debates. In T. Ellwein *et al.*, eds., *Yearbook on Government and Public Administration, 1987/88*, pp. 247–56. Baden-Baden: Nomos.

Offe, C., and U. K. Preuss. 1991. Democratic institutions and moral resources. In D. Held, ed., *Political Theory Today*, pp. 143–71. Oxford: Polity Press.

O'Halpin, E. 1989. *Head of the Civil Service: A Study of Sir Warren Fisher*. London: Routledge.

Oliver, P. E., and G. Marwell. 1988. The paradox of group size in collective action: A theory of the critical mass. *American Sociological Review*, 53: 1–8.

Olsen, J. P. 1976. Choice in an organized anarchy. In J. G. March and J. P. Olsen, *Ambiguity and Choice in Organizations*, pp. 83–139. Bergen, Norway: Universitetsforlaget.

———. 1983. *Organized Democracy*. Bergen: Universitetsforlaget.

———. 1990. *Demokrati på svenska*. Stockholm: Carlssons.

———. 1992a. Analyzing institutional dynamics. *Staatswissenschaften und Staatspraxis* 2: 247–71.

———. 1992b. Rethinking and reforming the public sector. In B. Kohler-Koch, ed. *Staat und Demokratie in Europa*, 175–278. Opladen: Leske & Budrich.

Olsen, J. P. 1995. Norway: Reluctant reformer, slow learner—or another triumph of the tortoise? In J. P. Olsen and B. G. Peters, eds., *Lessons from Experience. Experiential Learning in Administrative Reforms in Eight Democracies*. Pittsburgh, PA: University of Pittsburgh Press, in press.

Olsen, J. P., and B. Aardal. 1989. Under Publikums Årvåkne Øyne. In J. P. Olsen ed., *Petroleum og Politikk*, pp. 167–92. Oslo: Tano.

Olsen, J. P., and B. G. Peters, eds. 1995a. *Lessons from Experience: Experiential Learning in Administrative Reforms in Eight Democracies*. Pittsburgh, PA: University of Pittsburgh Press, in press.

———. 1995b. Learning from experience? In J. P. Olsen and B. G. Peters. *Lessons from Experience: Experiential Learning in Administrative Reforms in Eight Democracies*. Pittsburgh, PA: University of Pittsburgh Press, in press.

O'Reilly, C. A. 1983. The use of information in organizational decision making: A model and some propositions. In L. Cummings and B. Staw, eds., *Research in Organizational Behavior*, pp. 103–39. Greenwich, CT: JAI Press.

Organ, D. W. 1988. *Organizational Citizenship Behavior: The Good Soldier Syndrome*. Lexington, MA: D. C. Heath.

Orlie, M. A. 1994. Thoughtless assertion and political deliberation. *American Political Science Review*, 88: 684–95.

Orren, K., and S. Skowronek. 1994. Beyond the iconography of order: Notes for a "new institutionalism." In L. C. Dodd and C. Jillson, eds., *The Dynamics of American Politics*, pp. 311–30. Boulder, CO: Westview Press.

Oster, G. F., and E. O. Wilson. 1984. A critique of optimization theory in evolutionary biology. In E. Sover, ed., *Conceptual Issues in Evolutionary Biology*, pp. 271–88. Cambridge, MA: MIT Press.

Østerud, Ø. 1979. *Det Planlagte Samfunn*. Oslo: Gyldendal.

Ostrom, E. 1990. *Governing the Commons*. Cambridge: Cambridge University Press.

Page, B. I., and R. Y. Shapiro. 1993. The rational public and democracy. In G. E. Marcus and R. L. Hanson, eds., *Reconsidering the Democratic Public*, pp. 35–64. University Park: Pennsylvania State University Press.

Pateman, C. 1970. *Participation and Democratic Theory*. Cambridge: Cambridge University Press.

Pennock, J. R. 1979. *Democratic Political Theory*. Princeton, NJ: Princeton University Press.

Perry, M. J. 1988. *Morality, Politics and Law*. Oxford: Oxford University Press.

Peters, B. G. 1988. Introduction. In C. Campbell and B. G. Peters, eds., *Organizing Governance, Governing Organizations*, pp. 3–15. Pittsburgh: University of Pittsburgh Press.

———. 1995. Learning from experience about administrative reform: The United States. In J. P. Olsen and B. G. Peters, eds., *Lessons from Experience. Experiential Learning in Administrative Reforms in Eight Democracies*. Pittsburgh PA: University of Pittsburgh Press, in press.

Petracca, M. P. 1991. The rational choice approach to politics: A challenge to democratic theory. *The Review of Politics*, 53: 289–319.

Pitkin, H. 1967. *The Concept of Representation*. Berkeley: University of California Press.

———. 1981. Justice: On relating private and public political theory. *Political Theory*, 9: 327–52.

Polanyi, K. 1944. *The Great Transformation*. Boston: Beacon Press.

Polanyi, M. 1962. The republic of science: Its political and economic theory. *Minerva*, 1 (1): 54–73.

Powell, W. W. 1978. Publishers' decision-making: What criteria do they use in deciding which books to publish? *Social Research*, 45: 227–52.

Powell, W. W., and P. J. DiMaggio, eds. 1991. *The New Institutionalism in Organizational Analysis*. Chicago: University of Chicago Press.

Powell, W. W., and L. Smith-Doerr. 1994. Networks and economic life. In N. J. Smelser and R. Swedberg, eds., *Handbook of Economic Sociology*, pp. 368–402. Princeton, NJ: Princeton University Press.

Pressman, J. L., and A. Wildavsky. 1973. *Implementation*. Berkeley: University of California Press.

Quarantelli, E. L., and R. R. Dynes. 1977. Responses to social crisis and disaster. *Annual Review of Sociology*, 3: 23–49.

Rawls, J. 1971. *A Theory of Justice*. Cambridge, MA: Harvard University Press.

———. 1980. Kantian constructivism in moral theory: Rational and full autonomy. *The Journal of Philosophy*, 77 (9): 515–72.

———. 1985. Justice as fairness: Political not metaphysical. *Philosophy and Public Affairs*, 14: 223–51.

———. 1987. The idea of an overlapping consensus. *Oxford Journal of Legal Studies*, 7: 1–25.

———. 1988. The priority of right and the ideas of the good. *Philosophy and Public Affairs*, 17: 251–76.

———. 1993. *Political Liberalism*. New York: Columbia University Press.

Reich, R. B., ed. 1988. *The Power of Public Ideas*. Cambridge, MA: Ballinger.

Rice, E. F., Jr. 1970. *The Foundations of Early Modern Europe, 1460–1559*. New York: Norton.

Riker, W. H. 1962. *The Theory of Political Coalitions*. New Haven, CT: Yale University Press.

———. 1980. Implications from the disequilibrium of majority rule for the study of institutions. *American Political Science Review*, 74: 432–46.

———. 1982. *Liberalism Against Populism*. San Francisco: W. H. Freeman.

———. 1984. The heresthetics of constitution-making: The presidency in 1787—with comments on determinism and rational choice. *American Political Science Review*, 78: 1–16.

———. 1986. *The Art of Political Manipulation*. New Haven, CT: Yale University Press.

———. 1993. *Agenda Formation*. Ann Arbor: University of Michigan Press.

Rodger, J. J. 1985. On the degeneration of the public sphere. *Political Studies*, 33: 203–17.

Rogowski, R. 1993. Comparative politics. In A. W. Finifter, ed., *The State of the Discipline*. Washington, DC: American Political Science Association.

Rokkan S. 1970. *Citizens, Elections, Parties*. Oslo: Universitetsforlaget.

———. 1975. Dimensions of state formation and nation-building: A possible paradigm for research on variations in Europe. In C. Tilly, ed., *The Formation of Nation States in Europe*, pp. 562–600. Princeton, NJ: Princeton University Press.

———. 1987. *Stat, nasjon, klas*. Oslo: Universitetsforlaget.

Romer, P. 1986. Increasing returns and long-run growth. *Journal of Political Economy*, 94: 1002–36.

Romzek, B. S., and M. J. Dubnick. 1987. Accountability in the public sector: Lessons from the *Challenger* disaster. *Public Administration Review*, 47: 227–38.

Roper, J. 1989. *Democracy and Its Critics*. London: Unwin, Hyman.

Rose, R. 1993. *Lesson-drawing in Public Policy*. Chatham, NJ: Chatham House.

Ross, L. 1977. The intuitive psychologist and his shortcomings: Distortions in the attribution process. *Advances in Experimental Social Psychology*, 10: 174–221.

Rothstein, B. 1992. Labor-market institutions and working class strength. In S. Steinmo, K. Thelen, and F. Longstreeth, eds., *Structuring Politics: Historical Institutionalism in Comparative Analysis*, pp. 33–56. Cambridge: Cambridge University Press.

Rozelle, R. M., and J. C. Baxter. 1981. Influence of role pressures on the perceiver: Judgments of videotaped interviews varying judge accountability and responsibility. *Journal of Applied Psychology*, 66: 437–41.

Sabatier, P. A. 1991. Two decades of implementation research: From control and guidance to learning. In F.-X. Kaufmann, ed., *The Public Sector: Challenge for Coordination and Learning*, pp. 257–70. Berlin: deGruyter.

Sabine, G. H. 1952. The two democratic traditions. *The Philosophical Review*, pp. 493–511.

Sagan, S. D. 1993. *The Limits of Safety: Organizations, Accidents, and Nuclear Weapons*. Princeton, NJ: Princeton University Press.

Salancik, G. R. 1977. Commitment and control of organizational behavior and belief. In B. M. Staw and G. R. Salancik, eds., *New Directions in Organizational Behavior*, pp. 1–54. Chicago: St. Clair.

Samuelson, W., and R. Zeckhauser. 1987. Status quo bias in decision making. *Journal of Risk and Uncertainty*, 1: 7–59.

Sandel, M. J. 1982. *Liberalism and the Limits of Justice*. Cambridge: Cambridge University Press.

———. 1984. The procedural republic and the unencumbered self. *Political Theory*, 12 (1): 81–96.

Sarbin, T. R., and V. L. Allen. 1968. Role theory. In G. Lindzey and E. Aronson, eds., *Handbook of Social Psychology*, 2nd ed., pp. 488–567. Reading, MA: Addison-Wesley.

Sartori, G. 1987. *The Theory of Democracy Visited*. Vols. 1 and 2. Chatham, NJ: Chatham House.

Sbragia, A. M., ed. 1992. *Euro-Politics: Institutions and Policymaking in the "New" European Community*. Washington, DC: Brookings.

Schattschneider, E. E. 1960. *The Semi-Sovereign People*. New York: Holt, Rinehart & Winston.

Schelling, T. C. 1960. *The Strategy of Conflict*. Cambridge, MA: Harvard University Press.

———. 1978. *Micromotives and Macrobehavior*. New York: W. W. Norton.

Schlenker, B. R. 1982. Translating actions into attitudes: An identity-analytic approach to the explanation of social conduct. *Advances in Experimental Social Psychology*, 15: 194–248.

Schlesinger, P. 1991. Media, the political order and national identity. *Media, Culture and Society*, 13: 297–308.

Schmitter, P. 1988. Corporative democracy: Oxymoronic? Just plain moronic? Or a promising way out of the present impasse? Unpublished manuscript, Stanford University.

Schmitter, P., and G. Lehmbruch, eds. 1979. *Trends Toward Corporatist Intermediation*. Beverly Hills, CA: Sage.

Schrader, S. 1991. Informal technology transfer between firms: Cooperation through information trading. *Research Policy*, 20: 153–70.

Schulz, M. 1992. A depletion of assets model of organizational learning. *Journal of Mathematical Sociology*, 17: 145–73.

Schumpeter, J. A. 1934. *The Theory of Economic Development*. Cambridge, MA: Harvard University Press.

———. 1942. *Capitalism, Socialism and Democracy*. New York: Harper & Row.

Scott, M. B., and S. Lyman. 1968. Accounts. *American Sociological Review*, 33(1): 46–62.

Scott, W. R. 1987. The adolescence of institutional theory. *Administrative Science Quarterly*, 32: 493–511.

Scott, W. R., and J. W. Meyer. 1994. *Institutional Environments and Organizations*. Thousand Oaks, CA: Sage.

Searing, D. D. 1991. Roles, rules and rationality in the new institutionalism. *American Political Science Review*, 85: 1239–60.

Selznick, P. 1949. *TVA and the Grass Roots*. Berkeley: University of California Press.

———. 1992. *The Moral Commonwealth*. Berkeley: University of California Press.

Sen, A. 1990. *On Ethics and Economics*. Oxford: Blackwell

———. 1992. *Inequality Reexamined*. Cambridge, MA: Harvard University Press.

Sened, I. 1991. Contemporary theory of institutions in perspective. *Journal of Theoretical Politics*, 3 (4): 379–402.

Senge, P. M. 1990. *The Fifth Discipline: The Art and Practice of the Learning Organization*. New York: Doubleday.

Shapira, Z. 1995. *Risk Taking: A Managerial Perspective*. New York: Russell Sage.

Shepsle, K. A. 1986. Institutional equilibrium and equilibrium institutions. In H. Weisberg, ed., *Political Science: The Science of Politics*, pp. 51–82. New York: Agathon.

———. 1989. Studying institutions: Some lessons from the rational choice approach. *Journal of Theoretical Politics*, 1: 131–47.

———. 1990. *Perspectives on Positive Economy*. Cambridge: Cambridge University Press.

Shepsle, K. A., and B. Weingast. 1987. The institutional foundations of committee power. *American Political Science Review*, 81: 85–104.

Sherif, M., and H. Cantril. 1947. *The Psychology of Ego-Involvements*. New York: Wiley.

Shklar, J. N. 1990. *The Faces of Injustice*. New Haven, CT: Yale University Press.

Sills, D. L. 1957. *The Volunteers*. New York: Free Press.

Singh, J. V. 1986. Performance, slack, and risk taking in organizational decision making. *Academy of Management Journal*, 29: 562–85.

Sitkin, S. B. 1986. Secrecy in organizations: Determinants of secrecy behavior among engineers in three Silicon Valley semiconductor firms. Ph.D. dissertation, Stanford University.

Skinner, Q. 1989. The state. In T. Ball, J. Farr, and R. L. Hanson, eds., *Political Innovation and Conceptual Change*, pp. 90–131. Cambridge: Cambridge University Press.

Skowronek, S. 1982. *Building a New American State*. Cambridge: Cambridge University Press.

Slagstad, R. 1981. Liberalisme og demokrati. *Historisk Tidsskrift*. (60): 283–305.

Smirich, L., and G. Morgan. 1982. Leadership: The management of meaning. *The Journal of Applied Behavioral Science*, 10(3): 257–73.

Smith, A. 1776. *An Inquiry into the Nature and Causes of the Wealth of Nations*. London: Printed for W. Strahan and T. Cadell.

Smith, A. D. 1991. *National Identity*. London: Penguin.

———. 1992. National identity and the idea of European unity. *International Affairs*, 68: 55–76.

Smith, D., and Ø. Østerud. 1994. Nation-state, nationalism and political identity. Unpublished manuscript, Arena Project, Oslo.

Smith, R. M. 1988. Political jurisprudence, the "new institutionalism" and the future of public law. *American Political Science Review*, 82: 89–108.

Sörlin, S. 1994. *De Lärdas Republik*. Malmö: Liber-Hermods.

Spradley, J. P., and B. J. Mann. 1975. *The Cocktail Waitress*. New York: Wiley.

Spragens, T. A., Jr. 1990. *Reason and Democracy*. Durham, NC: Duke University Press.

Spring, J. 1992. *Images of American Life: A History of Ideological Management in Schools, Movies, Radio, and Television*. Albany: SUNY Press.

Staw, B. M. 1976. Knee-deep in the Big Muddy: A study of escalating commitment to a chosen course of action. *Organizational Behavior and Human Performance*, 16: 27–44.

Staw, B. M.; L. E. Sandelands; and J. E. Dutton. 1981. Threat-rigidity effects in organizational behavior: A multilevel analysis. *Administrative Science Quarterly*, 26: 501–24.

Steinmo, S. K. 1993. *Taxation and Democracy*. New Haven, CT: Yale University Press.

Steinmo, S.; K. Thelen; and F. Longstreeth, eds. 1992. *Structuring Politics: Historical Institutionalism in Comparative Analysis*. Cambridge: Cambridge University Press.

Stinchcombe, A. L. 1965. Social structure and organizations. In J. G. March, ed., *Handbook of Organizations*. Chicago: Rand McNally.

Stone, D. A. 1988. *Policy Paradox and Political Reason*. Glenview, IL: Scott-Foresman

Sugden, R. 1986. *The Economics of Rights, Co-operation and Welfare*. Oxford: Basil Blackwell.

Sunstein, C. 1990. *After the Rights Revolution*. Cambridge, MA: Harvard University Press.

Szporluk, R. 1994. After empire: What? *Dædalus*, 123 (3): 21–39.

Tajfel, H. 1972. La catégorisation sociale. In S. Moscovici, ed., *Introduction à la Psychologie Sociale*, vol. 1. Paris: Larousse.

———, ed. 1978. *Differentiation Between Social Groups: Studies in the Social Psychology of Intergroup Relations*. London: Academic Press.

————. 1981. *Human Groups and Social Categories: Studies in Social Psychology*. Cambridge: Cambridge University Press.

Tamuz, M. 1988. Monitoring dangers in the air: Studies in ambiguity and information. Thesis, Stanford University.

Taylor, C. 1985. *Philosophy and the Human Sciences*. Cambridge: Cambridge University Press.

————. 1992. The politics of recognition. In A. Gutman, ed., *Multiculturalism and "The Politics of Recognition,"* pp. 25–73. Princeton, NJ: Princeton University Press.

Taylor, M. 1975. The theory of collective choice. In F. I. Greenstein and N. W. Polsby, eds., *Handbook of Political Science*. Vol. 3, pp. 413–81. Reading, MA: Addison-Wesley.

————. 1987. *The Possibility of Cooperation*. Cambridge: Cambridge University Press.

Taylor, S. 1984. *Making Bureaucracies Think*. Stanford, CA: Stanford University Press.

Taylor, S. E., and J. D. Brown. 1988. Illusions and well-being: A social psychological perspective on mental health. *Psychological Bulletin*, 103: 193–210.

Tetlock, P. E. 1983a. Accountability and the complexity of thought. *Journal of Personality and Social Psychology*, 45: 74–83.

————. 1983b. Accountability and the perseverance of first impressions. *Social Psychology Quarterly*, 46: 285–92.

————. 1985. Accountability: A social check on the fundamental attribution error. *Social Psychological Quarterly*, 48: 227–36.

————. 1992. The impact of accountability on judgment and choice: Toward a social contingency model. *Advances in Experimental Social Psychology*, 25: 331–76.

Tetlock, P. E., and R. Boettger. 1989. Accountability: A social magnifier of the dilution effect. *Journal of Personality and Social Psychology: Attitudes and Social Cognition*, 57: 388–98.

————. 1994. Accountability amplifies the status quo effect when change creates victims. *Journal of Behavioral Decision Making*, 7: 1–23.

Tetlock, P. E., and J. Kim. 1987. Accountability and overconfidence in a personality prediction task. *Journal of Personality and Social Psychology: Attitudes and Social Cognition*, 52: 700–709.

Tetlock, P. E.; L. Skitka; and R. Boettger. 1989. Social and cognitive strategies of coping with accountability: Conformity, complexity, and bolstering. *Journal of Personality and Social Psychology*, 57: 632–41.

Teubner, G. 1992. De collisione discursuum: Communicative rationalities in law, morality and politics. Bremen/Firenze: Paper for the conference

"Jürgen Habermas: On his Recent Contributions to Legal Theory," Cardozo Law School, New York, September 20–21.

———. 1993. *Law as an Autopoietic System*. Oxford: Blackwell.

Thelen, K., and S. Steinmo. 1992. Historical institutionalism in comparative politics. In S. Steinmo, K. Thelen, and F. Longstreeth, eds., *Structuring Politics: Historical Institutionalism in Comparative Analysis*, pp. 1–32. Cambridge: Cambridge University Press.

Thigpen, R. B., and L. A. Downing. 1987. Liberalism and the communitarian critique. *The American Journal of Political Science*, 31 (3): 637–56.

Thomas, G. M., *et al.* 1987. *Institutional Structure: Constituting State, Society, and the Individual*. Beverly Hills, CA: Sage.

Thompson, D. F. 1980. Moral responsibility of public officials: The problem of many hands. *American Political Science Review*, 74: 905–16.

———. 1987. *Political Ethics and Public Office*. Cambridge, MA: Harvard University Press.

Thompson, J. D. 1967. *Organizations in Action*. New York: McGraw-Hill.

Thompson, M.; R. Ellis; and A. Wildavsky. 1990. *Cultural Theory*. Boulder, CO: Westview Press.

Tilly, C., ed. 1975. *The Formation of National States in Western Europe*. Princeton, NJ: Princeton University Press.

———. 1993. *Coercion, Capital, and European States*. Cambridge, MA: Blackwell.

Tribe, L. H. 1972. Policy science: Analysis or ideology? *Philosophy and Public Affairs*, 2(1): 66–110.

Turner, B. S. 1990. Outline of a theory of citizenship. *Sociology*, 24 (2): 189–217.

Turner, J. C. 1975. Social comparison and social identity: Some prospects for intergroup behavior. *European Journal of Social Psychology*, 5: 5–34.

———. 1985. Social categorization and the self concept: A social cognitive theory of group behavior. In E. J. Lawler, ed., *Advances in Group Processes*, 2: 77–122. Greenwich, CT: JAI Press.

Turner, J. C.; M. A. Hogg; P. J. Oakes; S. D. Reicher; and M. Wetherell. 1987. *Rediscovering the Social Group: A Self-Categorization Theory*. Oxford: Blackwell.

Tussman, J. 1960. *Obligation and the Body Politic*. London: Oxford University Press.

Tyre, M. J., and W. J. Orlikowski. 1994. Windows of opportunity: Temporal patterns of technological adaptation in organizations. *Organization Science*, 5: 98–118.

Van Maanen, J. 1973. Observations on the making of policemen. *Human Organization*, 32: 407–18.

Van Maanen, J. 1976. Breaking in: Socialization to work. In R. Dubin, ed. *Handbook of Work, Organization, and Society*, pp. 67–130. Chicago: Rand McNally.

Viljoen, S. 1974. *Economic Systems in World History*. London: Longman.

Viroli, M. 1992. *From Politics to Reason of State*. Cambridge: Cambridge University Press.

von Hippel, E. 1988. *Sources of Innovation*. New York: Oxford University Press.

Wagner, P., *et al.* 1991. *Social Sciences and Modern States*. Cambridge: Cambridge University Press.

Waligorski, C. P. 1990. *The Political Theory of Conservative Economists*. Lawrence: University Press of Kansas.

Walzer, M. 1983. *Spheres of Justice*. New York: Basic Books.

———. 1984. The resources of American liberalism: Liberalism and the art of separation. *Political Theory*, 12 (3): 315–30.

———. 1989. Citizenship. In T. Ball, J. Farr, and R. L. Hanson, eds., *Political Innovation and Political Change*, pp. 211–19. Cambridge: Cambridge University Press.

Watkins, S. C. 1991. *From Provinces into Nations: Demographic Integration in Western Europe, 1870–1960*. Princeton, NJ: Princeton University Press.

Weaver, R. K., and B. A. Rockman, eds. 1993. *Do Institutions Matter?* Washington, DC: Brookings.

Weber, M. 1978. *Economy and Society*. Eds. G. Roth and C. Wittich. Berkeley: University of California Press.

Weiner, S. 1976. Participation, deadlines, and choice. In J. G. March and J. P. Olsen, eds., *Ambiguity and Choice in Organizations*. Bergen: Universitetsforlaget.

Weingast, B. R., and W. Marshall. 1988. The industrial organization of Congress. *Journal of Political Economy*, 96: 132–63.

Weiss, C. H. 1979. Efforts at bureaucratic reform: What have we learned? In C. H. Weiss and A. Barton, eds., *Making Bureaucracies Work*, pp. 7–26. London: Sage.

Wendt, A. 1994. Collective identity formation and the international state. *American Political Science Review*, 88 (2): 384–96.

West, R. 1988. Economic man and literary woman: One contrast. *Mercer Law Review*, 39 (3): 867–78.

Whyte, W. H., Jr. 1957. *The Organization Man*. Garden City, NY: Doubleday.

Wildavsky, A. 1979. *Speaking Truth to Power: The Art and Craft of Policy Analysis*. Boston: Little Brown.

———. 1987. Choosing preferences by constructing institutions: A cultural theory of preference formation. *American Political Science Review*, 81: 3–22.

Wildavsky, A. 1988. *Searching for Safety*. New Brunswick, NJ: Transaction Press.

Wildavsky, A., and E. Tenenbaum. 1980. *The Politics of Mistrust*. Beverly Hills, CA: Sage.

Willke, H. 1989. Disenchantment of the state: Outline of a systems theoretical augmentation. In T. Ellwein *et al.*, eds., *Yearbook on Government and Public Administration*, pp. 225–45. Baden-Baden: Nomos.

Wittrock, B. 1992. Discourse and discipline: Political science as project and profession. In M. Dierkes and B. Biervert, eds., *European Social Science in Transition*, pp. 268–307. Frankfurt-am-Main: Campus.

Wolff, R. P. 1970. *In Defense of Anarchism*. New York: Harper & Row.

Wolin, S. 1960. *Politics and Vision: Continuity and Innovation in Western Political Thought*. Boston: Little, Brown.

———. 1981. The new public philosophy. *Democracy*, 1 (4): 23–36.

———. 1989. *The Presence of the Past: Essays on the State and the Constitution*. Baltimore: Johns Hopkins University Press.

Wood, B. D. 1992. Modeling federal implementation as a system: The Clean Air case. *American Journal of Political Science*, 36: 40–67.

World Bank. 1991. *The Reform of Public Sector Management. Lessons from Experience*. Washington, DC: The World Bank, Country Economics Department (PRS, 18).

Wrong, D. 1961. The oversocialized conception of man in modern sociology. *American Sociological Review*, 26 (2): 183–93.

Yack, B. 1985. Concept of political community in Aristotle's philosophy. *The Review of Politics*, 47 (1): 92–112.

Zhou, X. 1993. The dynamics of organizational rules. *American Journal of Sociology*, 98: 1134–66.

INDEX

285

ABOUT THE AUTHORS

James G. March is the Jack Steele Professor of International Management and a professor of political science and sociology at Stanford University. He is the author and co-author of numerous books and hundreds of journal articles on organizations, decision-making, and leadership. His highly praised works *Rediscovering Institutions: The Organizational Basis of Politics*, co-authored with Johan P. Olsen (1989), and *A Primer on Decision Making: How Decisions Happen* (1994) are published by The Free Press.

Johan P. Olsen is research director of ARENA (Advanced Research on Europeanization of the Nation-State), a basic research program under the auspices of the Research Council of Norway, University of Oslo. He is also an adjunct professor, Department of Administration and Organizational Science, at the University of Bergen (Norway), and is a member of the Norwegian Academy of Science and Letters.